Divine Credence

Volume 1 Part 1

A Lost Friend

Timothy D. James

ISBN: 979-8-7146-7653-6
Email : jamestim2021@gmail.com
YouTube: Divine Credence Official

DIVINE CREDENCE

CONTENTS

	Chapter Name	#
E	Elilament Classifications	2
P	Prologue	9
1	Deception	15
2	Academy	23
3	Transition	27
4	Misugami's Mistake	35
5	Vacant	39
6	Entry	49
7	Carnage	61
8	Contention of Kuki Sosa	75
9	Partition	87
10	Serenity	99
11	Implausible Ambuscades	111
12	Shrive	125
13	Allocated Information	129
14	Admission from the Ranks	145
15	Intruding Dicipients	151
16	Taku's Directive	165
L	Lore	171
C	Character List	175

Text Key

" Name(thts): " > The thoughts of the presented character

" Name(m): " > The presented character is mumbling

" Name(w): " > The presented character is whispering to another character

" Name(M): " > The presented character is talking through a wireless transmitter

" Name(Y): " > The presented character is yelling to converse with another character who is farther away than the location the presented character is placed

" Name(T): " > The presented character is using Magic to nonverbally converse with another character

Seeing " (M)(Name): or (mTV)(Name): " Any character following is speaking from a Magic Device or communicator. When a character no longer has the "( )" means it is from the live area

" Name(m.t.l.): " > The presented character is nonverbally communicating to another character who can perceive the movements of their mouth into words

etc...

" *Text* " These Asterisks represent character's movement, a slight change of setting, the change environment, anything noticed or unnoticed by a present character,

" ^Text^ " These Carets represent any intention of violence or the setup of a violence act

" [Text] " These Brackets represent the main Protagonist deeply analyzing something

" :Word-, " > Ending of word is cut off short by the speaking character

": -Word " > The entire word is said really fast or with a swift, urgent matter by the speaking character

etc...

Hydro- Most common use is manipulating the air molecules around a given area. Can morph and shift larger bodies of water.

Denryoku- Allows the ability to sense and differentiate an aura from other auras, an individual from another individual. An individual from a Familiar. This only works if the target has a Sustain active. Every aura you sense and notify will always unconsciously be remembered and felt once in proximity to the user. The amount of auras that can be associated at once and the range of proximity increases with each stage.

Barre- An Elilament that is made for protective shields, can incorporate other Elilaments in it. The higher the stage, the stronger and more energy-efficient a Barre becomes.

Raito- A magnified version of electricity that focuses and amps energy into a single array.

Kuki Sosa- A sub-division of Pure Energy that can be used to make objects or weaker forms of other Elilaments. The higher the Atle the more energy-efficient it becomes.

Uhnyoi- Being able to sense what stage of an Elilament is being used for anything that can support that Elilament. Stage III means you can see up to Stage III. Stage I means that you can see Stage I and lower. Etcetera.

Kori- The most common use is Ice. Takes full control of anything that has been submerged or frozen over by water.

Sustain- The amount of pressure or force an individual is protected from objects that are made from Pure Energy/Oplitals. It can also protect the individual from objects that are not made from Pure Energy/Oplitals, but this causes more wear on the body which lowers overall stamina.

Kemuri- Most common use is the divergence of particles into a collapsed state, causing a dense fog or smoke.

Zoka Hearing- Allows the user to control how sensitive their ears are, and in what direction they want the sensitivity to amplify.

Dermal Armor- Most common form is a suit of armor that may or may not resemble metal. A body type Barre that can be used for a second Sustain. Just like a Barre, can incorporate other Elilaments, can inhabit offensive and defensive attributes. Dermals are fully customizable in a sense where they can be invisible from the naked eye but can be sensed with Magic.

Patchi Tekiyo- Direct healing of someone's body and stamina. This can be used to heal yourself from any harmful Elilaments.

Zoka Swiftness- A manual state of being that instantly increases the effective speed of the user in pre and active movement.

Personal Casting- Using Elilaments in a synced way that it has its sequence{creating a block with the block having a gravitational field: Kemuri and Atoskito}. Merging two Elilaments into one.

Reverse- Cancelation of a reasonable cast or summon. Everyone can undo or stop, but after a certain point of Oplitals, a certain Stage of Reverse is needed to stop the Cast or Personal Cast.

Zoka Vision- Allows more accurate measurements, counts, and color. Increases your ability to understand what one is looking at faster. Can counter the motion blur, and the instantaneous movement of Zoka Swiftness only for the user

Celestial Summoning- Pure Energy in the form of a weapon. Can be made as a *Sustain*, initial summon that is easier to summon later, *Hold*, a constant supply of energy to the weapon, or a *Carry*, the weapon is given a very low amount of Pure Energy.

Ikkasei- Visually expresses the user's aura of any Ikkasei Influenced Elilament, or the user's personal aura to increase the casting speed, or the effectiveness of the Stages of your Elilaments, but at the cost of using more Oplitals. Ikkasei uses more Oplitals because it enhances more every Stage increase. Ikkasei can be used as a combination of Ikkasei Influenced Elilaments or just a singular one. One's aura can be used as or in an Ikkasei to improve the overall performance of everything, while Pure Energy as an Ikkasei will decrease damage taken.

Psychokinesis- Allows the user to maneuver any desired object. Depending on the size, and the speed the object is going to move, Oplital drainage can be quite high.

Denki- A basic manipulation of electrons and protons in the air. Can pass through objects with little defects. Most common use is electricity

Extilamental- Allows the user to create extra inhuman limbs anywhere on their body. These limbs do have a faulting point like Dermals, but they are easily broken. If they are broken instead of naturally Reversed, a fixed amount of one-percent of Oplitals is instantly consumed.

Atoskito- Allows the user to create a fixed point on an object or plane that creates a new chamber of gravity. This gravity can be merged with Edasia's gravity or forged against it.

Suva- Allows the user to convert Pure Energy into another individual's Oplital supply. This Elilament can be dangerous depending on how low of Oplitals the receiver has.

Irrow- Creation of wings that spawn from the back of one's spine. These wings increase multiple different attributes while also increasing the effectiveness of Basic, Novice, and Pristine Elilaments

Konseitsu- Allows the user to create a geometric position into an area in which Elilament effectiveness is lowered.

Element Shield- Allows the user to increase the protection from certain Elilaments.

DIVINE CREDENCE

Telepathy- Allows multiple individuals to communicate verbally and or mentally over distance. The longer the distance the more Oplitals used. Can be initiated as a Magic Contract, or as a physical marking.

Ancestrial Summoning- Pure Energy in the form of another existence of static or active life.

Doku- Allows the user to create a constant anti-healing effect on an object or as an object. The most common usage is Poison Particles that disassemble Conjoined-Particles

Fukashi- Allows the user to create an array of Nano-Particles that masks the user from incoming light rays, while simultaneously inverting the light behind the user around them, making it seem like there is nothing there. However, the basic physical interaction with the user still exists, meaning, if something hits them, they will be moved, and sound still applies.

Fukashi Vision- Allows the user to see Nano-Particles, which cancels out the effect of Fukashi. Does not share any characteristics of Zoka Vision but will always consume twice the amount of Oplitals of the same intensity of Zoka Vision.

Neutrality- Allows the user to manipulate the Cast of a Personal Cast from another individual into Particles.

Elilament Adapt- For Dermals: For a short period after being hit multiple times with an Elilament, it becomes immune. For Celestials: After being hit by an Elilament, it absorbs a small dose of it, and can be used as a Multi-Cast or an attack.

Itiro Irrow- Non-Physical attached wings, bound by magic. Increases the casting speed, power, and efficiency of Advanced and Elemental Elilaments while decreasing the amount of Oplitals it takes to use those Elilaments.

Itilusion- Uses Particles that weaken themselves to a point where they can still be used to create objects but can easily be destroyed with a TINY amount of displacement. Itilusion is a focused ability, meaning the effect only applies to a certain person or persons.

Kenesu- The ability to see the personal aura of another individual. This personal aura can be tracked to the current location of the individual. Unlike Denryoku, there is no physical adaptation of the persons one is looking at, which means one only sees auras instead of a body, and there is no limited range. Although the target does not need to have a Sustain active to locate them, one can only focus on one specific aura even though they can see all others. The Efficiency of an individual's Sustain does not affect the ability of Kenesu to notate them.

MultiCast- The ability to Cast two sequences of Elilaments or Magic at once without having to Reverse one's previous cast or summon. (Kosai and Hydro in each of your hands at the same time)

Void- A dark purplish empty material that consumes anything it touches. (Imagine Pure Energy but instead of colorful spacious white, it is a purplish spacious black). A Void is the polar opposite of Pure Energy, but it cannot be converted into any known Elilament. A collision between Void and Pure Energy creates an inner Atoskito horizontal, and an outer Protojet vertically.

Fukashi Deamsou- A constant flashing of Pure Energy around the user's body which makes the user's Sustain and or Dermal incapable of taking damage. However, using this Elilament takes an immense amount of Oplitals per second. The user can opt whether or not to take knockback or not at the cost of using even more Oplitals.

Tekiration- Allows the user to teleport to any marked known location, or if given an assist in some way, anywhere around Edasia. Requires a great amount of focus and concentration for precision

Prologue – Commence

-Yashi was coming back from a mail station to get a weekly letter from his parents. The area is quite rural and silent. While walking, the letter gets blown out of his hands by a gust of wind into a tall tree. Being so young and barely able to use his Magic properly, he struggles to get the letter from between the leaves and branches only being able to jump-

Yashi: Come on . . . *Jumps* I can barely reach it . . . *Yashi waits for another strong gust of wind to make the branches lower. When that wind comes, he jumps and barely touches the edge of the letter. Landing on his feet he sighs* **Yashi**: Maybe if I'm careful, I can get it down with Magic? *Yashi looks behind him* Then again, I don't think any of the Magic I have can get it down without destroying the tree in the process, and I don't want to get in trouble either. Hmmm . . .

-Along the sidewalk, not that far away-

Dia: Here you are, Ms. Okama. *Dia hands Okama a Magic Sealed Package* **Okama**: Thank you two so much. **Dia & Kokoa**: No problem, Ms. Okama. **Okama**: I'll be sure to tell both of your parents how much of a help you all have been when I get the chance. You two go along now. **Dia & Kokoa**: Have a nice day. *Ms. Okama closes her front door. Dia and Kokoa walk out onto the sidewalk. Kokoa turns towards Dia* **Kokoa**: Whew~, that was fun. Well, Dia, my parents will be a little worried if I don't show my face in a bit. **Dia**: I know, I was going to head home as well. *Kokoa grabs Dia's wrists and smiles* **Kokoa**: I'll see you tomorrow, okay? **Dia**: Oh-, yeah, okay. *Kokoa lets go of Dia's wrists as she starts walking down the sidewalk waving at Dia* **Kokoa**: See you, Dia! *Dia waves back* **Dia**: Bye, Kokoa! *Dia turns around and starts walking. Multiple chariots pass her on her left. Dia stops to look at the large line of Balancers. Everyone else on the street does the same. As Dia turns the corner, she notices Yashi jumping under a tree* Hm? *Dia continues to walk, getting closer to Yashi without him noticing her. Dia stops next to him as Yashi lands on his feet* **Yashi**: I might not even get it back. I wonder if Neitseka would get it down for me. *Yashi looks to his right, making eye contact with Dia as she stops a few feet away. Yashi gets startled from the encounter. The two of them stare in silence as a brown leaf falls from the tree landing in the middle of them* **Yashi**(thoughts): Woah, how long has she been watching me? **Yashi**: Uh~. *Yashi bows* Good morning. *Dia chuckles* **Dia**: Good morning. *Yashi raises, making eye contact again. Dia is smiling at him* **Dia**: What are you doing? **Yashi**: Oh-, uhm. *Yashi blushes as he looks away* My letter . . . it got stuck in the tree. I was trying to get it. *Dia looks up, spotting the letter dangling between the branches* **Dia**: Would you like some help? *Yashi looks back at Dia* **Yashi**: I don't want to be rude, but you're shorter than me. How do you plan on helping? *Yashi moves from under the letter, standing next to Dia* **Dia**: I could get on your back? **Yashi**: My back? Okay. *Yashi moves back under the letter and crouches. Dia walks to him and puts her legs around his neck. Yashi holds onto Dia's legs as he slowly stands* **Dia**: Woah, I didn't think you'd be able to pick me up. *Yashi blushes* **Yashi**: Well, my brother and sister, they train my physical body without my Sustain from time to time. **Dia**: Cool. *Dia looks up at the letter, reaching her right hand out to get it. The tip of her index finger just grazes the edge of the letter* **Dia**: Move back just a tiny bit. **Yashi**: Okay. *Yashi takes a tiny step back. Dia grabs the letter between her index and middle finger* **Dia**: I got it! Wha- *A heavy gust of wind pushes against Dia and Yashi. Dia leans forward from the pressure against her back which causes Yashi to lose his balance. Yashi stumbles around before landing both himself and Dia in a pile of leaves next to the tree. Yashi crouches up, rubbing his side* Ah-ss. Are you okay? *Yashi turns around, Dia is nowhere to be seen* Huh? *Yashi stands* Where did she go? *Suddenly, the pile of leaves lifts from the ground. Yashi falls back on the ground. The leaves fall off Dia's body. Dia is rubbing the back of her head* **Dia**: Yeah, I'm okay. *Dia looks at Yashi* **Dia & Yashi**: Hahaha. *Yashi stands and reaches a hand out to Dia. Dia takes the hand, supporting her as she stands up. While Dia is dusting her skirt off, Yashi looks up at the letter. It is farther up in the tree* **Yashi**: What?! There's no way we can get that back now! **Dia**: Wait. *Yashi looks at Dia* **Dia**: I can use Magic. **Yashi**: I don't want to damage the tree though. **Dia**: Don't worry. I have a neat trick that I've yet to tell anyone. Stand back. *Yashi stands behind Dia* **Dia**: Okay . . . here I go. *Dia raises her hands at the letter. A dark blue aura surrounds her hands and makes its way up to the letter. A few moments later the letter begins to float up from in between the twigs and comes down* Open up your hands. *Yashi opens up his hands, the letter lands onto his hands* **Yashi**: Oh~, cool. That's, Advanced Psychokinesis? **Dia**: Yup, it sure is. **Yashi**: Wow, you must be really strong then? **Dia**: My mom told me that I had a lot of amazing Elilaments for my age, but she's not going to focus heavily on me till I'm ten. **Yashi**: Oh~. *Dia puts her hands down and moves closer to Yashi, touching his shoulder while looking down at the letter* **Dia**: What's inside the letter? **Yashi**: It's just a letter from my parents. **Dia**: Your parents? **Yashi**: Yeah, they live overseas, so they send mLetters to check on me. **Dia**: If you don't mind me asking, when will they be coming back? **Yashi**: I'm not sure, I just moved here a few months ago, but hopefully soon. *Dia notices a frown on Yashi's face as he stares at the letter* **Dia**: That's good. **Yashi**: Well, I don't mind you reading it with me, but you have to wait till Neitseka's shop is open. **Dia**: Neitseka? He's one of the mLetter parlors, right? **Yashi**: Yeah, just around the corner from here. Suppressor of Seals. **Dia**: Okay. *Yashi holds the letter tightly* **Yashi**: Thank you . . . **Dia**: No problem. *After Yashi turns around, Dia taps him on the shoulder* Excuse me . . .

Yashi turns back around **Yashi**: Ye-, yes? **Dia**: My name is Dia Kean, could you tell me yours? **Yashi**: Yashi Taramasu. **Dia**: Yashi? Almost like the 1st ever Hero's name, right? **Yashi**: No! It's nothing like his. *Dia backs away. Yashi takes a step back* I'm sorry! *Yashi quickly turns around and starts to jog away* **Dia**: I'll see you at Neitseka's! **Yashi**: Okay!

-A few hours pass before Neitseka shop is open. Yashi heads over to it after playing at a small park in the woods alone. Once he makes it to the shop-

Yashi stands in front of the door and gently opens it. Yashi scans the room and finds no one. As the door closes behind Yashi, a gray light flickers above him **Neitseka**: One moment! *Yashi walks up to the counter. A few seconds pass before Neitseka is seen coming from the back* Oh-, Yashi, good to see you. **Yashi**: Good to see you too. *Neitseka looks down at Yashi's hands* **Neitseka**: Have another letter for me? **Yashi**: Yes sir. **Neitseka**: Well, let's get started. *A few minutes later, outside the shop, Dia has just arrived* **Dia**(mumbles(m)): Hopefully I didn't miss him. *Dia reaches for the door, but as she does her Mangole appears in front of her* **Mangole**: From Kokoa, Urgent. *Dia swipes her Mangole to answer it* **Dia**: Kokoa? **Kokoa**(Mangole(M)): Dia! Have you seen the news?! **Dia**: No, what happened? **Kokoa**(M): It's terrible! It's about Alma!!! It's just been forwarded out to everyone! *Kokoa is heard sniffing and wiping her face. Dia swiftly scrolls through her Mangole till she gets to the news app. On instant discovery, Dia covers her mouth as she looks at the first picture. The picture's point of view is looking at an island from the ocean. The shot is about a five-hundred-mile-long picture of the right side of the island. A destroyed civilization is in full view on the screen of Dia's Mangole. Tall buildings and forests are seen on fire and collapsed. Several craters are scattered throughout the ground from large blasts or cannon shots. The Energy Dispositor that sits in Alma's capital is at an angle; broken. The destruction of Alma's Energy Dispositor deactivates the nation's protective Barrier. The remains of particles leave a thin layer of Pure Energy above Alma's sky* **Dia**: All of it . . . is destroyed. **Kokoa**(M): They were attacked by the Dark Army last night. Almost a hundred Dicipients invaded Alma. *Dia continues to look through the many pictures* **Dia**: This is horrible . . . all those innocent people. **Kokoa**(M): I know. The conflict between Alma and the Demon King, just gets worse and worse with every year, and I bet Korosi is just taking that advantage that the 6th Generation Hero is nowhere to be seen. **Dia**: Alma's so far away, they might not get support in time. **Kokoa**(M): That goes for all the other Seiras[Countries] as well. **Dia**: If only there was some way I could help. **Kokoa**(M): But we're too young, and that's way too dangerous. *Dia hears movement from the other side of the door* Maybe in-, **Dia**: Wait, Kokoa, I'll call you back. **Kokoa**(M): Okay. *As Dia vanishes her Mangole, she turns to look at the door. Right after, Yashi bursts through the door, and Dia falls onto her bottom* **Dia**: Yashi? *They make eye contact. Yashi is in tears. He quickly looks away and runs down the sidewalk. The mLetter falls in front of Dia* **Dia**: The letter? *Dia starts to read the letter. As she continues to read, tears start to drop from her eyes as well* **Dia**: His parents . . . where in Alma . . . *Neitseka steps outside the door* **Neitseka**: Yashi! *Looking to his right, Neitseka sees Dia chasing after Yashi. Yashi continues to run through Sadnius. Dia tries to focus on him through all of the people and markets. After a minute, Dia watches Yashi take a turn into a noncolonized forest. Only knowing it to be an attraction, Dia continues to follow Yashi anyway. Dia shields her head while wiping her eyes* **Dia**(m): Now where's he going? *After a while of trying to catch up to him, Dia ends up lost in a clearing* **Dia**(Yelling(Y)): Yashi!? Where did you go?! *Dia stops in the middle of the clearing* **Dia**: Mom told me not to, but I have no choice. *Dia puts her right hand on her chest closed and the other in the air with her palm opened while also closing her eyes. Dia's aura unseen flourishes throughout the forest looking for Yashi's aura* There you are. *Nearby, in Yashi's house* **Kato**: Are you positive, Yashi? Please tell me you're just kidding around. **Yashi**: No, brother, *Sniffs and wipes eyes* I'm not. *Kato sits on his bed, now being eye to eye with Yashi, Kato hugs Yashi. Yashi begins to sob, and Kato's eyes start to water as well* **Kato**(m): I can't believe it; there's no way mom and dad could be dead. *Moments Later* **Kato**: Yashi, I'm going to be the one to tell Akima, okay? *Yashi nods. Yashi leaves the room and walks downstairs. Upon reaching the bottom, he sits on the wall that leads up the stairs and falls against the floor, covering his face. Dia stands at the open front door to the right of Yashi* **Dia**: Yashi. *Yashi looks up to his right* **Yashi**: Dia, you followed me? **Dia**: Of course I did . . . I feel just as much pain as you do . . . I'm sorry about your parents . . . *An angry frown grows across Yashi's face as his tear covered hands turn into fists* **Yashi**: It's all because of Korosi! *Dia walks closer to Yashi* **Dia**: You're right. It will always be the Demon King's fault. *Yashi stands and wipes his face* **Yashi**: He terrorizes whoever he pleases. **Dia**: It's been like that for a few years now, and even worse ever since the 6th Hero suddenly vanished a few months ago. Every Seira in their right has been doing their best in trying to stop the Dark Army's movements. **Yashi**: Even Macadamia. **Dia**: I feel as though, we need more strong Elilament users, and I'm going to be one of them. *A small pause* **Yashi**: You're not alone. I also want to become stronger. *Another pause* At first, I was going to start when I got older, but this, *Yashi stares at his hand as he puts in up in front of him and squeezes his fist even harder* To get strong enough to avenge my parents, I'm going to have to start training seriously today. **Dia**(m): Hey! *Yashi looks up at Dia* You can't just steal the spotlight like that. **Yashi**: Huh? *Dia puts a fist towards Yashi* **Dia**: I'm going to train just as hard, to protect those who are innocent. I don't care how strong anyone might seem or how young we might be, I just can't tolerate it anymore. In our case, I guess that makes us partners, right? *Yashi smiles* **Yashi**: Yeah! **Dia & Yashi**: For Purification! *They fist bump. Dia lightly grins*

Interlude

Since that day, Dia and Yashi have worked together, training to improve their Elilament skills, techniques, and knowledge. Needing a better grasp at how to use their Elilaments, both of them enrolled into Jurono Magic Academy weeks later in Kietnas, Macadamia. At this time, Dia is at eight years of age and Yashi is at nine years of age. After three years of attending Jurono and intense self-training, Dia and Yashi's Elilament status had allowed them to join an Expisimist team. Finally being able to help defeat Dicipients, they immediately joined a fairly new Expisimist group by the name of Anzen. Each of the already existing members' ages ranged from theirs to ten years in advance. A year after joining Anzen, and devoting their lives together, Dia and Yashi's relationship became great enough to perform a Trants. This feat would allow each of them to gain Stage bonuses on Elilaments and even unlock some of their previously Locked Elilaments. Being the more combat conducive person, Dia chose to have the ability to undergo the form anytime. Two years after their Trants, Anzen was called in on a dangerous mission with three more Expisimist groups. Feeling as though their recent missions were too easy, and their Magic has greatly improved, they decided to accept the call to arms. The mission took place in Adlius, Macadamia. An extremely mountainous area in Macadamia near a neighboring Seira, Digona. The mission was to seek, capture, or kill three Dicipients that had fled into the area unannounced to the Macadamian public. Days had passed as they settled in and got a few good leads onto where the Dicipients may be hiding. However, on their fourth day at the time of dawn, they were ambushed by nearly a dozen Dicipients at their most vulnerable. Outnumbering the Dicipients three to one, the Expisimists were able to hold their own against them. The Dicipients started to withdraw as each party had lost almost half of their fighters who had their Sustains. While chasing the Dicipients, the three initial Dicipients that they had been looking for appeared. The Expisimists started falling back, trying to regroup at the base. However, the Dicipients managed to track them down before they were able to call backup. Everyone's lives were being threatened. With Dia being one of the most powerful fighters on the allied side, the highest-ranked Dicipient was going to kill her first. This is when the Hero of the 7th Generation was born. Yashi had unlocked it, the 1st ever Hero's Dermal. Yashi's newfound power allowed him to stand toe to toe with all the Dicipients alone. Although being one of the most gruesome battles Yashi's ever had to deal with, he managed to defeat all the Dicipients by himself and saved everyone in that mission, with no casualties. Now possessing the Dermal, Yashi preferred to slay undisclosed, meaning not letting the public know his original identity. This effect was a choice made between him and the Dermal. Giving him special feats alone, but also helps him maintain his life separately from the Hero's life. Unfortunately, breaking this inner contract would revoke his special feats and exposing his identity to his enemies. This contract can be dealt around, such as Yashi's bond with Dia, his family, Anzen, and other special exceptions. Dia was the first to know Yashi was the Hero. With every Hero, there is a Spawn or someone who the Hero can trust 100%. Usually, they meet by circumstance or Yashi's Seal that exists on the Yáshido Dermal starts to glow green. Emuna is an Alchemist, with her sub as someone who studies the nature of Magic and its capabilities. Alchemists are also the main name for anyone you would normally call a doctor or scientist. Dia, Emuna, and Yashi met in an exploration site that was controlled by Dicipients in North Macadamia. After taking control over it, Yashi noticed that his Seal would appear and start to glow when around Emuna, and so the three of them linked up. Knowing that they can trust each other, Emuna would help Yashi with anything he can only learn from her or needs help with something that far exceeds what he and Dia could do by themselves. This friendship causes Dia and Yashi to leave Anzen, after introducing them to Emuna. With no bad strings attached, they still visit from time to time, including Emuna. Four years after leaving Anzen, capturing Dicipients, learning Magic, and attending an Academy, Yashi believed it was finally time to attack the head of the Dark Army, also known as Daphoria, the Demon King himself, Lark Korosi. Yashi has only ever seen the Demon King once in live action but was bombarded by Dicipients and had to fall back, nearly dying in the process. Yashi kept this plan only to himself, Dia, and Emuna. They would be the only three going to the Demon King's castle, located in Darku Mat'u. The island is surrounded by hundreds of miles of ocean. The closest other landmasses would be a recently captured island named Yato; Lark renamed the island to Darku Yat'u after taken complete control over it. Emuna would carefully teleports Dia and Yashi to Darku without causing any alarms. After succeeding, the two would carefully navigate through the harsh terrain. They make it to Lark's castle unnoticed and unattended. Being in his unbelievably massive castle for the first time, it takes them a while before they find Lark's throne room. Obviously shocked by their arrival without any notice, Lark becomes immediately angry. The three of them begin to fight soon after a minor dialogue. At Yashi's current state of power as the 7th Generation Hero, his power already levels with the records he had on the 6th Generation Heroine. Maybe this power gap will help in this major battle. Chapter One starts at the end of this battle.

Chapter 1 – Deception

Lark: Hahahahaha . . . . . . good job, Hero . . . an attempt yet failed by your simple-minded brain. Hmph, you almost impressed me, that is something I must say about you. You started off on good grounds. Built your path all the way up just to die by my will. It was your fate, people like you don't deserve to live, you deserve to be eradicated. Which is why you're pitiful. It doesn't matter the era. How strong, how smart, how influential you were, every last Hero all came to a stop. All of you. Especially the 'Macadamian' kind. Haha, yes, the 1st, 4th, and now the 7th. How does it feel to originate from the birthplace of the first ever Hero? And die before you could even change the world as he did? It's time for me to take over, Yáshido. It's time for you to die, but hahaha, but it seems you will die . . . in the most humiliating way ever and the fastest, death by fall. Wonderful . . . just wonderful . . . * Lark Reverses his sword as Yáshido hangs off the edge of the platform they have been fighting on* **Yáshido's**(thoughts(thts)): Ah, my Oplitals are nearly gone. Another hit and this Dermal is going to be done for too. *Small rocks fall off of the platform next to Yáshido's hands* **Yáshido**: You, bastard! Why did you have to go this far! First Alma, then Yato, now this! *Yáshido's hands slip more. Lark laughs* **Lark**: Your arrogance is what's going to get you killed. Let's go, Dia. **Dia**: Yes, Korosi. *Lark turns around and starts walking towards his throne. Dia who was standing next to Lark makes slight eye contact with Yáshido before she turns around* **Yáshido**: So, this is it Dia?! Is this really how it's going to end? All of this work we've put into getting here and you're just going to betray me! *Dia stops in her tracks. Lark immediately feels this with his back toward her. Lark also stops* **Lark**: Dia, remember why you came here for. You succeeded at your mission, while the one over there, sweaty in that skintight Dermal, all out of Pure Energy, is about to fall to his death. If he can't even go out by my sword, who has the right to call themself a Hero? **Yáshido**: You pushed me off, you coward! *Dia clenches her fists* Dia, you and I are together! We have always been together! We Trantsed Dia. You were there in the beginning. Why are you turning against me! It doesn't make any sense! *Dia turns halfway towards Yáshido, squeezing her fists even tighter. Lark turns around with aggression. Dia's eyes are focused in front of her. Both the Hero and Demon King stare at her* **Lark**: Dia-, stop . . . If you go back now, there won't be any second chances with me. **Yáshido**(Y: All those times we spent together! *Yáshido's hands slip even more* Doesn't that mean anything to you! Ahh- *Yáshido's hands completely slip off, but a loud burst of a Cast happens, and something catches him. Yáshido looks up to see Dia in her Trants form holding on to his hand* **Dia**(m): Eeh~! I got you. **Lark**: You're about to fail, Dia! **Dia**: It's okay, Korosi. *Dia pulls Yáshido up. Once on his feet, Yáshido takes a couple of breaths while staring at Lark* **Lark**: For the love- a *Lark summons his sword back. Dia looks back over at Lark* **Dia**: Wait. Please . . . * Lark, with an angry expression, halts his movements as he they stare at each other. Dia turns back to Yáshido* Yes, Yashi, those memories, our Trants. All of those things I hold dear to my heart. **Yáshido**: I know they do. *Dia hugs Yáshido tightly, Yáshido hugs her back* **Dia**: But it's too bad . . . that I've had my own goal. *Yáshido feels a sharp pain in his stomach* **Yáshido**: Wha-, ah. ^Yáshido looks down and there is a knife going through his Dermal into the left side of his abdomen. Yáshido feels the blade cutting his muscle inside his stomach. As Dia pulls it out, a burst of Pure Energy and a heap of blood comes from the intersection^ **Yáshido**: Dia . . . you, you stabbed me. *Dia is looking at Yashi with a frown and a tear coming from her left eye* **Dia**: I'm sorry, Yashi. **Dia**(Whispers(w)): I'll see you soon. **Dia**: Bye, Yashi. ^Still holding on to him, Dia moves back to the edge of the platform where Yáshido fell. While doing so, she kisses him on the lips. As soon as Yáshido feels the platform end with the heel of his boots, Dia gently pushes him off^ **Yáshido**(Y): Dia!!! *As Yáshido is falling, he sees Dia stare down at him before darkness covers his vision. A strong force starts to pull him down even harder* **Yáshido**(thts): This can't be happening. I must be dreaming or something. I have to be dreaming, there's no way Dia would ever do this to me. *Yáshido feels tears drop down his face in his helmet* But this feels so real though. The pain, the words, the Demon King. *While Yáshido is falling, he passes multiple small drawbridges with dim orange lights that brighten his view from time to time* I can say I tried, mom and dad. I believe that anyways. There are so many people on Edasia that I've helped. So many villains stopped. And so many wars subdued. But in the end, I couldn't repay you. I'm sorry. *With an image of his parents invading his mind, tears seep through the cracks in his helmet. Yáshido continues to fall. His body is numb and the pressure against his stomach builds. The Atoskito pulling him downward would ignore any efforts that Yáshido would make due to his low Oplital count. With every consecutive drawbridge being more spread apart, and nothing to save his life, Yáshido closes his eyes accepting his fate* **Voice**(Y): Catch!!!!! *Yáshido instantly becomes reactive as he searches around. Yáshido spots a flame attached to the end of a rope rushing towards him from above. Yáshido reaches tries to reach for it, but the Atoskito doesn't let him unparallel from the ground below. Using the last of his Oplitals, he uses a light burst of Zoka Strength and grabs the rope. His Oplitals just below one-hundred. Once Yáshido has the rope, the rope itself starts to curl around his body. As the flame rubs against his Dermal, it gets extinguished. Yáshido then feels a strong tug on the rope as he continues to fall. With another strong tug, Yáshido sits motionless in the air before he starts to ascend. Looking up, Yáshido can see the rope being pulled from someone out of sight on the inside of a drawbridge. **Yáshido**(thts): There's no way. Oh my gosh, whoever this is a lifesaver. And they don't feel like a Dicipient. *Yáshido looks down and feels a dark aura of Familiars* So if I didn't die from the fall, he was going to use Type One Familiars to finish me off. *With the adrenaline leaving his body, the pain from the stab reemerges* Ah-! This wound hurts so bad. *Yáshido feels his back going against the wall and over it onto the ground* Voice: Good, I managed to get you. You're not a Dicipient are you? *Yáshido on his back leans up a little. With the orange lights being so dim, Yáshido can't make any distinct features on the individual* Stranger: Oh geez, are you okay? You look badly hurt. *The person walks over to Yáshido* Stranger: Lay back down. *Yáshido lays back down, the stranger puts their hand over his wound. Yáshido's body twitches and aches as they do* Stranger: This is bad, it went straight through your Dermal. I think my Magic is enough to heal you though. You don't have any aura coming off you either, I'll give you some of my Pure Energy, so stay still, okay? *Yáshido nods at the stranger. With them being closer, Yáshido can make more accurate features* Yáshido(thts): A girl? *Their hands glow a pinkish-red over his wound* Oh yes, this person is an expert. They must have Aced Patchi Tekityo or at least Stage I. *Once Yáshido's wound is successfully healed, the girl moves from sitting next to Yáshido's stomach to sitting next to his head. She places her hand above his helmet* Girl: Now for the energy. *A spacious white substance comes from her hand and begins to go inside of Yáshido. The girl pauses as the white glow illuminates Yáshido's Dermal* Wait a minute, that armor looks familiar. *Gasp* Ah-, no way-, you're the Hero . . . aren't you? Yáshido(thts): Oh~, yes, I am . . . *A minute later of Pure Energy replacement. Yáshido sits up* Yáshido: Thank you. Girl: Oh, it's fine. Sorry if it wasn't perfect. Yáshido: No, you did an excellent job. Yáshido(thts): I wonder . . . if I should go back. *Yáshido looks at the girl, now being able to use Zoka Vision* [She has black shoes with red and white patterned stockings, the left one being higher than the right one. There is a small brown back attached to her right leg, she has jean blue shorts on with a lot of gadgets going around her waist, most noticeably a small pack of bandages. She has a white shirt with a denim jacket over it. She has red fingerless gloves, and pink hair] I don't know. Would that be the right call? She shared her Pure Energy with me, almost ten percent of my max actually. Even if then, Lark would most likely just tell his Dicipients to take her on. I don't know how strong her Elilaments are, but I don't want to take that chance and have two people killed today, myself included. Girl: Wha-, what's wrong? *Yáshido down at his* Yáshido: Nothing. Yáshido(thts): Wait a minute, what is she doing here!? *Yáshido quickly turns towards her* Yáshido: What are you even doing here?! Girl: What do you mean? *Yáshido stands* Yáshido: You do realize you're in the Demon Kingdom, right? In his actual palace? Girl: The one in Darku right? Yáshido: You don't think this is dangerous?! Girl: I uh~, thought it'd be a good spot for exploring, and you yelling like that will get us noticed. *A loud bell starts to ring, and the walls start to vibrate. A steady force begins to push them downward* Yáshido: That's not good, we need to get out of here now! *Yáshido and the girl start to run in the corridors away from the center* Yáshido(thts): Did you really have to make every single part of this place look like the rest! *Girl*: Follow me! *Yáshido*: What? *The girl grabs Yáshido's hand and runs in a set pattern. Right as they are about to cross an intersection, she slams both of them against the wall and covers the helmet part of Yáshido's Dermal. She activates Fukashi and both of them glow a gray shade across the edges of their bodies, both connected to one another before Yáshido can no longer see himself or the girl. Two people come from the left side of the intersection and stop in the middle* *Yáshido*(thts): Vekfla and Doridan. Both fairly strong Dicipients. *Yáshido activates his Fukashi Vision, now being able to see himself and the girl as she looks at him. Her also using Fukashi Vision* *Girl*(Moving Their Lips(m.t.l.)): Do you want to attack them? I'm all for it if you are. *Yáshido*(m.t.l.): No, even if we do, we'll be stuck fighting them, and others will just show up and then it'll be bad. *The girl looks over at the Dicipients* *Doridan*: I'm not seeing anyone or anything. *Vekfla*: I'm telling you I saw their potency outputs coming right into this intersection. It's obvious that one of them has Fukashi. *Doridan*: Oh, you're right. There's no point in trying to scout them out with Vision then. *Both of the Dicipients stand back-to-back* *Doridan & Vekfla*: Hyah! ^A circular blast of fire and electricity rush outwards, hitting the walls while hitting Yáshido and the girl. As the girl gets hit, she flinches a bit. The electric wave clicks around their gray shade, outlining their bodies. Vekfla points at them* *Vekfla*: There! *The girl instantly Reverses her Fukashi and jumps to the opposite side of the wall. Yáshido holds out his hand^ *Yáshido*: Jeshika! ^His sword does not summon^ *Yáshido*(thts): What?! ^Doridan casts a Barre in front of himself and Vekfla^ *Vekfla*: Perfect! ^Vekfla puts her palms on the interior of the Barre^ *Vekfla*: Shadow Strike! ^Large balls of Void shoots from outside the Barre at the girl. The girl uses Zoka Swiftness as she dodges each ball. When the balls full of dark substance hit the ground or wall behind her they explode rumbling the castle^ *Vekfla*: You're mine! Ha! ^A larger and faster Void Ball gets fired towards the girl^ *Girl*: Ha! ^The girl points her hand at the incoming attack and fires a small ball of Pure Energy at it. As the two blasts touch, a powerful shockwave immediately hits everyone and creates a horizontal line in the walls on the plane of the collision. Everyone slams against the closest vertical wall to them^ *Girl*: Let's go! *Yáshido and the girl quickly get up and run through the intersection. The Atoskito pulling them down is much harder to fight against. To counter, Yáshido activates his Zoka Strength* Good thinking! *She does the same. After a few more corridors and stairs, the girl finally brings them out to the exit. The large platinum doors are open. As they are running out it is sunset. Both of them are now running side by side* *Yáshido*: Protojet out of here! Stage II! Aim for those rocks! *Being on a slight cliff, Yáshido points at a group of rocks that sit in between the forest and the castle* Once you're there, use your Fukashi! *Girl*: Got you! *Yáshido Reverses his Zoka Strength. He points out his right arm with a fist at the rocks and holds it with his left arm* *Yáshido*(thts): Here . . . WE . . . GO!!! ^As Yáshido dives, a blast of Pure Energy releases from in front of him shooting behind him. The extreme force causes him to move at two hundred miles per hour. He holds this speed for nearly seven seconds before almost missing the rocks. Yáshido lands and rolls to soften the impact. Once down, he goes back first against the rocks and activates his Fukashi, a gray shade goes over his outline^ **Yáshido**: So much action in so little time.

-Thirty minutes pass before the bell stops ringing. A few Dicipients start to look for them, without knowing who they are-

Yáshido(thts): Okay, this has been long enough. Time to see where she landed. *Yáshido activates his Fukashi Vision Elilament Stage II, allowing him to see people using Fukashi of the same Stage or lower. The eye sockets in his Dermal turn gray while he looks around the rocks* Well, she's not on this side. *Yáshido carefully gets up and walks to the other side of the rocks* She's not here either. *Yáshido then climbs to the top of the rocks and searches the area* Other than seeing a few Dicipients, I don't see her at all. Could she be using a higher Stage Fukashi? **Voice**(w): Down here. *Yáshido turns around and looks down before seeing gray collapsing Particles going upward and disappearing. The Girl's figure starts to become clear. Her eyes are also gray. As Yáshido tries to descend off the rocks, his body feels insanely heavy, and dizziness fills his head. He sits on the rock and slides down instead, but as he lands it gets even worse* **Yáshido**(thts): Oh no, I'm going to pass out, I need to get out of this Dermal. *Yáshido Reverses his Fukashi based Elilaments. He puts his hands up in front of him and they both are shaking drastically; he sets them down next to his waist* **Girl**: You're not looking too well. Then again, you were holding down Fukashi for half an hour, and you were using someone else's energy, so I'll give you the benefit of the doubt. **Yáshido**: Thank you, it would have been a really different scene if you had not shown up. **Girl**: Ye-, yes, Hero. Of course. I'm quite surprised we got out of there. **Yáshido**: You did save my life back there, I'll let you see my actual identity. **Girl**: Oh, that's nice, I guess. I'm sure I'm not the first, so it's not that special. **Yáshido**: Yeah, technically you are the first. **Girl**: Oh really? Yeah okay, this will be more fun then. *Yáshido's Dermal shimmers off of him starting from his head* **Yashi**: Oh~, my body feels like it's being crushed by a giant hand. *The girl scans Yashi's body as she Reverses her Fukashi Vision* **Girl**: So, this is the body of the one who's always inside that Dermal and protecting the world. **Yashi**: Yes, that's me. **Girl**: Brown hair, still taller than me, and your muscular. Pretty cool. **Yashi**: I guess that means I would have to tell you my name as well, right? *Yashi looks at the girl and she is smiling at him. Yashi sighs* Yashi, Yashi Taramasu. **Girl**: Really? Can I do it please? **Yashi**: Yes, fire away. **Girl**: So, is it like, Y O S H I, but the O has an accent? **Yashi**: You know, that's the best one I've heard. **Girl**: Who did I top? **Yashi**: Trust me, you don't want to hear it. *Yashi scans behind him* We should probably leave this island. **Girl**: SO impolite. **Yashi**: My bad, what's your name? *The girl clears her throat* **Girl**: Niola. **Yashi**(thts): The adventurer Niola? *Yashi looks at the girl closer* Woah, that is her. She has that same energetic tone and style; How did I not notice that sooner? **Yashi**: Nice name. **Niola**: So is yours. **Yashi**: Seriously, we should go. There's a teleporter here waiting for me. **Niola**: I'm following your lead. **Yashi**: Hold on to my back. *Niola puts her right hand on Yashi's right shoulder. Yashi activates Fukashi again. While they are walking towards the shore, they enter through a forest* **Yashi**(thts): This is going to be awkward. **Yashi**: So, what do you do? **Niola**: Adventurer. You're not telling me you've never heard of me, Hero? We met once before. Remember? **Yashi**: Yeah, I know. Just trying to make conversation. *After a few more minutes of walking, they get the scent of sand through a now denser forest* You like what you do? **Niola**: I LOVE what I do. **Yashi**: By where we are, I see that. *Yashi takes them both on a path to the ocean* **Niola**: This has been bothering me this whole time. **Yashi**: Yes? **Niola**: What happened to you? Why were you falling? If I were taking a guess, I'd say you fought Lark, right? **Yashi**: Yes, yes, I was fighting Lark. Then something unexpected happened. Before even that happened, he was already a tough fight, and so mischievous. I've never seen such an evil character before. **Niola**: So, how'd it turn-, **Yashi**: We're here. *The both of them walk out of the forest and a beach resides just a few yards from them. Yashi Reverses his Fukashi as he walks out onto the sand* Emuna? *Yashi turns to the sound of another Fukashi being Reversed. Emuna stands in the releasing Gray Particles* **Emuna**: Hero. *Yashi turns behind him looking for Niola* **Yashi**: What. **Emuna**: What's the matter? **Yashi**: There was a girl with me. **Emuna**: A girl? You mean Dia, right? *Yashi turns and looks at Emuna directly in her eyes* Something happened to Dia? *Yashi nods. Emuna faintly looks at the ground* **Voice**: Exceeded Fire! ^Yashi sees a fireball heading straight for Emuna. Emuna immediately gets covered in a light blue aura as she turns her head towards the ball and raises her hand. The ball of fire hits her hand doing no damage. They look up to see Vekfla^ **Emuna**: Flash Screen! ^A white light comes from Emuna's hands towards Vekfla's. Emuna jumps over to Yashi as Vekfla falls to the ground covering her eyes^ **Emuna**: A-7 Core! *Emuna teleports them to her lab. While in the shift* That was a close one.

-Ten seconds pass before the Particles around them fade away and they rest inside of Emuna's lab in Macadamia-

Yashi instantly falls down as his body is irritated from the different sources of Magic **Emuna**: Hero! *Emuna takes a knee by Yashi* **Yashi**: I'm fine Emuna, my Oplitals are just low. **Emuna**: Yes, it is . . . extremely low. *Emuna picks up Yashi* **Yashi**: Oh no, Emuna, no Chamber. **Emuna**: Your safety is more important. **Yashi**: Emuna, please. **Emuna**: Fine, as you wish. *Emuna takes Yashi to a lab dedicated just for him. She sets him down on a bed in the middle of the room. Emuna opens a case that sits on the left of the bed and takes a glowing white tube out. Inside the tube is Type X Potency. This potency is universal Pure

Energy allowing those who are compatible to replenish part of their Oplitals* Here. *Yashi takes the tube and starts to drink it. Instantly, Yashi feels his body soothing itself* **Yashi**: Much better. Thank you, Emuna. **Emuna**: Part of your Pure Energy is restored, but your body is still sore, and your stamina has dropped. A lot. It's near night time right now. You're going to have to rest as much as you can before tomorrow. *Emuna looks down at Yashi's stomach as she notices the large bloodstain. She slowly moves up his shirt* You've already been healed? **Yashi**: By that girl, I was talking about. Oh yes, wait, Niola? The one you used to adventure with. **Emuna**: She was with you? In the Demon Kingdom? She honestly never changes. *Emuna raises both of her hands around Yashi. A pinkish-red aura surrounds Yashi's entire body* Let's talk about what happened with Dia, Yashi. *Yashi leans up, looking in front of him* **Yashi**: We were doing well, fighting wise. Of course, it's the first time I've ever gotten into a fight with him. I honestly don't know how the other Heroes defeated their Demon King by themselves. It was tougher than I imagined, but maybe that's just because I'm the youngest one to fight my opposition. I felt more excited than nervous, even when I took a massive hit. It was just the realization that I am the Hero fighting the biggest threat on our planet. The man that killed my parents, destroyed homes, killed families. And that started to push me harder, but near the end of the fight, all of our energies were low, and we were actually going to win. Korosi kind of tricked me by making me activate my Seal earlier than him. If Dia wasn't there, the fight would have ended in a loss for me. But before, Korosi activated his Seal a couple of seconds after me and the three of us clashed; Dia was in her Trants form around this time. Yet somehow, this could work. I finally got Korosi low enough for one of my special Personal Casts to end him. I pulled out Jeshika and cast the attack. I stunned him and stood back to make sure this attack was a hit regardless of my low stamina. As I'm running towards the defenseless Korosi, Dia hit me on my side with her Hammer. So perfectly that my Seal was completely deactivated along with my attack. I hit the ground far from both Korosi and Dia. Since I had put everything into the attack and just having it taken away with a powerful hit, I couldn't move. Dia walked up to Korosi and instead of attacking him, then started talking to him. I had no idea what was emerging. Korosi stood up and then they talked for a good two minutes before he turned towards me. Around the time where I was able to stand, he appeared in front of me and just started pummeling me with Aced Zoka Strength. Dia was just sitting by letting this happen to me. Blow after blow, my Dermal and Sustain were just fading away. There was no way I could win at that point. A minute later and I'm pushed off of the platform hanging onto the edge with almost nothing left. I'm pleading to Dia as she and Korosi were walking away, and she came back to me. Genuine as ever. Once she pulled me up. *A tear drops from Yashi's eye, Emuna stops her Patchi Tekiyo and puts her right hand on Yashi's shoulder* She hugged me, and . . . while she was . . . she stabbed me . . . right through the Dermal . . . right in my stomach.

Then told me, 'But, it's too bad that I've had my own goal. I'm sorry Yashi. I'll see you soon. Bye, Yashi.' *Emuna moves her hand from his shoulder to the back of his head and lays him onto her chest as Yashi starts to cry. Emuna wipes her eyes and tries to compress her emotions* **Emuna**: I know this hurts you, Yashi. It hurts me as well. I wouldn't believe Dia of all people, who has been beside you before even I, could do this. I never once sensed any bad intentions from her. **Yashi**: Right? It doesn't make any sense. After so many years, and so suddenly. *Emuna holds onto Yashi tighter* We're going to get her back. **Yashi**(thts): I will get her back. *Yashi slowly falls asleep while laying against Emuna* **Emuna**: See you soon? *Emuna looks at Yashi as she sits him back onto the bed* What could that have meant?

-After a few hours, Emuna takes Yashi back to his house. The next morning, Yashi wakes up only to realize that the day before was not a dream. Not wanting it to stress him out more, he prepares to go to his Academy-

Chapter 2 – Academy

-Jurono Academy is a couple of paths and small towns away from his home; A few select people know where he lives. His school starts at around 6 pm. Once inside the school, Yashi gets everything he needs from his locker and puts on his required bracelet. Walking to his classroom, which is on the second floor, he goes to sit at his desk. In front of the classroom farthest to the left by the windows. Three minutes until his class starts. Yashi's Major is The Seven Elements Kosai, Hydro, Raito, Kori, Kemuri, Denki, and Doku. This class has been Yashi's Major since he began attending Jurono Academy with Dia-

Yashi pushes the button on his desk to open the Academy Mangole. Yashi swipes through the applications until he finds notes from the three days ago. A couple of students walk in, one being the class president *Iragaru*(w): Pres, look, Yashi is back. *Aosra stops as she spots Yashi, and sighs* *Aosra*: The day has barely started, Iragaru, and you're already trying to cause trouble. *Latarea*: Oh~, come on, Aosra, you~know~you~miss~him~. *Latarea pats Aosra on her back. Aosra blushes before shaking her head* *Aosra*: You're delusional. I'm just worried. *Aosra leans over to Latarea* *Aosra*(w): You know we haven't seen him in days. *Latarea leans back* *Latarea*: You for one should know he's been on vacation. *Latarea starts walking to her desk while looking back at her two friends* Whatever you say. *Latarea takes her seat* *Iragaru*: Hm, hm. *Iragaru takes her seat as well. Three more students walk in* *Tirahi*: Uh, what is that smell, I think I smell a Classroom full of Stage I users. Hahaha. *The other two students with him laugh as well* *Aosra*: Good morning, Colduiat, Sutherland, Yetirsere. *Tirahi*: Heh? Someone's in a good mood. *Haraku looks over at Yashi. Haraku taps Tirahi on the shoulder* *Haraku*(w): Look who's here, Tirahi. *Tirahi looks at Yashi* *Tirahi*(w): Let's let him breathe for a while. *Aosra takes her seat, the three other students do the same. A few minutes later, the teacher walks in* *Pehegima*: Good morning, students. Open your provided Mangoles and sign into today's attendance. *Yáshido taps the button on his desk and another Mangole appears in thin air. He puts in the required information to sign into attendance* *Student*(A)(w): Hey, you notice Dia isn't here? *Student*(B)(w): Yeah, I've noticed. *Yashi feels something blowing on the back of his neck. Yashi turns around* *Yashi*(w): What do you want, Deven? *Deven*(w): I don't want to be a bother, but do you perhaps know where Dia is? I mean, you two are so close together, you would be the only one to know. *Yashi*(w): Maybe she just decided not to come today. *Deven*(w): But that would be a whole week, Dia has never missed a whole week before. She would at least stop by to tell what she has been doing. *Yashi*(w): Look Deven, I'm not sure what you want to hear, but I know just as little as you. *Deven sighs* **Deven**(w): Okay, Taramasu. **Pehegima**: Okay class, let's get started with today's lesson.

-After Yashi's first period is over, he goes to the library to return a few things-

A few of the students Yashi recognizes are also in the library. One of them looks at him as he closes the door behind himself **Mokea**(w): Good morning, Yashi. *Yashi walks over to the shelf that Mokea stands by* **Yashi**(w): Good morning, Mokea. What are you up to? **Mokea**(w): Haha, I actually kind of forgot. I've been here since halfway into the first period. I've just been looking at some different books that I might want to study later on. Especially since Mr. Lamarck hasn't said anything to me. **Yashi**(w): Oh, okay. **Mokea**(w): Hey Yashi, why don't you come after school to do some sparring with me, Mavrik, and Xiciriah? **Yashi**(w): On what? Elilaments, or physical training? *Mokea puts the book she was reading back into the shelf before looking at Yashi with a smile* **Mokea**(w): Does it really matter? You've been gone for a few days; Anything can be beneficial for you. Am I right? **Yashi**(w): True. *Mokea looks down at Yashi's arm and sees a scar on his wrist. She quickly grabs his hand looking at it* **Yashi**(w): Wha-, what are you doing? **Mokea**(w): How'd you get this scar? You never had one on your wrist before. **Yashi**(w): Uhh~. **Voice**(w): Hey, Mokea! *Both Mokea and Yashi look down the aisle to the voice. Another girl is waving her hand* **Classmate**(Girl)(w): Quit your flirting and come back to class! Ms. Halthorne is looking for you! *Mokea quickly lets Yashi's hand go as her eyes widen* **Mokea**(w): Oh no. *Mokea starts to gently jog to her classmate while looking at Yashi* **Mokea**(w): You better show! And you can bring any friends of yours too! *Mokea disappears around the corner with her classmate* **Yashi**(m): Okay then. *Yashi walks to Mr. Lamarck who sits at the main desk. As Yashi opens his mouth placing the books on the rack* **Lamarck**: I don't even want 'ta hear it boy. Saying sorry ain't gonna cover how late 'ya are this time. **Yashi**: Hah, sorry? **Lamarck**: You're lucky you're a good kid or I'd be charging 'ya *Ca* every minute behind the hour. **Yashi**: Thank you for your generosity, Mr. Lamarck. **Lamarck**: No problem boy. I see you don't have your supplies with 'ya. You might want to hurry back to your class before those hooligans finesse your possessions. **Yashi**: Right. *Leaving the library and entering his class once more, Yashi sees that none of his belongings have been tampered with. Despite the crowded room. Reaching his desk, Yashi starts to pack his things. Tirahi, Tamari, and Haraku walk over and surround him* **Tirahi**: What's up, Yashi? **Yashi**: Hello. *Yashi locks his books between his hands and picks them up. Tirahi puts his hands on the top of Yashi's Mangole and pushes it back down on the table* **Tirahi**: Not so fast now. *Yashi lets go of his things and looks Tirahi dead-on* That's more like it. **Yashi**: Tirahi, I just got back from a vacation. I'm not trying to start any trouble with you. **Tirahi**: I'd say you're doing the exact opposite. *Tirahi and Yashi stare at each other* **Yashi**(thts):

He has that same smug look on his face just like Korosi. Maybe I should take him out here, to save me some time. He's so lucky I'm not granted the right to carry a usable bracelet in here. *Tirahi*: Where's your 'girlfriend' Dia? *Yashi clenches his fist* *Tamari*: Yeah, the one that makes you feel less lonely? *Yashi*: Dia and I aren't dating, and why does it matter to you? *Tirahi*: Hey, I'm just asking you a question. No need to act all hostile on me. Besides, you say the same thing every time, what else was I expecting? *Tirahi steps back* I don't even understand how she can be friends with people like you anyway. It's kinda annoying that she's so nice. *Haraku*: I bet she's forgotten about you too, along with everyone else in this Academy. Hahaha. *Tirahi*: It's amazing to remember that she fights alongside the Hero. *Tamari*: You're not even worth her time anymore. She's probably out with him now, while you're just in an Academy. *Yashi feels a small bit of anger rise as he balls his fists. Yashi looks down, trying to hide his face* *Tirahi*: Not so confident now, are we? *Yashi*(m): No, it's just that you're pushing the wrong buttons. *Tamari*: What was that? Speak up, Tirahi can't hear you. **Voice**: Hey, leave him alone! *The three boys turn to the voice. Everyone in the class freezes as they watch the encounter* *Tirahi*: What is it, Aosra? Mind your business. *Aosra*: You must not forget Colduiat, you have two offenses, one more and you're out of Jurono Academy. Doesn't matter if your Elilaments are strong or not. So I recommend you step away from Taramasu right now. *With her hands on her hips and a fierce expression, Tirahi is startled before looking at Yashi with an annoyed face then looks at Haraku and Tamari* *Tirahi*: Come on guys, let's get out of here. *They walk past Aosra and out of the classroom. Aosra walks up to Yashi* *Aosra*: Are you alright, Taramasu? *Yashi sighs* *Yashi*: Yes, Aosra, I'm alright. *Yashi picks his books back up and Reverses his Mangole. He walks next to Aosra, parallel to her* *Yashi*: Thank you. *Yashi continues to walk* *Aosra*: You-, you're welcome, I'm just doing my job. *Right before Yashi leaves the room, the intercom comes on. The sign above the door changes into an exclamation mark while flashing red* *Intercom*: This is a Code Four Halo! This is a Code Four Halo! All classified personnel please prepare for battle! The target is-, *The intercom fizzles out as a loud explosion is heard on the other end. Some of the students start to freak out. Yashi turns and sees Pehegima stand up. Pehegima puts his hands to his side and a gust of energy comes off of him. A Dermal whiffs around onto Pehegima and a staff appears in his right hand* *Aosra*: Everyone please calm down! *Pehegima*: Listen to your Class President. If you all go mad, people may get unnecessarily hurt. *Pehegima looks at Yashi* Move out the way, Mr. Taramasu. *Yashi nods as Pehegima glances out of the door. People are screaming while running through the halls. Pehegima exits the room* *Pehegima*: You all this way! *About fifteen students run inside of Yashi's class* I want you all to stay in here-, ah-, *Pehegima gets hit in his side by something and is knocked out of sight. Aosra runs up to the door* *Aosra*: Shuttle! *The door shuts and locks with a Barre, Aosra turns around to the classroom* Everyone, get to the other side of the classroom, and move the desks up to the front! *The students follow Aosra's orders. As they are, they hear an explosion outside, and the walls start shaking. **Yashi**(thts): This isn't good, I don't want to go Hero mode in front of everyone. It only feels like one Dicipient. *Everyone sits at the back of the classroom completely silent while a lot of fighting is heard outside. Suddenly it stops. The power lights on the ceiling slowly dissipate before the Barre on the door disappears and the lights turn off. Aosra casts a katana. She stands up and slowly walks to the door* **Iragaru**(w): Aosra, what are you doing?! *Aosra looks at Iragaru and puts her finger over her mouth* **Aosra**(w): Ssshhh!~ **A *voice from outside the door***(w): Yashi? Is Yashi in here? **Students**(w): Yashi? What do they want with him? **Yashi**(thts): Yeah, what do they want with me? **Aosra**(w): What if he is? Why do you need him? **Voice**(w): Oh, Aosra, it's you. No time to explain, just please if he is in here, tell him to come out. **Aosra**(w): Who are you? *A head pokes from around the door as it opens all the way* **Person**: It's me, Ro. *Yashi makes direct eye contact with Ro* **Ro**: Yes, he's here, Yashi, follow me. Please. *Yashi looks around him and everyone is spectating him* **Yashi**(thts): This seems sketchy, it would be better for me to go anyway. I can use the Dermal if it comes down to it. *Yashi stands up* **Iragaru**(w): You're gonna go? *Yashi looks back at her* **Yashi**(w): What choice do I have? *Yashi walks up to the door. Aosra is watching him* **Ro**: Come on, quick. *As Yashi walks passes Aosra* **Aosra**(w): Be careful. *Yashi nods. Now in the hallway, Yashi scans around, there are multiple dents in the walls and floors. Patches of fire and water puddles lay in the ground* **Yashi**(thts): There was clearly a fight, why did it get so calm all of a sudden? And where have all the teachers gone? Code Four Halo means a Dicipient has attacked, it's no way they could have wiped out all of them so quickly. *As Yashi is being taken to a room* **Ro**: We're here. Go inside. **Yashi**: Rosken. **Ro**: Yeah? **Yashi**: Who's in that room? *Rosken looks in a full rotation around him and then walks up to Yashi's ear* **Ro**(w): It's Taku. *Yashi clinches* **Yashi**(w): Taku? I've heard rumors he was no longer a Dicipient. **Ro**(w): Same, it's just a rumor though, he is gathering up students for something. I believed this was the best choice for everyone. I did good right? **Yashi**(w): Yeah. *Rosken sighs* **Ro**: Good. That's all I know, good luck. *Ro walks away. Yashi propels his hand towards the already cracked door and opens it. There are three other students inside* **Keshio**: Taramasu's here, haha, what? *Keshio and Namari are sitting on the left side and Otara is standing on the right next to two empty desks. Yashi looks past them to see Taku sitting in a chair staring at him* **Yashi**(thts): Woah, he really is here. *Yashi looks to the right of him and his partner, also Trants, Savanna, who is holding a sword ready for combat* They're both here. **Taku**: Take a seat and close the door. *Yashi slowly pushes the door closed behind him and walks to an empty seat next to Otara. Yashi looks at her as he sits down. Otara doesn't pay any attention to Yashi's arrival. Yashi then looks back at Taku* **Yashi**(thts): Otara's here, Namari, Keshio as well, he's gathered up all of the strongest ones in Jurono. Especially

Otara. **Taku**: I don't have all day before the Balancers arrive. **Keshio**: Alright, all four of us are here. 'You mind starting off on why you attacked the school? *Savanna moves forward slightly, but Taku instantly puts his hand in front of her* **Savanna**: But, Taku. **Taku**: If the kid wants to know, he can know. *Savanna nods before going back into position* **Taku**: I know you've heard quite a few rumors that I'm a Fallen Dicipient, correct? Well, that is true. Now, I wouldn't go as far as saying I attacked you. It was more like me walking in here with Savenna, requesting for you four, and then getting attacked myself, so, Keshio, I don't recommend you start calling names, alright? **Keshio**: Yeah, whatever. **Taku**: As you know, by looking at the ones around you, that you all have some of the highest Oplitals and Elilament ratings at this school. **Keshio**: 'Bout time someone noticed what I'm capable of, but uhm . . . *Keshio looks at Yashi* **Taku**: As hard as your pride deceives you, you are the strongest. **Savanna**: Taku, the sensors have just been activated. We need to get going. **Taku**: Before we leave, are there any of you who want to stay? I'm not forcing you to come with me. *Taku casts a box in his hand* I'm sure you know, once you come with me, you won't be able to attend this Academy anymore. If you're coming, stand. **Yashi**(thts): Well, if I want to learn more about what he is planning~, better go. *With Otara already standing, Yashi stands, then Keshio, following Namari* **Taku**: Nice. *Taku throws the box at the ground in the middle of everyone. The door gets kicked open and slides just behind Otara's legs. A Balancer stands at the entrance entering slightly* **Balancer**: Stop! **Taku**: Hey Balancer, tell your Generals I got some new-recruits, but what I'm doing shouldn't concern them. They will end up thanking me! ^Spirals from the box cover all of them. The Balancer fires a spear at the spirals. Savanna casts a Barrier on the outside of the spirals, and it takes the blow. The spear and Barrier explode into Particles^

-They teleport away-

Chapter 3 – Transition

Yashi scans his surroundings as soon as they are done teleporting **Yashi**(thts): We are in just a normal house. **Taku**: OH, FINALLY, SAVENNA, WE DID IT, IT TOOK US SO MUCH PLANNING, AND SO MUCH TIME, BUT FINALLY, WE DID IT. *Savanna's body shines brightly before she is out of her Trants Dermal* **Savenna**: Yes, I know Taku, calm down. ^A Dermal is heard equipped and a spark of electricity rushes at Taku. Taku's body glows in a light blue aura before knocking the shot away. Taku dashes behind the person in the Dermal, he has a katana around their neck. It's Keshio, and everyone is frozen* **Taku**: I highly recommend you not to do that again. **Keshio**: Stress testing okay. I was only stress testing. ^Savenna walks up to Keshio and points her sword at his feet* **Savenna**: Please don't forget who you are dealing with. Although we want to change, stay mindful of that. *Keshio Dermal vanishes. Taku Reverses his katana and moves from behind Keshio* **Taku**: We did our best not to hurt anyone that attacked us. Well, only slightly wounded, but we did our best. *Yawns* Well, I see you guys tomorrow. Savenna will take you to your dorm. **Namari**: Dorm? **Taku**: Yes, a dorm. She went out of her way and made a dorm especially for you four. *All four of the students look at Savenna. She has her arms crossed and eyes close looking away* **Savenna**: If I didn't, Taku would have had you all sleeping outside on the ground, and I couldn't allow that. **Namari**: Thank you? **Taku**: Now, begone, I must sleep. *Taku looks at Otara before turning around and walking inside of a room, closing the door behind him* **Yashi**(thts): It's quite funny how, if we wanted to, I and Otara could most likely take them both down. And now, he's leaving us alone with Savenna, that's a four versus one, why would he do that? He must have high hopes for us not to attack them. **Savenna**: Alright kids, follow me. *Savenna goes to a door and opens it, everyone follows. Yashi scopes around and he sees nothing but trees. In the direction Savenna is walking, there is a small dorm, enough for about seven residents. As they are walking, Savenna sighs before looking back in front of her. Once they stand at the dorm's entrance* **Savenna**: I don't know too much about you four, but no funny business, okay? *Everyone but Otara shivers* **Keshio**: Don't expect that from any of us. **Namari**: I don't know about those two, but me and Otara are off-limits. *Keshio looks at Namari* **Keshio**: What do you mean by those two?! **Namari**: Hey, I'm just saying, haha. **Savenna**: GOOD, no funny business. See you in a bit. *Savenna starts to walk back to their house* **Keshio**: Wait, Savenna. *Savenna stops* **Savenna**: Yes? **Keshio**: Why does Taku call you Savenna? **Savenna**: Well that's because-, **Otara**: Savanna is what Taku chose to call her for her Trants form, Savenna is her actual name. *Everyone looks at Otara* **Savenna**: Oh-, someone knows their research. But yes, that's why. Any more questions? *Silence* **Yashi**: Uhm, if you don't mind me asking, why did Taku specifically choose us four? **Savenna**: That's information for another day, but all of you are very important for his plan. **Otara**: I don't take it that you mean wrong? **Savenna**: Not at all. Anything else? **Keshio**: Yeah, do you guys have thick blankets? *Namari laughs* What, I'm serious. If I'm going to stay here, I want to be warm. It's freezing out here. **Savenna**: Then the only way to find out is to go in and check for yourself, right? **Keshio**: Yes, ma'am! *Keshio opens the door and walks inside, it closes by itself* **Savenna**: If you still are having trouble figuring out whether or not you should join us, we are in that passageway between Distome and Ruby, so, if you want to go out for a walk, you can. Just don't go past the line I drew out of Kuki Sosa. See you later. **Yashi**: Wait, one more thing. *Savenna stops with a huge sigh* **Savenna**: Yes? **Yashi**: What are we doing here? **Savenna**: Oh, that's right. Today Taku is going to let you all relax today. Tomorrow is when he will explain a few more things to you. As a heads up, you'll be training. *Savenna eyes each one of them* See you later. *Savenna walks to her and Taku's house, entering it. Namari sighs* **Namari**: Well, this day turned in a completely different direction than I was hoping for. **Yashi**: Oh, did it? **Namari**: Yeah. You see, I was supposed to be participating in the Zoka tournament in Adenine, but oh well. *Namari smiles as she walks over to the door. She opens the door* You two coming in? *Otara shakes her head* **Namari**: Yashi? **Yashi**: Yeah. *Otara sits on the bottom of the stairs. Yashi walks up and enters the house behind Namari* **Namari**: Nice, it looks like an actual dorm. *Namari faces Yashi* It's kind of already night, guess it wouldn't hurt to sleep early. Goodnight, Taramasu. **Yashi**: Night. *Namari walks down the left hall from the entrance. Namari looks to the right and gasps as she walks around the corner out of sight* **Yashi**(thts): You know, I need to tell Emuna about this. *As Yashi starts to walk down the hallway in front of the entrance. As he takes his first step, he hears a faint cast outside* That's Otara. *Yashi slowly walks back to the door and slightly creeks it open, Otara is no longer there* Did she teleport? *Yashi opens the door and walks out of it* Forest . . . *Yashi chooses a direction in the forest and starts to walk. After about five hundred yards into the forest* This should be good. *Yashi transforms into the Hero Dermal*

-Somewhere else in the forest, a couple seconds prior-

Otara closes her eyes **Otara**: Ola Transa. *Other than a faint spark of Otara's gray aura, the Cast does nothing* **Tatsumi**: Are you sure you're putting enough Oplitals into it? I never seen it so dull before. **Otara**: Tatsumi, I did this many times before without even trying, and you know that. **Tatsumi**: That's the point. You think maybe you've . . . become . . . you know? **Otara**: Become what? Say it . . . *A noise is heard in the distance; they feel a surge of aura cross over theirs* **Tatsumi**: You heard that right? **Otara**: I felt it too, someone just equipped a Dermal. **Tatsumi**: That's convenient. Do you want to check?

Otara squeezes her palms as she looks in the direction it came from **Tatsumi**: That's your 'obvious' face, so I will assume yes. *By Yáshido, he opens his Mangole. Looking at his contacts trying to find Emuna's name, he scrolls across Dia's first* **Yáshido**(thts): Maybe later . . . I could try calling her. *Yáshido scrolls back down to Emuna and taps the screen. Instantly, it is answered. Yáshido turns his Mangole into an earpiece and attaches it to his ear* **Emuna**(M): Yes, Hero? Are you alright? I've seen the news. **Yáshido**: Yes, I'm alright. It seems that Taku is no longer a Dicipient. **Emuna**(M): Good to hear. **Yáshido**: But I don't know what he is planning still, I'm going to be staying here until I get a good clue, okay? **Emuna**(M): Alright. *Yáshido feels someone near him* **Yáshido**(w): Emuna, I'll call you back, okay? *Feeling the awareness in his voice, Emuna doesn't question Yáshido* **Emuna**(M): Emhm. *Yáshido Reverses his Mangole. He turns to the side where he feels the aura* **Yáshido**: If someone is over there, I advise you to come out. *The area remains desolate before Gray Particles start to vanish upwards a few feet in front of him* **Yáshido**(thts): Otara, what's she doing here? **Otara**: Hero? Is that you? **Yáshido**: Yes, it's me. Misugami, what are you doing out here at such a late hour? **Otara**: It really is . . . *Otara mischievously smiles* **Yáshido**: Are you going to answer? **Otara**: No, Hero, I have a demand for you. **Yáshido**: A demand? What would that be? **Otara**: You're going to fight me. Ola Transa. *A bright golden light illuminates from Otara's body. Covering her appearance entirely. The light fades away starting from her now golden greaves. As the light fully fades away, Otara's is equipped with a thick, golden Dermal* Apara Lance! *Otara holds out her right hand as a lance is summoned in it, she points it towards Yáshido. Yáshido just watches. After a couple of seconds of staring* What are you waiting for, aren't you going to cast your sword? **Yáshido**(thts): Otara's being aggressive. It's scarier than what I seen on the news years back. **Yáshido**: What do you mean? **Otara**: Where's your weapon? *Yáshido holds out his hand* **Yáshido**(thts): Why won't you summon. Wait, that's right. When I got pushed off, my cast-assist fell off the platform. I can't summon Jeshika directly without it. **Yáshido**: It's quite the story, Otara. I lost it. *Otara's guard drops a bit* **Otara**: You . . . lost it? **Yáshido**: Yup, pretty funny right? **Otara**: The 7th Generation Hero has lost his sword. *Otara puts up her lance* Behind you, Yáshido. **Yáshido**: Feels like a Familiar. What about your friend? *Tatsumi comes from behind a tree* **Tatsumi**: This is not how I wanted my first encounter with you, but hey, Yáshido. **Yáshido**: Nice to meet you. *The sound of trees collapsing is heard behind Yáshido* **Otara**: Hero, catch. Apara Lance Duel! *Yáshido catches the second lance, they hear a growl as a giant figure is standing amid the trees. Tatsumi joins them. The Type One Familiar stands in front of them. Staring down at them it roars with might* **Otara**: Definitely an Epsilon. **Yáshido**: Compress it right? **Otara**: Of course. **Yáshido**: Alright let's go. ^Yáshido activates his Zoka Swiftness and dashes towards the Epsilon. The Epsilon tries to stump Yáshido, but he easily dodges. Yáshido daps the Epsilon in its front leg. The Epsilon then jumps to Tatsumi who shoots a beam of water right into the bottom of the Epsilon in response. The pressure of the water knocks the Epsilon over its side into the air. While in mid-air, Otara gets a clean hit right into the side of the Epsilon with her Lance. The Epsilon roars in pain. Once the Epsilon falls onto its feet, it charges at Yáshido. The Epsilon claws spark in a flame as it tries to strike Yáshido with them. Yáshido aims the Lance at the Epsilon^ **Yáshido**: Momentum Gear! ^The Lance goes right through the claw of the Epsilon and into the air. In pain, the Epsilon falls flat on its stomach^ **Yáshido**: One more. ^Before Yáshido could say anything else, Otara is already above the Epsilon using one of her Personal Casts^ **Otara**: Tatsumi! **Tatsumi**: What, oh-, yeah got it! ^Tatsumi summons a Barre around them to stop Otara's attack from damaging anything else^ **Otara**: Bow Down! To the Lance of Apara! ^Otara's body and Lance glow in a magnificent aura, blinding even, as she comes down on the Epsilon's head. Otara's Lance penetrates through the Epsilon and a beam of light comes from out of the Epsilon's mouth. The Epsilon's Sustain vanishes off of it allowing them to compress it. Otara Protojets from out of the Epsilon's mouth and lands next to Yáshido^ **Otara**: Go, Tatsumi! **Tatsumi**: Untangle, from the dark spirit! ^A yellow aura starts to surround the Epsilon as it cries in pain. Its Pure Energy starts to evaporate from it as it gets smaller. Once all the Pure Energy is gone, what remains is a statue of a dog^ **Tatsumi**: Oh man, it had that corrupted energy for too long and its body couldn't handle it. *Yáshido walks to the dog and takes a knee. The dog statue starts shining before it comes back to life and starts barking* **Yáshido**: We rarely get these situations anymore. **Tatsumi**: Woah, I've never seen someone do it up close, that's awesome. **Yáshido**(thts): I'm hoping she still doesn't want to fight. *Yáshido looks at Otara and Tatsumi* **Yáshido**: That was pretty nice how we all worked together. *Yáshido focuses his attention on Otara* Despite your introverted style, no one can deny how intelligent you are, Otara. Just seeing you in any battle, there's not a lot of people who can comprehend the level you think at. *Otara looks at Yáshido* **Yáshido**(thts): Oh no. **Yáshido**: Here. *Yáshido hands Otara the dog* **Otara**: Me . . . **Yáshido**: Sure, why not? You did help, and I'm sure you'll take better care of him than anyone else here. And besides, we don't want to let him loose again. *Yáshido turns around* You two stay safe. Oh, wait, here's your lance back. *Yáshido turns around and hands Otara the lance. Otara turns to her side* **Otara**: You, you can keep it. **Yáshido**: What? **Otara**: Keep it, you don't want to be defenseless would you? Use it until you get your sword back. **Yáshido**: You're right, thank you. *Yáshido holds up the Lance* Apara Lance. *The lance vanishes into Particles* You two get home safely. *Yáshido turns around and starts walking away* **Otara**: Wait, Yáshido. **Yáshido**: Emhm? *Yáshido turns his neck to look at Otara. Otara briefly sighs, before losing eye contact with Yáshido* **Otara**: Never mind. *Yáshido nods as he continues to walk away* **Yáshido**(thts): I think she was going to tell me about Taku . . . but I'm finally free. I need to beat her back to the dorm. I don't want to run into her on my way back. She wanted to fight me though. That would be interesting, although it's not fair once I use my Seal. I don't think even Otara can handle that. And that's the first time I ever saw or heard her break character since she moved here. She's normally quiet and emotionless. I guess she just decides not to show it. I wonder what that was about. *By Otara* **Tatsumi**: There he goes, I guess you never did get what you wanted. **Otara**: It's irrelevant now. The time will come when it needs to. *By Yáshido* **Yáshido**(thts): This time I'll summon a Barre around me. *Yáshido summons a Barre around himself to transform back to his normal state. After he Reverses the Barre* **Yashi**: Now it's time to get back.

-Yashi finds the dorm. He quickly walks through the halls, trying not to wake anyone. Once he finds a suitable room, the one third farthest down the central hall, he enters and closes the door-

Yashi lies down in the bed **Yashi**(thts): Now I'm the one undercover lurking in the enemy's territory. Well, I'm not sure I want to classify them as enemies now. I have a good feeling they seem like they are trying to do something good for a change. Who knows? It's weird though, being in the creation of someone who was just attacking villages a couple of years ago. Then again, that's why it is so surprising, Taku's been on the low for a few months. And like he said, he's been planning this forever, and he's just now pulled it off. I'll just have to wait and see. Besides, I've been staring at this ceiling for too long, I think it's time for some sleep. *Yashi turns and faces the wall*

-Yashi falls asleep-

Yashi wakes up. Attempting to grip onto his surroundings but can't manage to find anything to grip on to. Yashi feels as though he's being pulled down. He then hears flames above him. Looking up and Yashi sees his left hand holding onto a ledge. Yashi has his Hero Dermal equipped. Dia stands on his gauntlet with a flame aura around her. Dia's face is blacked out from the heat waves and smoke surrounding her. Her right arm slowly reaches out to Yashi. Yashi tries to move his other hand out to her but it is constrained by something. Looking down, another hand holding onto his right arm. The hand is inhuman, having multiple fingers grasping onto him, and a ghostly gray color. The gray color peels off the disfigured hand like a snake sheds its skin. Yashi tries to shake the hand off, but his struggle makes it pull harder. Yashi feels something wet drip onto his helmet. He looks back up and tears are coming from Dia's face. Dia lifts her foot and Yashi becomes extremely heavy. Yashi's hand slips and he starts to fall, as he is falling Dia walks away from the edge. Right before Yashi's vision gets fully covered in darkness. Yashi jumps up out of the dream. His heart is beating fast, heavy breathing and sweat is all around his forehead **Yashi**(thts): A dream? Oh my . . . *Yashi smashes his face together. He looks at the bright god rays coming from the curtains* It's morning. *Yashi leans up, putting his feet onto the floor. He notices the closet door is open. Standing up, he walks to it and opens it all the way* They gave us clothes too? *Yashi gets fully prepared before heading outside. Keshio is positioned against the wood that's connecting the stairs to the roof, Namari is sitting on the bottom of the stairs* **Yashi**: Good morning, Namari, Keshio. **Namari**: Oh, good morning, Taramasu. **Keshio**: Taramasu, what's up? **Yashi**: You all don't have to call me by my last name. **Keshio**: Until you show me some latent strength, you're gonna be a Taramasu. **Namari**: Keshio, apologize to Yashi, that was uncalled for. **Keshio**: Nah, don't feel like I need to hear that from a Katsuni either. *Yashi sighs* **Yashi**: Are we waiting for something? **Keshio**: Taku said something about making a training ground, so I think he's getting it set up or something. **Yashi**: Okay. *Yashi looks out into the field* Has anyone seen Otara? She wasn't inside. **Namari**: Behind you. *Yashi turns around and Otara is standing against the wall next to the door with her arms crossed and eyes closed* **Yashi**: Good morning, Otara. *Otara opens her eyes, staring at Yashi* **Otara**: Good morning, Taramasu. *Yashi sits on the top stair. Keshio turns to Namari and Otara* **Keshio**: So~, what are you guys' opinions on those two? **Namari**: I feel awkward, being here in general. **Keshio**: I feel you on that. Taramasu? *Keshio looks down at Yashi* **Yashi**: I'm more worried about what they might do to us than anything else. **Keshio**: Sounds like something you'd say. Misugami? *Keshio and Otara look at each other at the same time* **Otara**: I'm neutral. **Keshio**: I see. Well, I think that our opportunities to be great have arrived. **Yashi**: What do you mean by that? **Keshio**: Who knows, we'll just have to wait. ^All of them look to the forest on their right as they feel a wave of Hydro being shot at them from that direction. Keshio gets off the pillar^ **Keshio**: What was that? ^The four of them see multiple trees collapsing as a thin flat disk made out of water cuts right through the bottom of the tree line closest to them. The spinning disk flys past the dorm. Namari and Yashi get up^ **Yashi**(thts): Feels like Taku and Savenna, but they're not aiming at us. ^More trees start to collapse as a clear area is seen behind the fallen trees, Taku and Savanna are standing in the clear area, both looking at the students. A large Magical Circle appears above the falling trees and goes down on top of them. The circle and the trees disappear as the mCircle touches the ground. Taku starts waving at them^ **Keshio**: Time to see what this is all about. *They walk over to them* **Taku**: Good morning, recruits. **Students**: Good morning. **Taku**: So, how do you like it? *They all look around the space. It is layered with a brittle beige metal in circular form and to the left from the dorm's view, a bench with three levels sits* **Namari**: This is the training ground you mentioned? **Taku**: Precisely. Savenna, go and bring our guest. *Savanna nods as she starts walking towards their house* **Yashi**: I have to say, it's nice. **Taku**: Thank you. Okay, so, today, I brought someone to continue teaching you. **Keshio, Namari & Yashi**: Teach us? **Taku**: I know right, I was just as surprised as you when she agreed. *Taku tilts his head past them* There she is now. *The students turn around, a girl stands next to Savanna* She needs no introduction, but here is Kamira Exna, your new teacher. *Keshio, Namari & Yashi*: WHAT?! *Taku*: That's right, so, behave yourselves. *Otara*: One of the three Exna sisters, how? *Taku*: She was actually looking for an opportunity to teach. *Kamira approaches behind Savanna waving with a smile* *Kamira*: Hello you all, it's nice to see you all so excited to see me. *Kamira scans the students* Oh. Ms. Misugami, it's nice to meet you in person. *Otara*: You as well. *Taku*: You have it from here, Kamira? *Kamira*: Yes. *Taku*: Then I will leave you to it. Thank you again. *Kamira*: No, thank you, Taku. *Taku and Savanna walk away* *Keshio*: Wow, I can't believe he got a hold of you. *Kamira*: Really? Believe me when I say that he was almost attacked. But I held my composure, and had a nice, civilized chat with him, and he seems completely clean to me, and considering when I was by myself when he approached, it could have ended really bad if he was still, you know 'evil'. BUT enough of that, let's get started with what I have planned for you today. Ancestrials, any of you have one? Well, you attended Jurono, so you wouldn't have any Ancestrials, my apologies. Who wants to be the first to learn how to summon a Familiar? *Keshio*: Right here. *Keshio puts his hand up* *Kamira*: Keshio Revalorese, I assume you already have Ancestrial Summoning, right? *Keshio*: Yeah, but I don't use it at all. *Kamira*: No worries, you're up first. Everyone else please stand back a bit. *Namari, Otara, and Yashi stand back a couple of yards* Good, now, what kind of Ancestrial do you want to summon? Type One Ancestrials are based on animals. They normally have a Sustain one to five times of their summoner, depending on the rank you can cast it at. The ideal Type One Familiar will take 50,000 Oplitals for the initial summon and 8,000 afterward. Type One Ancestrials under the Charlie rank can only hold two dominant Elilaments and three interchangeable Elilaments. Type Two Familiars are human-based. They take the most Oplitals on the first summon, ranging up to 100,000 at moments, but after that, it'll take about 20,000. Type Two Familiars have the same Sustain as their summoner or lower. They can be equipped with as many Elilaments as you have Oplitals to give. They are the only Familiar type that doesn't have a proximity range before automatically Reversing themselves. The final type of Familiar is Type Three. Type Three Familiars are a little special. They can be made from anything. A jacket, a chair, basically anything. *Keshio*: I've always wanted a Type Three Familiar. *Kamira*: Okay, close your eyes, and make sure that you keep a stable release of your Pure Energy. *Keshio's light green aura covers his body like a shade* *Keshio*: Okay, done. *Kamira*: Get a good idea of how you want your Familiar to operate, free-ranged, or bound. Once you do that, sense your Familiar, what types of Elilaments do you want it to hold, how much strain it will put on your body while trying to keep it as effective as possible. How much of your Pure Energy would it take to use it? Do you want it to be a *sustain*, let your Familiar free roam until you cast it away, a *hold*, whenever you cast it, you will supply it with a steady source of Pure Energy and as soon as you stop it gets Reversed, or a *carry*, you cast it and it Reverses itself seconds later? Once you have what type of summoning you want, feel it as if you were holding it, and how you would see it. Finally, give it a cast. *Keshio stands still for a couple of seconds* **Keshio**: Scheetz . . . Aperta! *Sparkles appear around Keshio, it all combines in front of him into a small pen* **Kamira**: Perfect. **Keshio**: Yeah, I actually did it! **Kamira**: What kind of Familiar is it? *Keshio walks over to the pen and picks it up. Keshio clicks the end of it and his ears point up* **Kamira**: Zoka Hearing, I see. Pretty well thought out. **Keshio**: Wonderful teaching skills. **Kamira**: Thank you. How about you Namari Katsuni, do you have Ancestrial Summoning? **Namari**: Yes, please! *Keshio and Namari switch places. Keshio sits on the bench, opposite of Otara and Yashi, toying with his new Familiar* **Yashi**: Hey, Otara. **Otara**: Yes, Taramasu? **Yashi**: I've seen a lot about you, but I have never seen you with a Familiar of your own. Have you ever summoned a Familiar before? *Otara looks at Yashi confused* **Otara**: Have you not heard? **Yashi**(thts): Yes, Yáshido's heard. **Yashi**: No? **Otara**: Do you want to know the story? **Yashi**: Sure. **Otara**: Give me your hand. *Yashi gives Otara his hand* **Yashi**: And? **Otara**: Otara. *Instantly they vanish into a dark space* **Yashi**(thts): Woah, what's this, I've never felt anything like this before. *Suddenly they are standing in the air looking over a village* **Otara**: This is where I used to live. **Yashi**: This is Watashimono Delshigo. **Otara**: Yes. How did you know? **Yashi**: Re-, research?~ But Otara, what Magic is this? Is this a Personal Cast? *Otara ignores Yashi's question* **Otara**: It's also where I cast my first Familiar. *Yashi looks at the village* I was eight, today was the village's Hero Day. We were speaking in our native tongue so refrain from trying to loosen my grip on your hand. I'm only translating it into Atiro for you. **Yashi**: Got it. **Otara**: Also, yes that is me you're about to see.

Chapter 4 - Misugami's Mistake

Otara: Watch and listen. *Otara squeezes Yashi's hand as she activates Zoka Hearing and Vision*

-Inside the village-

Ota'Nomi: Otara, come on. *Otara*: Where is Kufa? *Ota'Nomi*: Good question, maybe she's still changing, go and see. Tell her to come on so we can get started. *Otara*: Okay! *Yashi*(thts): Oh, this is pre-emotionless Otara. Kind of weird. *Otara runs inside of a house* K., are you in here? We need to get started. *As Otara walks past a door, something covers her mouth from behind and pulls her into the room* *Kufa*(w): Otara, ssshhh~. *Kufa lets go of Otara* *Otara*(w): You could have just told me to come in here, you didn't have to nearly suffocate me. *Kufa*(w): You're over-exaggerating, we both know you would have hurt me if you were in pain. *Otara cools down* *Otara*(w): Kufa, what are you doing in here? Iroas Day is about to start. *Kufa*(w): I found the Enchanted Book Grand Euvex is always talking about. *Otara*: The Enchanted Book? *Kufa*(w): Shh~, you know what I'm talking about. The book our family tree has been passing down. *Otara*: The Book of Apara, seriously?! *Kufa*(w): Whisper, Otara, whisper. *Otara*(w): Oh, I'm sorry like this? *Otara giggles* *Kufa*(w): You're too playful. Follow me. *Kufa leads Otara to a hidden passage. A door with Magical bound locks around it. A small amount of Kufa's Pure Energy flows into the door as she raises a hand towards it. The door opens and a chest sits at the end of a small tunnel* *Otara*: This is what you've been doing this whole time? You're so nosy. *Kufa*: I just happened to stumble across it. *Otara*: How do you stumble across a chest tha-, *Kufa*: Never mind that, it's just as I said, I stumbled across it. *They look at the chest* *Otara*: How do you know the book is inside? *Kufa grabs Otara's wrist and sets it next to the front of the chest* *Kufa*: It has the same marking on your wrist, your mom's, Grand Euvex's, Tafia's, and her dad's. *The chest starts making a sound, both Kufa and Otara jump back away from it* It didn't do that before. I'm actually glad you were the one who came, I think you have to be one hundred percent Misugami to open it. *Otara*: So, I can try? *Kufa*: Go for it. *Otara moves back to the chest and reaches out to the handle. Otara's hand gets pulled down onto the chest. Pure Energy starts to ooze from her marking into the marking on the chest. Suddenly, the chest opens, and the book floats up. Multiple lights shine outward from the pages. The text on the pages glitter in hundreds of colors. Both Kufa and Otara stare at the amazing scene. Although being able to see the scriptures, Yashi cannot understand any of it* *Kufa*: Woah, I never imagined it would look

like this. **Otara**: That's because you're too old. **Kufa**: I'm fifteen, Otara, in seven years, you'll be the same age as me. **Otara**: Haha, but then you'll be even older hahaha. **Kufa**: I'm going to ignore that. Try summoning one of the Familiars. **Otara**: You sure? **Kufa**: If you don't want to, you don't have to. But you're so talented, I don't see you not being able to summon one. And you'll just show Grand Euvex more of your potential. *Otara grabs the book and starts looking through it with Kufa* **Otara**: I don't understand any of this. **Kufa**: Maybe because you have it upside down. *Otara flips the book right side up* **Otara**: Oh yeah, haha. **Kufa**: You're hopeless. Look here's one. *Otara looks at the words above Kufa's finger* **Otara**: Isn't that a Gamma? **Kufa**: Yeah? Do you want something stronger? **Otara**: Yes. **Kufa**: Let's see. *Kufa scans through many different pages* I don't know Otara; these look pretty complicated. I think you should just stick with the Gamma, okay? **Otara**: Fine. *Otara looks around* We need to get in a more open spot. **Kufa**: There're three different casts, choose one and memorize it so we can get going. [Otara puts her other hand on Yashi's head] *Otara looks over at the page on the left* **Otara**(thts): I'll try this Charlie instead, Apara P-, pjerd Alstaen. Ok, got it. [Otara removes her hand] **Otara**: I'm ready. *Kufa leads Otara to a more open room* **Kufa**: You summon it, and I'll watch the door just in case you need to cancel the cast okay. *Otara nods. Kufa looks away then back at Otara* You DO know how to stop summoning it right? **Otara**: Trust me, I know what I'm doing. **Kufa**: Somehow, I doubt you, Otara. **Otara**: Just get to the door. *Otara squints her eyes and smiles* **Kufa**: Okay, Otara, I'm going. *Kufa walks to the door. Otara is on the opposite side of the room. **Otara**(m): Here I go. **Otara**: Apara! Pjerd! Alstaen! *Instantly a large amount of Pure Energy gets extracted from Otara's body and flows into an orb in front of her. Otara falls from the subtle grab but quickly stands back up watching the creature form* **Kufa**: Wait did she just say pjerd? That's a Charlie! (Y): Otara, what are you doing?! **Otara**(Y): Summoning a Familiar, you?! *Kufa runs back to Otara. The outline of a horse starts to form and absorb more Pure Energy coming from Otara* I did it, K.! **Kufa**: No, Otara you didn't. This is dangerous, you need to Reverse the cast. **Otara**: NO. **Kufa**: What do you mean NO. You need to cancel the cast, or we need to get out of here. *Kufa grabs Otara's arm, but Otara shrugs away using a light Protojet* Come on, Otara! **Otara**: No! I'm tired of being treated like a weakling! **Kufa**: That's only because you're eight, Otara! **Otara**: Well too bad, I'm going to stay here! *Otara turns back to the Alstaen and raises her hands towards it, feeding it more of her Pure Energy. The Alstaen's size increases exponentially* **Ota'Nomi**: What's going on in here?! *Ota'Nomi runs to the two girls* **Kufa**: Otara won't come. *Ota'Nomi looks at the Charlie Alstaen* **Ota'Nomi**: Who's summoning this thing?! **Kufa**: Otara. *Ota'Nomi stands in front of Otara, her eyes are grayed out, but her hands are still pointed towards the Alstaen at her stomach level* **Ota'Nomi**: It's already happened to her. **Kufa**: The Trivilation? **Ota'Nomi**: Yes, stopping her now can damage more than just this building. *Ota'Nomi puts her hands on Otara's shoulders*

Ota'Nomi(w): You got this, Lil sis. *Ota'Nomi*: Let's go, Kufa. *Ota'Nomi lets go of Otara and starts to jog towards Kufa* *Kufa*: What about Otara? Can't we do anything? *Ota'Nomi*: Not even I know the Reverse to a Charlie Cast. Someone higher up will have to do it. We can at least get out since my sister will be protected. *Kufa*: O-, okay. *Ota'Nomi glows light blue as she picks Kufa up and dashes through the building to the exit. As they're just getting out of the building, the Alstaen starts breaking through the ceiling. Outside the building* *Grand Euvex*: Are you all alright? *Kufa*: Grand Euvex, I thought you were asleep? *Grand Euvex*: I was, but then I felt that Charlie's aura, I couldn't just ignore it. It's demolishing that building. Fascinating isn't it? *Otara's mom and dad arrive* *Tera*: Father, I called the Balancers. They should arrive any minute. *Toby*: Is everyone out of the building? *Ota'Nomi*: Otara's still inside. *Tera*: Otara! You left your sister in there! *Ota'Nomi*: Mom, she was already in a Trivilation when I arrived, I couldn't do anything but get Kufa out. *Tera*: No excuses, Ota! *Tera charges towards the house activating multiple Zokas, but Toby gets in front of her also with his Zokas* *Toby*: You know better than I do not to go in there. *Grand Euvex*: Stand aside, Toby, let her go. *Toby*: But. *Grand Euvex*: You should be getting prepared to fight, with the rest of the Misugamis with potency. *Toby*: Yes sir. *Tera*: Where is she?! *Ota'Nomi*: Guidance Room. *Tera beams right through the front door. Not a moment after, the Alstaen breaks part of the wall. The rubble blocks the entrance. When Tera finds Otara, she is laying on the ground. Otara's body is engulfed in her aura as Pure Energy is still being sucked from her into the Familiar. Tera dashes to her* *Tera*: Otara! Otara! *Tera starts gently shaking Otara while healing her body. Otara slowly retains her consciousness* *Otara*(m): Mo-, mom? *Tera Reverses her Zoka Swiftness* *Tera*: Oh, sweetie! You're back! *Tera holds on to Otara* *Otara*(m): I'm sorry mom, I thought I could do it. I thought I could control the Familiar. *Tera*: It's okay, Otara. *Tera aims one of her hands at the Alstaen* Apara Contract! ^The Familiar stops accepting energy from Otara and starts to become opaque. The Alstaen's hind legs kick against the walls behind it while loudly squealing. The wall crashes against Tera's floor causing it to drop down multiple levels. Tera covers Otara and summons a Barre around them as the large bricks and wedges slam against them. Outside, as the Alstaen disconnects from the building^ *Kufa*: No~No~Noo!~ *The world around them begins to fade back into darkness after a sudden flash* *Otara*: Namari is done. I'll have to show you the rest another day. It will take a while before we're back. *Yashi*: Okay, thanks for showing me. *Otara*: No problem. *Yashi*(thts): How can she still see what's going on in the real world? It's clear she's using either Ace or Stage I of Kuki Sosa. Maybe even Elemental Void, but how can she replay memories? If I could take a guess, maybe she's always using Zoka Vision. I know it has something to do with that. *Yashi slowly glances at Otara's face. He sees a tear come down from Otara's right eye* *Yashi*: Otara? * Otara's eyes widen as she realizes she's crying. Otara wipes her eye* *Otara*: It's just that, my emotions come back whenever I visit this memory. It's fine.

Don't worry about me. **Yashi**(thts): I feel bad now. But her eyes, they have always been light blue. That means it's a possibility.

-In the training grounds-

Namari: It's so cool! **Kamira**: Good Namari, you did an excellent job. **Namari**: Blazing Lfow! *Namari Reverses her Familiar* **Kamira**: Couldn't you have come up with a more original name other than wolf backwards? Hahaha. **Namari**: What? I think it sounds cool. La~, fow~. Lfow! **Kamira**: Haha, yeah. It's 'cool', Namari. *Kamira looks over to Otara and Yashi* But it seems as though two of our students fell asleep. **Namari**: What? *Kamira walks over to Otara and Yashi. Kamira starts snapping her fingers in front of their faces* **Kamira**: Hello?! You two wake up. *Otara and Yashi come back to themselves* **Yashi**: Huh? *As Yashi's vision comes back, the entire of his field of view is filled with Kamira's face* **Kamira**: I can't believe you two actually fell asleep. Especially you, Otara. **Otara**: I wasn't sleeping, look. *Otara holds up Yashi's hand* **Kamira**: What does that mean? You fell asleep while holding hands? **Otara**: I'm sorry, I forgot you're an Exna, not a Misugami. Delta Wolfarus, right? **Kamira**: Oh, so you did see. **Otara**: Good job, Namari. **Namari**: Thank you. *Kamira turns towards Yashi and leans forward* **Kamira**: How about you, Yashi Taramasu, did you see it? Yashi(thts)(Otara): Her cast is Blazing Lfow. *As Yashi hears this, an electric surge runs through his arm. In reaction, Yashi lets go of Otara's hand and leans away from Kamira* **Yashi**: No, sorry. *Kamira stands straight up* **Kamira**: Come on then. Namari loves the cast so much, I'm sure she will show you up close. *Kamira turns around and starts walking towards Namari* **Yashi**: Okay. *Yashi stands up* ^Right before Yashi takes a step, he feels something move below him. Yashi looks down and a noticeable dent has formed in the ground at the tip of his shoes, about a yard long. Another dent is parallel to that one. The distance between the two lines is also a yard long. Kamira turns around and looks at Otara. Yashi does the same. Otara is looking in their direction but not at them, then Otara looks at Yashi. Yashi turns and looks at Kamira, who then looks at Yashi and smiles before turning around and starts back walking^ **Yashi**(thts): What was that about? ^Yashi continues to walk before he feels the pressure below him again. This time, the dent deeper into the ground and stretched out in front of him more than last time. Yashi looks at Kamira who has stopped walking. Kamira turns back around with a competitive face^ **Yashi**(thts): She's looking at Otara, right? *Yashi turns around to Otara, she is looking at Kamira* **Otara**: Yashi, walk around her. **Yashi**: Around her? *Yashi turns to Kamira, she is smiling while staring at Otara* **Kamira**: I don't know what she's talking about. Do you, Yashi? *Namari stands next to Kamira* **Namari**: What's going on? **Kamira**: Yashi's coming to see you summon your Familiar. **Yashi**: Hey, uhm, why do I feel like I'm surrounded by both of your auras. ^The line in the ground moves towards Otara instead of Kamira^ **Kamira**: Well this . . . turned out . . . fiercer than I intended. *Keshio

41

joins them* *Keshio*: You guys alright? *Yashi*: I think they're having a competition or something. *Keshio*: I don't think you should be standing in the middle of them then. *Yashi moves out of the way. Otara looks completely calm while Kamira looks like she's struggling. The line deepens towards Kamira* *Kamira*: I can't believe she's stronger than my Barrier and Psycho. *Otara*: Do you want me to stop? *Kamira*: No, keep going. ^The line gets really close to Kamira's legs. Gray particles collapse where the lines settle. There is a Barre with Denki, electricity, flowing around it* *Yashi*: Wait, I was going to walk into that? *Kamira*: Well, it's too late now. *Otara*: Are you sure, Kamira, if I go any further, you might get hurt. *Kamira*: Trust me. You're not going to win this. ^The Barre moves towards Otara slightly^ *Otara*: I know you're stronger than this. *Kamira*: Just let me work my way up, okay? ^The Barre moves closer to Otara. Now equidistant between them; Their auras start to become visible as each of them activate Ikkasei^ *Keshio*: Woah, they are serious about this. *Otara stands* *Voice*: Hey! What are you doing?! *All of them turn, except Otara and Kamira, to see Savenna walking up to them* *Savenna*: You two, calm down with that aura. People miles away can feel that. *Kamira*: You first. *Otara waves her hair* *Kamira*: Oh, okay fine. *Both of their auras disappear and so does the Barre* *Namari*: Well that was something. *Kamira*: Why do you have to be so strong? *Otara*: Why did you have to put up an invisible Barre for Yashi to walk into? *Kamira*: You know why. *Sighs* So much of my Pure Energy wasted. That was fun though, it was the first one I've ever done. *Otara*: I see, and you enjoyed it? *Kamira*: Yeah? *Silence. Kamira looks at Yashi* Well, Mr. Taramasu, do you want to summon a Familiar? *Yashi*: No thanks. *Kamira*: That's it? Just a no? *Yashi*: I'm not an Ancestral type of person. *Kamira*: Oh, okay then. Today's lessons are over. I'll see you all tomorrow. *Kamira turns to Savenna* Make sure to tell Taku I'm gone. *Savenna*: We-, sure. *Kamira walks away* Oh, minors, always into trouble. *Savenna facepalms* We have food, come and eat it while it's hot. *Keshio*: Well deserved. *Namari*: Haha, we did one thing and now she's gone. *Yashi*: It's Kamira Exna, what do you expect? *Voice*: I guess you guys don't want to eat then; I'll just throw it away. *They turn to see Savenna nearly at the dorm* *Keshio*: Hey! *Keshio activates his Zoka Swiftness and starts running* *Namari*: I am a bit hungry. *Yashi*: Let's go then, I think she might be serious. *All of them prepare for dinner*

Chapter 5 – Vacant

-After dinner, Yashi is standing outside of the dining room. Namari and Keshio are still inside. Otara and Savenna have gone to their rooms. Taku walks up to Yashi-

Taku: Hey, Yashi, you got an hour? *Yashi*: An hour? *Taku*: Yeah, an hour or two possibly. I need to head to a market to get some more supplies. *Yashi*: Yeah, I understand. *Taku*: I want to go to a side market; They don't really look into who you are. *Yashi*: I know, I've been to one. *Taku*: Okay, then let's go. *Yashi*: Which one exactly? *Taku*: I figured you'd know a few, that's not so far. *Yashi*(m): We are pretty far from Dreium, so maybe~. *Yashi*: Okay I know one.

-Taku and Yashi leave his base. Yashi starts walking along a path to a foreign market. During the walk, Yashi notices that Taku looks quite anxious, and a conversation is non-existent. Inside the market-

Yashi: Not that many people here. *Taku*: That's good. *Yashi*: So, what are you looking for? *Taku*: Let's see, hmmm~. We need meat, some sauce for Savenna, and I don't know, uhm, water? *Yashi*: You came here not knowing what you wanted? *Taku*: Well, we especially need that sauce. It's called Noi Sauce. *Yashi*: We would be extremely lucky if we found it. *Taku and Yashi walk down multiple aisles trying not to have any contact with other civilians* *Taku*: Oh-, here it is. *Yashi looks at the can* *Yashi*: So, this is what I was tasting, interesting. *Taku*: Savenna is fairly new to this, 'cooking phase'. Not too long ago, she had dark auras coming from everything she made. Ha, one time, I think it spoke to me even. Don't tell her I said that. *Yashi*: My lips are sealed. *Taku reaches for the can. As he does, someone bumps into him causing him to drop the can. Taku turns to the stranger* *Taku*: Hey, watch who you're shoving, pal. *The stranger is in a hood; they stop walking and turn towards Taku* *Stranger*: Ta-, Taku? *Taku stops and looks at the figure* *Taku*: Kata? *The stranger takes their hood off* *Kata & Taku*: It is you!! *Yashi takes a step back* *Yashi*(thts): Kata, another Dicipient?! Please don't tell me this was a setup. Does he know I'm the Hero? I'm so confused right now. *Kata*: What a pleasure meeting you here mate. *Taku*: I wouldn't say that. *Kata*: Come on, don't be like that. Remember the good times? *Taku walks up next to Kata* *Taku*(w): I'm not a Dicipient anymore Kata and you know that. *Kata*(w): Indeed. *Kata puts his hand on Taku's shoulder* A Fallen Dicipient, that's what you are. *Taku*(w): You can't attack me with the treaty in place. *Kata*: Attack you? I'm not that foolish. And speaking on the treaty, Lark is planning on breaking it. *Both Taku and Yashi jump a little* *Yashi*(thts): What did he just say?! *Taku*(w): He wants to do what?! *Kata*(w): I know right, I was quite surprised as well. *Taku*(w): But he can't just go do that. *Kata*: It doesn't matter, think about it. People like you will actually be a threat, well you're already a threat. But if you don't go rogue, other Seiras could use you. *Taku*: That's been the case for the longest of times. *Kata makes eye contact with Yashi. Yashi holds his guard* *Kata*: Who's the fellow? Part of that army you were talking about? *Taku*: Could be. *Kata*: Taking your plans seriously I see. *Kata walks over to Yashi* Hmph. *Taku*: What are you even doing here? *Kata puts his hood back on and turns back to Taku* **Kata**(w): You see, Yáshido actually attempted to attack Lark, and lost, really, really pathetically. At least, that's what I'm getting. **Taku**(w): Wait, so the Hero is dead? **Kata**(w): That's the problem. When Lark went looking for him at the bottom of that abyss, he found nothing. Like Yáshido had escaped. No traces in his Familiars either. The same day, there was a report of a break-in, two people. So, it could have been Emuna with him and they managed to leave. Now we have been ordered to go looking for him. *Taku rubs his head* **Taku**: And you chose to come to Macadamia of all places? Why not Regra, Makatama, maybe even Yat'u? **Kata**: Who knows. That's information you don't have the right to know anymore. *Kata bends down and grabs the can from before and hands it out to Taku. Taku takes the can* Well my old friend, I'll be on my way. Tell Savenna I said hi, hahaha. *Kata walks down and around the aisle* **Taku**: Okay, that's our leave. *Taku and Yashi get the rest of the supplies they need. Once they pay for it, they carefully go back to his base, trying not to look suspicious while at the same time trying to make sure they are not being followed*

-Back at the base. Inside Taku's house-

Taku: You can set it right there. *Yashi places the bags down* Thanks. **Yashi**: No problem. *Taku looks down the hall at his room* **Taku**: Savenna, are you here? *No answer* Hmm~. It's night so she might be asleep. *Taku looks at Yashi and continues to stare at him* **Yashi**(thts): Oh. **Yashi**: Got you. *Yashi leaves Taku's house and heads over back to the dorm. Yashi stands outside the dorm* **Yashi**(thts): Well, Dicipients are looking for me. I should stay even quieter then. *The door of the dorm opens. Yashi turns to see Namari walking out* **Namari**: Oh, hey, Yashi, you're back. **Yashi**: Yup, just catching some fresh air. **Namari**: Okay. *Namari stands next to Yashi* **Yashi**: You ever think we will be found? **Namari**: What do you mean by that? Do you want Taku and Savenna to be caught? **Yashi**: No, I'm just saying, from a general view. **Namari**: Taku was right about choosing a discreet place such as this one, but remember, Macadamia does checks randomly. And if he hasn't found a way to live here, it could cause issues. **Yashi**: True. *Namari yawns before looking away* **Namari**: Anything happened while you two were out? **Yashi**: We did run into . . . another Dicipient . . . *Namari gasps* **Namari**: Really? What happened? **Yashi**: They were whispering, but I heard a few things. *Namari moves close to Yashi* **Yashi**(w): You know the treaty between Dicipients and the Demon King, right? **Namari**(w): Yes, if a Dicipient so chooses to no longer be one anymore, they turn into a Fallen Dicipient and other Dicipients cannot hurt them unless the Fallen Dicipient attacks them first. Something like that right? **Yashi**(w): Right. Well, what I heard is that Korosi is planning on breaking that treaty entirely. **Namari**: You're kidding? **Yashi**(w): They were whispering so I could be wrong, but Taku was also startled when Kata said this. **Namari**(w): Oh-, so Kata was the Dicipient you ran into? *Yashi nods* **Namari**: He didn't follow you back, did he? **Yashi**: We did our best to make sure no one was following. **Namari**: Good. *Namari looks back over the porch* I wonder what he was doing here, and how he got in Macadamia. **Yashi**: Same goes for Taku. *Both of them laugh* Alright, I'm going to sleep, Namari. **Namari**: Okay, goodnight. **Yashi**: Goodnight. *Yashi ventures to his room, he lays in his bed and summons his Mangole. He taps onto his contacts and goes to Dia's name. Yashi hesitates to pull up Dia's profile* **Yashi**(thts): Why is this so difficult for me? *Yashi separates the Mangole into two earpieces as he pushes her name. With a moment of silence after pushing the call button, it begins to ring* Please answer . . . *The Mangole continues to call for a while before it just turns off* Her Mangole could sense my call, but she chose not to answer it at all. *Yashi Reverses his Mangole and turns towards the wall* Hm, I'm not gonna think about it too much. Maybe she's just busy right now. If she really turned against me completely, it wouldn't have picked my call up at all, nor would I have seen her on my list.

-Yashi falls asleep. Once he walks up, he prepares to start another day of training. After a shower, Yashi heads to the dorm's exit-

Everyone else is standing on the porch, they all turn to Yashi as he opens the door **Yashi**: Good morning. **Keshio & Namari**: Good morning. *Otara does an unenergetic wave at Yashi* **Keshio**: Someone woke up late. **Yashi**: At least I'm up. **Keshio**: That's one thing you're right about. **Namari**: We are waiting for Kamira's arrival. **Yashi**: I see. You all ate breakfast too, right? **Keshio**: What do you mean breakfast? **Namari**: What, you didn't check the kitchen, Keshio? **Keshio**: There's FOOD in there? **Otara**: It's too late now, Kamira's here. *Kamira is coming from Savenna and Taku's house while conversing with them* **Keshio**: She didn't see me yet. Tell her I'm uhh~, taking a shower. *Keshio runs inside. After Keshio enters the dorm, Kamira ends their conversation. Looking at the dorm's location, Kamira motions the students to the training ground. Once they all are there* **Kamira**: Good morning, everyone. **Students**: Good morning. **Kamira**: Where's Keshio? *Namari and Yashi look at each other* **Otara**: He went to eat before you arrived before training. *Namari and Yashi look at Otara* **Kamira**: Oh okay, we can wait. While we're waiting though, I want you to get to know you all a bit better. Let's start with you Mr. Taramasu. **Yashi**: I used to attend Jurono Academy, as you all may know. *Kamira and Namari chuckle* I like using Pure Energy-based weapons, swords for the most part. My Elilaments are mainly Basic and Novice, while I have a few in Pristine. **Namari**: What's your favorite Elilament? **Yashi**: I would say, Kosai would be my favorite. **Kamira**: Alright good. Ms. Katsuni. **Namari**: Well, similar, I also happened to attend Jurono Academy, until Taku came and got me. *Yashi smiles while Kamira laughs again* **Kamira**: All of you are going to keep this up I bet. **Otara**(m): Please stop saying that. **Namari**: I am a direct combat user, so no weapons for me. Other than these fists. *Namari raises a fist up before putting it down* My favorite Elilament would be Ikkasei. It's a huge help when it comes to people that use nothing but Magic to fight me. *Kamira*: Splendid. I have been attending Yothos Academy for six years. My weapon is a staff for the six elements alongside Kuki Sosa and False Kuki Sosa. *Keshio arrives* *Keshio*: Good morning. Sorry teacher, I'm late. *Kamira*: Just follow along. *Clears throat* My favorite Elilament is Reverse. It's always nice to cancel something when you see an opportunity to use something better, and that's all for me. Ms. Misugami. *Otara crosses her arms* *Otara*: My name is Otara Misugami. My weapon is the lance. My Elilaments range up to Elemental. My favorite Elilament would be . . . Zoka Vision. Knowing what your opponent is doing is a big part of strategy. Much like Kamira's opinion, you can cast something that will deal with it. *Kamira*: You understand what to do now, Keshio? *Keshio*: I'll take a shot. My name is Keshio Revalorese. My weapon of choice is also a sword; longer than a standard one, I suppose. My Elilaments, Pristine is what I am most comfortable using. My favorite in that range would be . . . Denki. I like just going right through people's defenses, and, just the feeling of using it makes me feel good about myself. *Kamira*: Fantastic, that's everyone. Are you all ready to start training? *Students*: Yes. *Taku*: Wait, wait, wait, wait. *Taku is standing next to them. Alongside him, Savenna stands* *Kamira*: Yes, Taku? *Taku*: Okay, since everyone is here, I want to make this as simple as possible. Huddle around me. *Everyone huddles around Taku. Except for Savenna who remains a couple of feet behind him* So, when Yashi and I went out for supplies, we ran into another Dicipient, Kata. *Kamira & Keshio*: Kata? ^Otara summons her lance and points it at Taku. Everyone stands back except for Taku^ *Kamira*: Otara, what are you doing? *Otara*: This is my final time asking, are you planning on doing something that needs to be taken care of? *Savenna stands in front of Taku and casts her sword* *Taku*: Calm down. I told you before that I'm not planning anything bad. Please both of you, put down your weapons. *Namari*: Otara, calm down. *Otara and Savenna stare at each other* *Otara*: You show up in Macadamia somehow, requesting the strongest obtainable students you could find. You say you plan for something, but yet you don't tell us at all what it is. And then the next day, you just so happen to run into another Dicipient? *Otara tightens her grip* It's really hard to believe you're doing something good, Taku. *Taku*: Hmph. I told you myself, I just had managed to get all of you. I want to publicly express my intentions to everyone, so I will on my own time. That's why I don't want to tell you anything, not until I'm in front of more than just Academy students. And yeah, it just so happened that Kata was there, Yashi was the one who chose the silly market in the first place. If you, yourself, are going to cause trouble, I suggest you leave. But if you really don't believe me, and want to fight me, I'm here, Otara. *Otara continues her glare at Taku without moving an inch* But right now, I believe that the information I'm about to tell you is more important than your feelings. *For a split-second Otara's face changes to a surprised look before closing her eyes* *Otara*: Hmph. *Otara Reverses her lance and turns around. Namari holds Otara's shoulders* Kata told me that Yáshido attempted to fight Lark and lost. **Keshio**: He lost?! **Namari**: Are you serious?! *Yashi puts his hand over his mouth. Otara turns back around* **Savenna**: Listen, there's more. **Taku**: It seems as if he managed to escape before dying though. This means he is still out there somewhere recovering possibly. *Namari lets go of Otara's shoulders and walks next to her, facing Taku* **Namari**: You want to go searching for him, don't you? **Taku**: Precisely. **Savenna**: The flaw in Taku's plan is that he is not exactly sure where Yáshido is and is relying on my sword to find him. **Taku**: Yup. Savenna has Elilament Adapt and Denryoku on all of her Celestials. With that, there's a good chance that we'll be able to find him if the Hero is in Macadamia. If there's no luck today, Savenna and I will have to go out alone. Maybe even find Emuna. **Keshio**: Don't you think that's a bit much? **Taku**: No, I don't. *Savenna Reverses her sword and turns towards their dorm* **Savenna**: We will be ready after your training. **Kamira**: I have more time today, so is it okay if I come with you? **Taku**: Sure. *Taku and Savenna walk away* **Yashi**: The Hero fought the Demon King already? That's insane. **Namari**: It really is, not even mentioning that Kata's saying that Yáshido lost the fight. **Otara**: I am only getting more agitated. **Namari**: Why are you acting so furious, Otara? **Otara**: I cannot understand why you all are taking this so lightly. Taku was a Dicipient, we are a part of a plan that we know nothing about. Isn't it also strange how . . . he meets a Dicipient and then wants to find the Hero on the same day? I find that ridiculous. *Kamira walks in front of Otara and grabs both of her hands, putting her fingers through them and lifting them to Otara's chest level* **Otara**: Wha-, what are you doing? **Kamira**(w): Calm down, Otara. There has to be a certain part of your life when you just have to trust. Believe me, when I say that he isn't planning to harm anyone, but to actually help. Fallen Dicipients are rare. Just think about it. There have only been nine in all of the generations before Taku, and only two had the power to change their hearts. Let Taku be the third. **Otara**(w): O-, okay . . . I understand. Now please, let go of my hands. **Kamira**: Not until you promise. *Otara's eyes open wider as she becomes more embarrassed* **Otara**(w): I . . . promise . . . **Kamira**(w): Thank you. *Kamira lets go of Otara's hands and turns to everybody else. Otara stares at her hands before placing them by her sides* **Kamira**: Today, we will work on your Celestials. Laito, you can come out now. *Next to Kamira, a flask of Gray Particles appears and vanish, and a boy stands there* **Keshio**: Laito? You seriously brought him here? **Laito**: Hey, you don't want me here? Fine. *A gray shade goes over Laito's outline before he's gone* **Kamira**: Laito, I won't bring you back if you leave now. *Laito Reverses his Fukashi* **Laito**: YOU DO KNOW I WAS JOKING RIGHT? **Kamira**: I am teaching, I don't need unnecessary distractions. *Laito crosses his arms* **Laito**: Fine, my bad. **Kamira**: As you all might know, Laito is a close friend of mine. **Laito**: So, we're friends now? That was a fast downgrade. *Kamira looks at Laito* **Kamira**: When I'm teaching, everyone is my friend. Now shush. **Laito**: I know, I know. *Kamira clears her throat* **Kamira**: Because I know two of you have your own personal Celestial, one of you will have a spar with Laito. So, who wants to be a volunteer? *Otara steps forward* **Laito**: Wait, Otara's here?! *Otara stares at Laito. Laito looks at Kamira* **Keshio**(w): You telling me you didn't feel her aura before you walked in here . . . how . . . *Laito looks at Keshio* **Laito**: Didn't want to waste Oplitals on Denryoku, obviously. *Laito quickly looks at Kamira* SO I am going to fight her?! **Kamira**: I mean, she volunteered, so what's the problem? *Laito walks up to Kamira* **Laito**(w): This was all planned as a punishment for something I did isn't it? **Kamira**: Hahaha, it's just a spar. I'm sure Ms. Misugami wouldn't hurt you. **Otara**: Apara Lance. *Otara holds her Lance to her side* You would be right in a sense. *Laito sighs as he looks at Otara* **Laito**: Guess I have no choice. **Kamira**: Everyone else, sit on the bench. *Once everyone else is on the bench, Kamira stands in front of Laito and Otara* Your spar works like this. I will summon a Barre with Konseitsu. This obviously will lower your overall output on your Elilaments and stamina. Recently, I also just started to practice my Itilusion skills, I will try my best to put a fair feeling for both of you. So even though you know you're not doing and taking a lot of damage, it will not feel like that. That means you can get hit by a full-wave of Pure Energy and still be OK, okay? *Laito and Otara nod* **Laito**: I'm pretty sure we know how Konseitsu works. *Kamira rolls her eyes* **Kamira**: You might also know this affects the way you sense auras, especially if you have Uhnyoi. You may start ten seconds after I cast the Barre. *Kamira walks in front of the bench and raises her hands at Laito and Otara* Magica! Barre! *Half of a clear sphere forms in the middle of the two. The hemisphere spreads out until it stops in front of Kamira. Nearly fifty feet in diameter, Laito and Otara are on opposite sides. Inside the Barre* **Laito**: First one who submits? **Otara**: First one who gets knocked unconscious. **Laito**: That's a bit creepy but okay. Dasu Blade! ^Particles coil down Laito's arms and form two long daggers^ **Laito**: What about your Dermal? **Otara**: Don't need it. **Laito**: Quick question, are you going to go full out? ^Suddenly multiple waves of wind expel from Otara's body. Using Ikkasei, the aura of Zoka Strength, Zoka Swiftness, and Zoka Hearing creates a never-ending change of colors around her body. Kamira's Barre slightly cracks behind and above her^ **Laito**: -Wow, literally everything you just activated is Stage I, maybe even Ace. *Otara points her lance at Laito* **Otara**: Your turn. *One large powerful wave of wind comes from Laito as she leans towards Otara* **Laito**: Whew, let's go! ^Laito rushes towards Otara^ **Otara**: Extinlina Oyado! ^A wall of Pure Energy forms in front of Otara. Otara hits the wall at an insane speed, and it flys towards Laito. Laito slows his sprint down, allowing him to aim at the center of the fast-moving blockade. With a Protojet, Laito rockets towards the wall twice as fast. Right before Laito hits it, a hole opens up in the spot where he was about to intersect, and Otara is floating just behind the hole^ **Otara**: Lance Syosa! ^The length of Otara's Lance increases as she points the metal end towards Laito. Laito stops his Protojet and tries to move to the right of the wall, but Otara's Lance reaches and pierces his

Dermal through his chest plate before Laito manages to dodge. Pure Energy explodes from Laito's back from the shock. Laito immediately removes himself from the Lance^ **Laito**: Kosai Tunnel! ^A massive sphere of fire forms in front of Laito and rushes towards Otara. From Laito's view, Otara, although blocking, takes the hit and gets consumed in the flames. The Lance in front of Laito retreats as he continues to shoot Kosai. After seeing this, Laito Protojets diagonally towards the ground. After Laito lands against the ground, three Particle-Lances strike the location in the air that would have hit him if he was in that same position. Each of them coming from different angles. Once the remains of Laito's blast hit the Barre, Otara stands in the air with her arms and Lance covering her chest for protection^ **Otara**: Hmph. **Laito**(Y): How was that, Otara?! Caught you off guard didn't I?! ^Otara says nothing while staring at Laito. She starts to descend towards the ground. While Otara is floating down, Laito aims his daggers at her^ **Laito**(m): She'll never see this coming. ^Laito starts running towards Otara's landing spot before using Fukashi. Then he uses Zoka Swiftness and zips behind Otara. Otara turns and blocks, but Laito moves slightly faster and lands a few strikes on her. Laito slashes Otara across her stomach twice before kneeing her in the stomach. As Laito's Fukashi fades away, Otara tries to intercept Laito's next slash, which is aiming for her head, but Laito knocks Otara's Lance downward with his other dagger and still gets his initial move off. Otara gets stunned as she takes the massive hit in the face. Laito then Protojets above Otara and kicks her to the ground with the bottom of his shoes. A platter of dusk explodes into the air from Otara's collision with the surface. Laito catches his breath as he sees Otara lying motionless on the ground below him^ **Laito**: Nice! ^Still spectating Otara, her body slowly fades away into Particles^ **Laito**(m): What? **Otara**: Engulf! In the Power of Apara! ^Everyone notices Otara's reappearance behind Laito. Otara's Lance and Dermal is emanating a magnificent golden aura of light filling everyone's vision. Laito covers his eyes being so close to Otara. Simultaneously, Otara charges down at Laito while an Atoskito pulls him towards Otara. Laito prepares to block before turning around to face Otara, but Otara's Lance penetrates him in the side before he completes his turn. Laito gets knocked to the ground in a near second with a large amount of Pure Energy trailing him. On impact, a small explosion occurs on Laito's Dermal, so hard that he deepens into the crust. Kamira's Barre cracks even more^ *Outside as this happens* **Keshio**(Y): Did you all see that?! Otara just handled him. **Kamira**: Yes, Keshio, we saw. **Yashi**: What's wrong, Kamira? You don't like seeing Laito get hurt? **Kamira**: No, not at all. **Namari**: Are you sure he's going to be okay, Exna? **Kamira**: He will be fine. Use Denryoku or Uhnyoi. You can see their actual levels. **Yashi**: Still, that really does look like it hurt, a lot. **Keshio**: I like how she just returned the favor. **Namari**: That had to be Itilusion on top of a Particle Magic clone. **Kamira**: Good eye. You would be right, Ms. Katsuni. Although that first couple hits Laito actually landed. Otara teleported after being hit in the stomach. *Keshio puts his hands together, one in the other* *Keshio*: That just shows how strong and overpowered having an Elemental Elilament is, but it just makes me more excited for when I'm gonna be in there. *Kamira*: Good. *Yashi*: How about your Barre? It looks like it's going to shatter. *Kamira*: I've noticed, don't worry. Continue watching. *Inside the Barre* ^Laito rolls the rocks off of him and stands up rubbing the back of his head. Laito's Dermal is no longer summoned^ *Laito*: Ow, that was . . . quite the hit. ^Otara lands behind him. Laito jumps up and tries to attack Otara. Otara dodges backward before trying to attack Laito. Laito also dodges^ *Laito*: I'm not unconscious yet. *With a straight face, Otara tilts her head to the right confused* *Otara*: That was only a joke. You didn't notice the sarcasm? *Laito*: What? Really? I don't think anyone can tell when you're being sarcastic, Otara. ^As Laito finishes his sentence, without even seeing Otara move, Otara closes the distance between them and lands a slash against the left side of Laito's abdomen. Laito takes the blow and flys in the opposite direction. While in the air, Laito summons a Particle-Block further down his trajectory. Once Laito reaches it, he grabs onto its curved edges and swings downward, landing on his feet once more. Otara is standing in his previous location^ *Laito*: All of your attacks hurt. Geez, calm down. ^Otara takes a deep breath as she raises her right hand towards Laito^ *Otara*: Extinlina Buschco! ^A mCircle appears next to and on both sides of Otara. Laito summons a Barre around himself right as two thick metal pillars shoot out of the tekCircles at him^ *Outside the Barre* *Kamira*: Magica! Barre! *Kamira summons another Barre around the existing Barre* ^Laito's Barre breaks as the dense metal extensions hit it. Laito ducks under the pillars as they continue forward and hits Kamira's first Barre. Shattering it on impact. However, the pillars shatter as they hit Kamira's newly formed one. Laito places his left dagger on his right arm. Flames emerge around his whole arm and form a longer more powerful dagger^ *Laito*: Dabl! ^Laito aims his left arm up as another dagger-like his right one appears. Otara stands guard^ *Laito*: Xinau Losai! ^The flames of his dagger turn into a poisonous blackish-green color^ *Outside the Barre* *Kamira*: Here he comes. It's about to get interesting. *Yashi*: Doku blades, Otara isn't wearing a Dermal. *Namari*: That means if she gets hit, her Sustain is going to be constantly dropping. *Kamira*: Exactly. *Keshio*: Why doesn't she just cast a Dermal or something? *Kamira*: It's all about tactics, Otara could just be luring him into attacking and cast it right before she gets hit. *Yashi*: Because then, he will be stunned from that Pure Energy it gives off, and Otara will be able to get an easy shot. *Kamira*: Precisely. Or maybe Otara is conserving the max amount of Oplitals into her attacks rather than just defense. *Namari*: That makes sense also. *Kamira*: It's all about tactics, and I'm sure she is doing one of those I mentioned. *Inside the Barre* ^Laito aims his daggers directly at Otara^ *Laito*: Spiral Death! ^Laito's daggers instantly fire a spiral wave of dark green poisonous material right for Otara^ *Otara*: Hmph, Apara Lance Triklet! -Extinlina Jet! ^One of Otara's Lances forms next to her glowing a pinkish color then shoots through the spiral towards Laito. As the Lance passes through the center of the spiral, the poison turns into Particles. Otara with her other Lance holds it sideways, and as the Particles reach her, she spins her Lance in a circular motion. Redirecting them away from her. Laito moves out of the way as the incoming Lance almost hits him face first. The Lance loses momentum and hits the ground a few meters behind Laito before disappearing. Laito looks at Otara shocked^ *Laito*: I'm calling some type of cheat; There's no way you could have executed that so perfectly. *Outside the Barre* *Keshio, Namari, & Yashi*: Woah. *Kamira*: Impressed? *Namari*: Otara. I've seen a lot of Otara's fights and try to incorporate them into my fights in the 'No Limit' tournaments, but you can't get better than the original. *Keshio*: Laito better think of something quick cause uhm, he's not looking too good. *Kamira*: I can already tell, he's about to use his so-called ultimate attack. *Keshio*: Rising Finisher? *Kamira looks at Keshio* *Kamira*: How do you know that, Mr. Revalorese? *Keshio*: Well I fought him before, that's how. And against Otara, it might work, probably not, but hey. *Inside the Barre* *Laito*: Otara, if this doesn't work, I will happily submit for you, okay? *Otara*: I'm starting to consider the 'being knocked unconscious' part. *Laito*: That's if I don't get a direct hit on you. *Otara*: You're confident that three-quarters of this attack's power can fully wipe out an Aced Sustain? *Laito*: Oh~, yeah, you got a point, but it'll be funny if I *crit* you, wouldn't it? ^Otara stands guard^ *Laito*: Guess not. ^Laito crosses his daggers around his chest and starts to float upward. Otara floats up with him^ *Laito*: You know you're just making this easier for me by coming up here right? ^Otara slightly leans her Lance towards Laito^ *Laito*: It's quite sad you don't talk that much. (Y): Rising Start! ^Suddenly Laito vanishes as the hint of a red aura surrounding his daggers before he disappears. Everyone notices Otara immediately activating Zoka Hearing as her ears point up. With the combination of all her Zokas, Otara senses all of her directions. Otara turns in one direction as Laito becomes visible closer to her^ *Laito*: Three! ^Otara fires a Pure Energy blast at Laito, but he disappears again before it hits him. Otara turns to another direction as Laito becomes visible there, but closer to her^ *Laito*: Two! ^Once again, Otara fires another blast, but Laito disappears before it could hit him. Otara looks above herself and Protojets up. Laito becomes visible just under her. Otara quickly points her Lance down at him^ *Otara*: Extilina- Jet-! *Laito*: AH-! One-! ^Laito disappears again right before the lance hits him. Otara's Lance hits the ground, forming a small crater around it^ *Otara*: Apara. ^Otara's Lance rushes back up towards her and she catches it. Otara floats back down to where she was before. Abruptly, she disappears too. Otara then appears on the opposite side of the Barre. Otara continues to disappear and reappear in a different location, teleporting^ *Outside the Barre* *Keshio*: Uhm, is Otara okay? *Namari*: What's she doing? *Kamira*: Take a guess. *Yashi*: Because of the Konseitsu limiting her, Otara is trying to get the feel of what it feels like when Laito is moving. Laito can only move so fast to keep the power in his attack undetectable. If Otara stays in one spot, it's easy for him to change his direction of impact while getting closer at the same time. If she's far like she is now, then Laito cannot cross that speed limit and or stay invisible forever, forcing him to be nearly perfect, timing his Fukashi, Zoka Swiftness, and his attack. But still, if Otara senses what his aura is like in that state he's in, then it's pointless. **Kamira**: Right on. **Keshio**: Why doesn't she just activate Fukashi Vision? **Namari**: That's only because she doesn't have it. *They all look at Namari* **Namari**: From every battle I saw her fighting someone who used Fukashi, if you pay attention, her attacks are much more hesitant than her actually seeing her opponent. And, I've never seen Otara's eyes change into that gray Fukashi Vision color. **Keshio**: Interesting, an Elilament I now know she doesn't have. That's crazy. Wait so how did she almost guess where he was before? **Kamira**: Well, as Mr. Taramasu said, Otara's is basing her guess off the aura she feels on Laito's not being invisible. In theory, Otara's recognition is really good, so she can feel immediately when that aura reappears somewhere in the Barre. **Keshio**: So, she's making educated guesses? **Kamira**: From our view, most likely, but she probably knows more than we think. **Keshio**: Well, that doesn't explain how she knew about the invisible Barre you put up yesterday. *All of them pause and look at each other. Inside the Barre* ^Otara continues to teleport around. Every time she does, she focuses on a particular direction. Getting closer to a specific point. Otara Casts an Ikkasei before disappearing. Otara appears in the air facing a certain direction with an aura around her^ **Otara**: Ola Transa! ^Otara summons her golden Dermal^ **Otara**: Bow Down! To the Lance of Apara! ^Right in front of her, about three feet away and a foot down, Laito appears^ **Laito**: Rising Finish! ^Laito uncrosses his daggers towards Otara, there is a giant wave of redness and blackness in correspondence with his daggers. Otara's Lance has a magnificent aura as she beams down on Laito. As they collide, a lot of Pure Energy shoots away from the impact. Each of their visions is blinded by the white lights. However, Otara doesn't give up an ounce of strength as she feels Laito's blades drift away from her Lance. From a spectator's view, the entire Barre is filled with white lights and the addition of auras. Suddenly the pressure of the Barre intensifies, and all of their Magic disappears. Laito and Otara both fall down and land on a knee. The Barre gets Reversed. The remains of Particles fly up in the air^ **Kamira(Y)**: That's enough you two! *All four of them run to the competitors. Laito stands up* **Keshio**: Good job, guys! That was entertaining. **Namari**: Yeah, you did great! **Laito**: Easy. **Keshio**: You didn't even win. **Laito**: UH, she didn't win either. **Yashi**: Still, good fight. *Namari walks to Otara* **Namari**: Wonderful match, Otara. *Otara continues to stay on the ground as she struggles to get up* **Namari**: Otara, are you okay? **Otara**: I-, I'm fine. *Otara stands before crumbling back down to the ground on a knee. Everyone looks over at her* **Kamira**: Otara, are you sure you're alright? **Otara**: I told you already, I-, I'm fine. *Right before Otara stands back up, she falls chest down onto the ground*

Chapter 6 – Entry

Kamira runs over to Otara **Kamira**: What's wrong, Otara?! *Otara is unresponsive. Kamira sits on her knees and rolls Otara on to them. Otara's body is rapidly twitching randomly. Kamira holds on to Otara's arm. Otara looks like she's in a lot of pain. Keshio and Yashi walk over to her as well* Otara, can you hear me? *Otara does not answer; Kamira's hands start to glow a pinkish color around Otara* **Otara**: Hmm!!! *Otara rolls off of Kamira and lands on her back with her head facing Yashi and Keshio* **Keshio**: It's her body, she's proba-, **Kamira**: OH-, you're right, she's potency deficient! That explains it! Namari, help me! *Both Kamira and Namari's hands glow around Otara's head rather than her whole body. Otara's body stops spazzing* **Namari**: Oh, good she looks better. **Kamira**: Revalorese, hurry, and get Savanna. **Keshio**: On it. *Keshio leaves. Yashi crouches next to Otara. Kamira sighs* **Kamira**: It's my fault, I was too reckless with the Barrier, and I should have asked you all in the first place. **Namari**: It's okay, Exna, we could have never known. Us staying here and giving her the strength is our best option. **Yashi**: There's another name for it, uhm, Enecceptance. Her body cannot handle a mass influx of Oplital increase. **Kamira**: Yes, and because I had it at a quarter most, all of her Oplitals she was using under those conditions, at the end of the spare, was probably about twenty percent from out of eighty percent. When I increased the Konseitsu stage from Stage I to Ace, then deactivated the Barre, her Pure Energy potential went from almost forty percent to eighty percent . . . That is extremely deadly. If she gives out, Otara could die . . . *Kamira pauses as she looks down at Otara* And it's all my fault. *A tear drops from Kamira's eye* **Yashi**(thts): No, way. It makes sense, it makes so much sense. The vision she showed me about her past. The Familiar continuously absorbing her Pure Energy. Even after being unconscious for that long amount of time, that's how she got it. *One of Otara's eyes open and look at Yashi, it's a silvery blue color rather than the light blue it normally is. Otara coughs and a small amount of blood onto the ground before closing her eyes* Oh no, not now. There's no way Otara could be dying right now. *Yashi looks up at Kamira and Namari who are considerably focused on Otara* **Yashi**: Why do you need Savenna? **Kamira**: Because! I'm sure she knows something better than what I'm doing now, that's why! Not to mention, I will forever be under guilt. I would never be able to forgive myself! All of her life she still has yet to explore, and she gets killed by some stupid selfish mistake! *The aura around Otara's head starts to disappear on one side slightly* **Namari**: Kamira, stay focused. Please. *Kamira takes a deep breath* **Kamira**: Thank you, Namari. *Kamira looks back down to Otara. Not much time later, Keshio and Savanna arrive. Both of them using Zoka Swiftness before standing right next to the group. Savanna crouches next to Kamira* **Savanna**: How long has she been like this? **Kamira**: About two minutes. **Savanna**: She's been like this for two minutes? She's a strong girl indeed. *Savanna looks down at Otara* You hear, Otara? You're strong, and I need you to stay strong for me, okay? **Namari**: You know a better way of helping her? *Savanna places her hand on Otara's forehead. Savanna instantly takes it off* **Savanna**: Ha~ . . . *Savanna shakes her hand as a gray smoke protrudes from it* **Kamira**: What's wrong? **Namari**: Is it that bad? **Savanna**: The amount of Pure Energy leaking from her is absurd, and it's making her body extremely hot. If it all depletes . . . *Savanna stares at Otara* Yes, I know something. There is a Chamber inside of your dorm. If we are careful, we can place her in it. That should put less stress on her body by slowing the amount of Pure Energy that is leaking. Giving her body's core more time to obtain it back and cooling her body temperature down. Ultimately, putting her to sleep. **Kamira**: I understand. Yashi, take my place. *Yashi moves closer to Otara while placing his hands above Otara's head and activates Patchi Tekiyo* Only her head, okay? *Yashi nods. Kamira tries to remove her hand from Otara's arm, but Otara continues to hold onto it. Everyone looks at each other* **Yashi**(thts): That's her way of making sure she's still with us. **Kamira**(w): Namari? *Namari nods and gently uses one arm to trade places with Kamira's. Kamira stands with Savanna* **Savanna**: We need a Particle-Block with no fill. With that, we will place her inside it and fill it up with water. Once that is finished, we will carefully take her into the Chamber. All of these casts have to be *holds* not *sustains*, got it? *Everyone agrees with a nod* **Kamira**: Sounds good. *Savanna points a finger at Otara and Particles start to form with slightly bigger dimensions under her* Healers, I need you to support her all the way until she's fully inside the Chamber, got it? *Namari and Yashi nod* Please tell me, Kamira-, **Kamira**: Yes, I have Pristine Psychokinesis. **Savanna**: Good. Okay, we start with you, Keshio. Remember no *sustains*. You have to hold down your Magic until she is fully inside the Chamber. *Keshio holds both of his hands out towards Otara. Tiny water droplets start to fill up into a rectangular prism from Otara's neck to her feet. Once filled though, the bubbles of boiling water erode from it* Perfect, Keshio. Kamira. *Kamira aims his hands towards Otara. As Otara begins to rise into the air, Namari and Yashi stand to maintain their form* Slow and steady. *They carefully walk to the dorm. Keshio uses his elbows to open both of the doors* Tap the locks on the sides of the doors, Keshio. *Keshio finds the buttons on the lower part of the door. After pushing them inwards with his feet, the doors swing to the walls and they stay open. After entering the dorm, Savanna leads them down the left hallway. As they turn the corner, the floor is slightly elevated, causing Kamira and Keshio to slip. However, they catch themselves before completely falling* **Yashi**: You two okay? **Kamira**: Yeah, we're fine. **Keshio**: Totally didn't just almost break my ankle. **Namari**: I'm not taking the blame if you drop her, Keshio. You'll have to deal with that. **Keshio**: Hydro is easy.

Everyone feels Savanna's aura spread through the hall. Looking at her, Savanna does not look pleased **Savanna**: You two need to cut it out and focus. *Keshio and Namari get startled from Savanna's glare and tone of speech* **Keshio & Namari**: Yes, ma'am. *After reaching the end of the hall, Savanna opens a door* **Savanna**: In here. *The four of them bring Otara into the room. The room is empty except for a Horizontal Chamber with the advanced technology panel that comes with operating one. The blue faded lights embedded in the bottom of the Chamber is the only thing lighting up the room. The students look at the Chamber* **Yashi**(thts): Somehow, I'm not surprised they have one of the more up to date ones. It's just one series behind the one Emuna has for me. **Savanna**: I have to type some commands in, so please be patient. *Savanna walks over to the panel, keeping one hand aimed at Otara and using the other to type in the commands* **Keshio**(w): I wasn't going to say anything, but that Chamber though. **Namari**(w): What do you mean? *Keshio sighs* **Keshio**(w): Do you not know the flagship Chambers, Namari? **Namari**(w): Not a clue. *Savanna clears her throat* **Savanna**: I can hear you by the way. *Keshio jumps from the remark. A few seconds pass as the only thing heard is the beeping noises from the panel. Namari watches Otara's body lower slightly and a water droplet hits the ground* **Namari**: Kamira? *Kamira is staring at Otara* **Kamira**: I got it. We don't have that much longer, I can hold. *Yashi looks at Kamira. She is noticeably sweating* **Yashi**(thts): The first Barre she summoned was a *sustain*, but her second one was a *hold* because she could change the aspects of it. She's been holding an Stage II Psychokinesis this whole time too. That takes a lot of Oplitals to begin with. I can understand why she's struggling; she's running low on Oplitals to use as well. And I'm sure everyone else knows that. **Savanna**: Almost finished. *The Chamber starts to rumble as it is turned on. The blue lights on the bottom brighten. Kamira's arms start to shake* You're doing good, Otara. I can still feel your presence. Just give us a couple more seconds. *The door of the Horizontal Chamber opens upwards and a frosty blue smoke comes out* Let's go, we've come this far, no hiccups now. *Kamira slowly places Otara above the Chamber, Savanna notices the droplets on the floor as more of them appear* **Yashi**(thts): She's not going to make it. *Yashi feels another presence somewhere near them. As they continue to move Otara to the Chamber, no more droplets are seen on their path and Kamira's posture is more relaxed. Keshio lowers her into the Chamber. Savanna pushes a button, and the Chamber starts to close* **Savanna**: Okay, stop your Magic. *They all stop their *holds*. Everyone does a heavy sigh* **Keshio**: That was so tense. *The remains of Magic inside the Chamber exit through dedicated air holes as Particles. Savanna looks at all of the students* **Kamira**: We did it, oh thank goodness. **Namari**: Oh my. *Savanna scans around the room* **Savanna**: Otara will be here for the rest of today, and maybe tomorrow. All of you get some rest. I have to talk to Taku about this and see if he still wants to go searching. *Savanna walks next to Kamira* Please pay more attention, okay? Come up with a better routine if you have to. *Kamira*: I will. *Savanna looks around the room as she walks out* *Yashi*(thts): Savanna felt that too. Who was that, and why do I feel like I've felt that before? Strange. *A couple's minutes pass as Yashi walks outside and tries to feel that aura he felt in the Chamber room. With no hint of what it was, Yashi goes to his room and lays down*

-Half an hour later-

Yashi(thts): How am I going to do this? I can't 'not' do my role as the Hero, even if I'm here. Should I just randomly leave? I'm controlling the situation really because they ARE looking for ME. So, I can just come out whenever, to be honest. *Namari walks in* *Namari*: Knock, knock. *Yashi*: Hey, Namari. *Namari*: Hey, still sad too, huh? *Yashi*: Ah it's nothing. Have you checked on Otara? *Namari*: Surprisingly, her heart rate and body necessities are nearly back to normal. *Yashi*: Really, already? *Namari*: Emhm, Kamira has been watching the whole time. She saw her statistics go all the way up. Out of all of us, she's really the only one who is no longer gloomy. *Yashi*: I'm not gloomy. *Namari*: Taramasu, you're sitting in your room by yourself with the blinds closed and curtains up, you know what never mind. *Yashi*: Okay, I see your point. That's good though, she's already healing. *Namari*: Yeah, thanks to Savanna. I came to tell you that we are about to leave, Taku still wants to go searching. *Yashi*: On my way in a bit . . . *Namari*: K, meet us in his house. *Namari leaves. Yashi stands and walks over to a dresser and pulls out a shirt. He sits in his bed* *Yashi*(thts): A quick change, then I'll be ready. *As he lifts his shirt up someone knocks on his door. Yashi puts his shirt back down* *Yashi*: Kamira? *Kamira*: Oh-, so this is your room. *Yashi*: Yeah, it is. *Kamira walks in and sits next to Yashi* *Kamira*: How are you feeling? *Yashi*: Shouldn't I be asking you that? *Kamira*: Yeah, haha. I'm fine. *Kamira stares in front of her* What are you doing? *Yashi*: Well, I was going to change shirts, then you came in. *Kamira picks up Yashi's shirt that's next to her. Kamira lifts it up in front of her* *Kamira*: I don't understand how you all can wear such tight attire. *Yashi*: I, well, I'm actually quite small so~, it's not that tight. *Kamira places the shirt back down where she got it from* *Kamira*: How about your Dermals? *Yashi*: Don't have any. *Kamira*: What? You don't have a Dermal? *Yashi*: Nope. *Kamira*: Is it a Locked Magic? *Yashi*: No, just don't prefer using one. *Kamira looks up at the ceiling before looking at Yashi* *Kamira*: Sounds just like the Hero if you ask me. *Yashi*: Wha-, what? *Kamira*(w): Only uses Pure-Energy based weapons. Kosai is his favorite Elilament and if you were the Hero, you wouldn't need any other Dermal. *Yashi*(w): But I'm not the Hero. *Kamira*(w): Are you sure? *The two of them stare at each other* *Yashi*(thts): Could it be? She actually knows? But how? Kamira Exna, there's no way. She's just too busy to be focusing on things like this. And if she does know, why would she directly tell me . . . *Kamira*: I know, your secret, Yashi, and I think that's a very amazing job you have. *Yashi*: You mean. *Kamira*: Yes, but don't worry,

I'm not the type to tell. Just keep up the good work. *Kamira stands as someone walks past Yashi's door* **Kamira**: Laito? **Laito**: Oh-, there you are. Come on, both of you. *Kamira turns to Yashi. Yashi takes his shirt off. Laito gets confused and takes a step back* Hey, what's going on here? **Yashi**: I'm just changing shirts; I have no clue what Exna is doing here. **Kamira**: I was coming to tell him to come as well. **Laito**: Look, I was told to tell you to come back. We don't have time for misunderstandings. **Yashi**: Agreed. *Kamira walks out of the room. Yashi changes his shirt and walks out behind them. Once everyone is inside Taku's house* **Taku**: Kamira, I know you said you would stay with Otara, right? *Kamira nods* How about you, Laito? **Laito**: Well, I'm not going to be having lunch with someone because I got a tie, so sure. **Kamira**: Seriously, Laito? I was giving second thoughts, but since your attitu-, **Laito**: Really?! Yeah-, I'm definitely in. **Taku**: Good. Savenna's spectral says that he's been in Artea, so we'll lurk around there. **Yashi**(thts): Did you have to say lurk though. Wait a minute, that's where I live. That can't be good. **Taku**: Laito, Namari, and Keshio, there's a school section in Artea. It's a small section and they are just a little younger than you so it shouldn't be hard. There aren't any Balancers around this time, so it'll be a nice swipe. Savenna, Yashi, and I will be in the town section. Obviously, you all need to stay low and try not to be spotted. It's not like they've given up on trying to find you guys. **Namari**: How long will we be searching for? **Taku**: Yeah, that's right. I need all of you to give me a part of your arm. **Keshio**: Why can't you just make a pact or something? **Taku**: Everyone here has Telepathy? **Yashi**: I don't. **Taku**: Then you three make a Telepathy pact with me. *Keshio, Namari, and Laito stare at Taku before an aura appears in the middle of them. A spark of light from Taku goes into the aura and to each of them* **Taku**: Done. Yashi, I'll deal with you when we're there, okay? **Yashi**: Okay. **Taku**: Namari, you're the leader of your group. **Namari**: Smart decision. **Keshio**: What's with you and harassing boys? **Namari**: I don't 'harass' boys. **Taku**: Okay, let's go.

-Once all of them are in Artea, the two groups split ways. Artea is Macadamia's third to smallest city. Yet, one of Macadamia's more busy cities. However, the side of town they're on is fairly empty. Savenna, Taku, and Yashi sit in a tree line watching the few people travel. A couple Balancers are patrolling-

Savenna(w): I thought you said there would be no guards? **Taku**(w): Well hey, it wouldn't be that easy. *Savenna hits Taku on his shoulder* **Savenna**(w): Nothing we do is easy. **Taku**(w): So why complain? **Savenna**(w): I'm not complaining, I'm just stating the differences in your so-called plan. **Taku**(w): Savenna, really? *Savenna sighs* **Savenna**(w): Summon the Barre. *Taku summons a Barre to prevent any Magic from being detected. With the Barre being Personal Casted with Fukashi, it makes them and itself invisible. Savenna summons her sword. She holds it upwards and a red glare is aligned down the center. Savenna squeezes her offhand* Again, he's been here in the past few days. We wait and watch. *Taku*: Oh, before I forget, Savenna, put a pact symbol on Yashi. *Savenna*: Give me your hand. *As Savenna Trantses, Yashi reaches his hand out* Actually, your arm, right on your bicep. *Savanna draws a small circle with a line through it on Yashi's bicep. She then puts a tiny amount of Pure Energy in it and it shines white before fading away* *Savanna*: He's good. *Yashi*(thts): Nice, that's part of my body that'll take five minutes of concentration on getting rid of. *Taku*: Like Savenna said, 'wait and watch'. If you run into any problems, use our Telepathy bandwidth. You can also communicate with Namari, Laito, or Keshio if you have to, okay? *Yashi*: I got it. *Savanna*: Let's move out. *Right after Taku Reverses the Barre, Savanna instantly jumps to the top of the building across the street. None of the Balancers spot her as she jumps along the roofs. Taku turns invisible as Yashi sees bushes open and close next to him. Yashi starts moving opposite of the way they went. He stops in some bushes and goes prone* *Yashi*(thts): This is so dumb. I'm literally looking for myself. *Yashi crouches back up looking at the houses* A ground mCarrier passes loaded with six passengers* People actually can afford one of those. Now thinking about it, who don't I know that can't buy one. I could even buy one. *Yashi looks back at the house* My house is around the corner. Oh yeah, and my birthday is in a couple of weeks. *Yashi scans the top of the building* Savenna's probably far gone. Time to make my escape. *Yashi wanders into the forest. While walking* This should be good. *Yashi casts a Barre around himself. The Hero Dermal appears around him, and he Reverses the Barre* *Yáshido*: Now, I just wait till they show. Huh? *Yáshido feels the presence of someone behind him* *Yáshido*(thts): That was fast, they're almost moving like they're trying to be sneaky. ^Something grabs onto Yáshido's leg and drags him chest first into the forest^ *Yáshido*: Woah, what's the meaning of this? Extilamental? ^Yáshido deepens his hands into the ground, slowing him down. He comes to a complete stop as whoever is in control of the Extilamental has stopped their pull. Someone flips him over and sits on top of him. They use their Magical Limbs to grab his right arm and keep his waist from leaving the ground^ *Girl*: I got you! Time to see who you really are! *Yáshido*: What do you mean? ^The girl puts her hand around Yáshido's neck^ *Girl*: This will be so worth it! *Yáshido*: Hey, stop! ^Fire spreads down the girl's arms onto her fists. Her entire arms are dampened and a deep fiery red. The neck part of Yáshido's Dermal starts to turn red in response to the immense heat. Yáshido activates Aced Zoka Strength and tries to move her off, but as soon as he does she activates Atoskito. The force pushes Yáshido back down on the ground, canceling out his Zoka Strength^ *Yáshido*(thts): Aced Atoskito? How determined is this girl?! ^The temperature of the girl's flames only rises as the color of her flames are now yellowish. The entirety of Yáshido's helmet slowly turns red as the metal itself starts to disassemble into Particles^ *Yáshido*(thts): She's physically trying to burn it off! *Yáshido*: Stop! Now! *Girl*: I'm almost done! It's too late to stop now! ^Yáshido grabs her wrist with his loose hand and pulls it back, but then she also activates Zoka

Strength around her entire body* **Yáshido**(thts): ACE AGAIN? ARE YOU KIDDING ME?! Uhm, think, how can I get out of this?! Yes, Protojet! *Yáshido's Helmet starts to transition into Particles. Yáshido aims his hand at a nearby tree. Immediately, the Girl uses her other hand to pin it down. She tightens both of her grips^ **Girl**: No Protojet for you! **Yáshido**: Uhh!!! Get off of me! You do realize this is a serious crime, right?! **Girl**: Of course, I do! But I will never get this opportunity again! **Yáshido**: Is it really that important for you to know who I am?! **Girl**: Simple, Yes! ^The girl's Kosai elevates another stage of heat as her arms start to turn into bright white glares. More of his Dermal neck area starts to turn into particles. The heat is around his whole helmet at this point. Steam fills the interior of Yáshido's helmet, limiting his visibility^ **Yáshido**(thts): Man, I really don't want to do this, but it seems I have no choice. Fukashi Deamsou! ^A spacious white glow appears around Yáshido's body, but just before moving, the girl looks behind herself at something^ **Girl**: What? What's this feeling? *The girl turns back to Yashi* **Girl**: Woah. ^She suddenly gets knocked off of Yáshido. Yáshido leans up, not seeing her anywhere^ **Yáshido**(m): What. **Yáshido**(thts): Fukashi Deamsou. *The spacious white glow stops as Yáshido stands* Where did she vanish to? *Yáshido activates Denryoku, allowing him to sense auras. He scans in a circle around himself* I feel that same aura again from earlier today. Is someone following me? *Yáshido looks at the dent in the ground behind him* What just happened though, it had to be another person surely. A Protojet and maybe Konseitsu. *Yáshido slowly stands back up, still looking around* Fukashi for sure, I didn't see a thing. *Yáshido creates a wall of water around his Dermal and steams it, cleaning all of the dust and scratches off* That was scary, I got jumped out of nowhere. I know there are people like that, but really, you didn't have to nearly destroy my part of my Dermal. I guess it's not entirely immune to Kosai, only indirect pressure. Hmm~. Now I'm actually worried about her. *Yáshido looks in the direction he thinks the girl went in* Again, now the aura has vanished, and the girl that just assaulted me. *Yáshido instantly turns to his left and jumps a few feet back. Taku and Savanna stand in the middle of two trees staring at him. Savanna's sword is off to her side glowing red* **Taku**: Yáshido . . . **Yáshido**: Taku . . . *Yáshido makes eye contact with Savanna and she has an angry expression* **Yáshido**(thts): Really, Savenna? Why do you have to look so mean? I know we fought a lot, and hurt each other a lot, but you don't have to be so expressive about it. *Yáshido changes his focus to Taku* **Yáshido**: What are you two doing here in Macadamia? **Taku**: I came to find you, Yáshido. Assist in protecting you. I'm sure you've heard I am a Fallen Dicipient. **Yáshido**: And that means I'm supposed to instantly trust you? *A short pause* **Taku**: That would be appreciated. Hear me out when I say I want to help you . . . I actually want to help everyone. **Yáshido**: You want . . . to help? **Taku**: Yes, exactly how it sounds. I want to go against Lark. *Yáshido stands straight up, although still in a defensive posture* **Yáshido**(thts): What a bold claim. Looks like it was worth the wait. **Yáshido**: So, you're saying I can trust you? *Taku*: Yes. However, Savenna's a different story. *Yáshido*: I can tell. *Looking at Savanna, she angrily frowns, and a red glare crosses her eyes* *Yáshido*: I am willing to accept our differences, but only if you are as well, Savenna. *Savanna*: Do not call me by that name. *They continue to stare* *Taku*: It's way more difficult for Savenna than it is for me. Even though we share the same goal, I cannot force her under anything she isn't comfortable with. With that said, Savenna, I want you to shake Yáshido's hand. *Savanna turns to Taku* *Savanna*: You're joking? I can deal with him being in the area, but there's no I could do that. Not in a million years. *Shocked, Taku turns towards Savanna* *Taku*(w): Savenna? We've already talked about this. He is here. One of the final aspects of what you and I have been working on. *Savanna*: As much as I want to deal with it, it's hard trying to forgive someone who's put multiple scars on my body, Taku. *Taku*: If we're going to be joining the same side, it's going to be something you're going to have to deal with in its entirety. *Savanna*: What? You never told me that I would have to be buddy-buddy with the Hero if we were accepted. *Taku*: Come here. *Savanna walks right next to Taku* Give us one second, Hero. *Yáshido nods at Taku. Taku summons a Barre around him and Savanna* *Yáshido*(thts): Wow, I didn't know Savenna hated me that much. *Inside the Barre* *Taku*: This is one of the final aspects of our plan. The plan that we made and agreed on together, that no matter what, it will be accomplished. *Taku holds on to Savanna's shoulders and they stare directly into each other's eyes* It was you who said, 'I want to change'. It was you who gave me the heart to not do evil anymore. And now we made it to one of the things we really need. The Hero of the 7th Generation, and this might be our only chance of persuading him to believe us. We both know, if we don't, there's no way he would let us go free. Attacking him is no longer an option; I just can't go back to doing those things I did before, Savenna. If the only time in my life where I would plead . . . would be now . . . to the one I love. Please, Savenna. *Taku hugs Savanna. Savanna kisses Taku on the check* *Savanna*: Okay, I will throw my pride, everything, aside for you. *Taku*: Thank you. *Taku lets go of Savanna and she turns back to Yáshido's direction while Detrantsing. Taku Reverses the Barre* *Yáshido*(thts): They're out. *Savenna Reverses her sword and she sighs before walking towards Yáshido. Yáshido starts walking towards her. They meet halfway. Savenna stares at Yáshido. Yáshido raises one hand up in the shaking position* *Yáshido*: Truths? *Savenna clinches as she looks at his hand before raising hers and shakes it. When she grips onto it, a sphere of Pure Energy spins around their hands and shocks them both* *Yáshido*(thts): Woah, we've connected our hands together so many times during fighting, we naturally release energy when we grip onto each other's hand. That's crazy. *Savanna*: Truths. *They shake hands. After they let go, a surge of energy evaporates in the location where they separate. They lower their hands. Savenna turns to Taku and nods. Taku raises his hands up to his mouth* Yáshido(Telepathy(T))(*Taku*): Everyone, we have obtained the Hero. Head back to base.

(Namari): On it. (Keshio): YOU ACTUALLY DID? THERE'S NO WAY. *As this happens, Yáshido slightly rubs his ear. Savenna sees this* Yáshido(thts): I was not expecting that. (T)(Taku): Focus on getting back first. *The sound of heavy breathing echoes through the bandwidth* (Laito): I think-, I'm legit going to pass out. I've been walking in a loop since we started. Like three Balancers came up to me and I got so scared. Luckily, I got them off my case. Then like all of these students came up to me asking for pictures and my Mangole information. I had to say no to at least two hundred students. (Keshio): I like how he says that, yet I haven't seen a single student out here. (Namari): Same, and didn't you hear me when I said you didn't have to walk, Laito? (Laito): Nah, no thanks. I would rather walk than camp in a bush. All of your Pure Energy levels are probably toasted. (Taku): Didn't you all hear me when I said get back to base? (Laito): Haha, on my way. (Keshio): Be there in a bit. (Taku): Travel together. Namari, make sure you don't let them get off track. (Namari): They left me already, Taku. (Keshio): Halfway there too. (Taku): You know what it's pointless. Just make sure you all are around the table when you get there. You'll be introducing yourselves. *Taku lowers his hand from his mouth* Yáshido: Telepathy to~ ? Taku: The students from Jurono, they were also helping in finding you. Yáshido: I see. Taku: You mind teleporting back with me or walking? Yáshido: I'll walk. I want to hear some more of how you plan to help go against Korosi. I can cast a Fukashi over all of us as we walk. Taku: Sounds good. Yáshido: Did you think leaving them alone was a good idea? Macadamia is not a Seira under communism, but still private is private and public is public. Just two clicks of a button and they could find an aura of anyone. Taku: I'm not going to lie to you Yáshido, I thought it would be much harder to find you. *Taku awkwardly laughs* I was expecting to have to travel to another part of the world, just to hear that you've been seen completely opposite of where we were, but believe me, Savenna and I have been trying our absolute hardest on trying not to be arrested. The kids, on the other hand, it's all down to trust. Yáshido: Hmph, okay.

-The three of them walk back to Taku's hideout. Taku tells Yáshido about Jurono and what Korosi's next missions are. Once they cross the tree line to Taku's house, they start walking towards the entrance-

Yáshido: I see, that explains a lot. If he takes out the Energy Dispositors, and a com-tower. There's no way a Seira could signal an attack before it's too late. Taku: Much like Alma and Yato. Yáshido(thts): Attacking from the inside out, huh? Interesting. Yáshido: Do you know any Dicipients that are in Macadamia? Taku: Two, oh I'm glad you brought that up. Kata was here. He says that Lark sent a couple out to look for you. Yáshido: So, they have started searching for me. Taku: I'm glad I found you first. Wouldn't want you being attacked after what happened in Darku. Yáshido: Did he tell you? Kata? Taku: Not everything. I'm just happy you're still alive. When I heard that you lost against Lark, it seemed as if the world was collapsing in on me, but then I heard that you escaped, and I knew then what I had to do next. I'd be done for without at least having you. *Savenna*: Sorry to bud in, but, Yáshido, could you tell me how your fight went with Korosi? *Yáshido*(thts): Of course. Of course, you would ask that. Out of ALL the questions you could have asked, you decided on that one. Even Taku avoided asking me that. Shaking my head Savenna, shaking my head. *Savenna*: I would really appreciate it if you would. *They arrive at the door* *Yáshido*: That's a very personal question. *Savenna*: Could you at least tell me if you completely lost? Did you stand a chance at all? *Yáshido*(thts): Oh yes, I was standing alright. Over an empty cabin of nothingness. *Yáshido*: It was a close fight. Really close. Then an unexpected occurred. *Savenna*: What was it? *Taku*: It can wait, Savenna. We're here, I'll let you get your time with him once he's settled, okay? *Kind of annoyed, Savenna looks away* *Savenna*(m): Alright. *Taku opens the door and they walk inside. Kamira, Keshio, Laito, Namari, and Otara are sitting around a table* *Yáshido*(thts): Otara? She's out? But why? *Taku*: These are others who I picked up. *The five of them around the table have school uniforms on* *Yáshido*: Kamira Exna? *Kamira*: Greetings, Hero. *Kamira winks* *Yáshido*: Namari Katsuni, a tournament specialist. *Namari*: Hi, Hero. You actually watch some of my fights in the tournaments? *Yáshido*: I've caught a few. *Keshio*: Yáshido, how's it going? *Yáshido*(thts): It's actually quite sad how I know all these people. *Yáshido*: Denki master, Keshio. *Keshio*: I'm going to have to start calling myself that now. *Yáshido*: Laito, Kamira's man. *Laito points his fingers at Yáshido* *Laito*: You know it. *Yáshido makes direct eye contact with Otara* *Yáshido*: Otara Misugami, nice to see you once again. *Taku*: Are you feeling better, Otara? *Otara nods* *Kamira*: She woke up inside the Chamber, Savenna. I let her out once all the Nitrogenous was out. *Savenna*: Good. *Kamira*: Her potency is back to par, but her body physically has to recover. *Yáshido*: What happened to her? *Everyone looks at Kamira* *Kamira*: Hehe~. *Taku*: I heard they had an accident while training. *Savenna*: Can you speak, Otara? *Otara shakes her head left to right* *Kamira*: I gave her some paper if that'll help. *Otara hands Kamira a written piece of paper* *Kamira*: Okay. *Kamira looks at Yáshido* Yáshido, uhm, Otara wants to know 'do you still have it'? *Yáshido looks at Otara* *Yáshido*(thts): Do I still have it? What could she be-, oh the lance, that's what I have. *Yáshido*: Yes, I do. *Otara puts her hand out* You want it back? *Otara nods* Apara Lance. *Otara's Lance appears on the table. Otara grabs the lance by its handle. Otara's lance glows white before Pure Energy from the weapon starts to leak off into her body. Pure Energy from her also starts to go inside of the weapon. Otara takes a deep breath. After five seconds she stops* *Otara*: Much better. Here you are. *The lance moves towards Yáshido. Yáshido Reverses the weapon* *Laito*: Well miss O.P. girl, why didn't you do that before? *Otara*: My Pure Energy was tainted. That particular weapon still had an untainted form of my Pure Energy that I could use to naturally heal myself, but I only healed my mouth muscles. *Namari*: Otara has Personal

Casting at another level, but now you look like you're extremely mad for some reason. *Otara looks at Namari* **Otara**: Time will come when I don't, so don't mind it too much. **Keshio**(m): Even though she always looks like she wants to hurt someone. *Otara looks at Keshio being right next to him. Keshio looks away, pretending neither he nor Otara heard that* **Yáshido**: So, Kamira, Taku tells me you're the teacher here? **Kamira**: Emhm. *Yáshido looks at Taku* **Yáshido**: You've told me you've had them for? **Taku**: A while now, I'd say four days. Now, personally, I think you should stay here and support me while trying not to alert the public. Including any Dicipients around this area. **Yáshido**: I'm more concerned about you. You don't have the authorization to live here. **Taku**: That's one thing I need your help with. **Yáshido**(thts): Even if I do stay here, wouldn't his aura be sensed by any Dicipients that come lurking? **Yáshido**: I see, they can't attack you because of the treaty, so they'll never expect me to be with you. Is that what you're saying? **Taku**: Possibly, but, when I met Kata, he told me that Lark might break the treaty. **Yáshido**: He can't just do that. **Taku**: That's what I said. So, if he chooses so, they could appear here randomly to take me down. **Kamira**: Excuse me, but I don't understand how the treaty works exactly. *Everyone looks at Kamira* **Kamira**: I understand that in order to become a Dicipient, you form some type of seal with the Demon King, but when you become a Fallen Dicipient, what's exactly stopping a Dicipient from attacking you? **Otara**: The Demon King has a covering over everyone under him, Kamira. It-, **Taku**: I wouldn't want to interrupt you, Misugami, but it's much deeper than that. The Seal is more of an inner soul exchange. Once it's made, your intentions and whereabouts become one with the Demon King. It's not like you don't have free will, but that's what makes it so final. The Seals themself are like a fetus version of Yáshido's and Lark's Seals. That's why it grants so much power. Hence, a Dicipient. However, the Seals themself can be directly or indirectly manipulated. I guess you could put it in two different categories. The first being, a willing separation between the Demon King and the Dicipient. An agreement that destroys the seal. The other being, a forced breakaway without the other's consent. My case is the ladder. With Savenna's attempts at getting at me, and understanding what was happening, I forged enough power to escape from my own will. Now, what has been in your head Kamira; The seals on Dicipients never unregister another Dicipient, or Fallen Dicipient to clarify, without a direct encounter. If a Dicipient now tries to attack me, no damage will be done. A shield from their seal itself will withdraw all the damage done because it's made to not hurt allies. But if I were to attack, not having the seal anymore, that's when every Dicipient loses that bond with me on the spot, allowing them to attack me back. *With everyone in shock but Otara and Savenna, Kamira sighs* **Kamira**: That explains a lot. **Yáshido**: I always wondered why it felt like I'd hardly ever see friendly fire, it wouldn't occur regardless. **Taku**: But second parties like Savenna are still at risk, Yáshido. **Savenna**: I'm not protected by the seal, because I'm not a Dicipient. **Namari**: I guess that goes for everyone who's on

Korosi's side and not a Dicipient. **Keshio**: That's a huge tactical advantage. **Laito**: Yeah with that in mind, it's not like you can hold a Dicipient hostage when fighting another Dicipient. **Otara**: What a smart move the Demon Kings has made. **Yáshido**: Something I would have to agree on, Otara. You mentioned before that there were two Dicipients in Macadamia besides Kata. Who are they? **Taku**: Kasca and Lethica, but I don't think they're going to come out and even if they do, they'll probably retreat. **Yáshido**: Lethica? He's in Macadamia? **Taku**: Yes. Kasca was planned to traverse between Macadamia and Catalyst. Lethica is only patrolling in Macadamia, anywhere part of Macadamia he wants. **Yáshido**: If we need to fight anyone, in Macadamia, it would be him. **Taku**: But, if you fight, the word will spread that you're in Macadamia. Then Macadamia will be attacked as a whole. **Yáshido**: How are you so sure? **Taku**: There are about ten Dicipients on this island alone, not counting second parties. Another two I would worry about are in Digona. Povroca, and Nvonka. **Yáshido**: I've known that Dicipients are scattered around the place but ten? Zenni said that the highest was probably six or seven? **Taku**: Well, Lark has a way of doing things and because you escaped, he probably will send about five more here. To think of it, he actually will send them here. That explains why Kata is here. **Yáshido**: That does. **Yáshido**(thts): Lethica, Povroca, and Nvonka, all of them are dangerous. **Taku**: Macadamia is the largest Seira, Kata was only about three miles away from where I saw him. **Yáshido**: Wait, so how long have you been here? **Taku**: Almost a month here, in Macadamia for a few months. **Yáshido**: Okay. *They discuss and disclose information for a few more minutes* So, do you plan on joining the Macadamian Army? **Taku**: Something like that. *Taku stretches while looking at Savenna* I'm sure you're tired by now, Yáshido. **Yáshido**: Maybe just a little. *Taku points at the students while his hands are behind his neck* Show the Hero where he will be sleeping. **Namari**: I'll do it. **Taku**: Alright, see you all in the morning. *Taku starts walking to his room at the end of the hall. Savenna makes eye contact with Yáshido before turning around and walking towards the room as well. Keshio helps Otara, who's in a wheelchair, outside. Everyone else also goes outside* **Yáshido**: You all really fine with being here? **Kamira**: It could be worse, when he first encountered me, I was alone. And we all know how that could have gone. Oh, and yes, I'm fine with being here. **Laito**: As long as I can keep coming, I'm straight. **Yáshido**: How about you three? You feel like he's going to use your power for wrong? **Namari**: Otara has been kind of hawking him. **Otara**: I wouldn't say hawking, more of just forbidding any bad actions and thoughts I have against him that he does. **Keshio**: I'm not gonna lie, that didn't make any sense, Otara. **Otara**: I'm fine with being here. **Keshio**: Same. **Namari**: Me three. **Yáshido**: Well, that's moral for me. So, I'll do my best as well. **Kamira**: It was nice being here and all, but I have to go now. **All**: Bye, Kamira. **Kamira**: Oh, okay then. **Laito**: See you guys. Bye, Yáshido. *Yáshido nods at Kamira and Laito as they leave* **Keshio**: Otara, you want to go back and rest? **Otara**: Yes, that would be nice. **Keshio**: Okay, hold on. *Kamira and Laito leave.

Keshio helps Otara into the dorm and her room. Namari and Yáshido stand in the intersection of the hallways. Namari starts to walk down the center hallway and passes Yashi's room, she stops and looks at it* **Yáshido**: What's the matter? **Namari**: We're missing someone. **Yáshido**(thts): Now's my chance! **Yáshido**: Oh, could you be talking about Yashi? *Sporadically, Namari slams a fist in her left palm* **Namari**: Yeah, that's who's missing. I haven't seen Yashi. *Namari looks at Yáshido* How'd you know? **Yáshido**: Well, he was actually the first to meet me, but he told me he wasn't going to be coming back. **Namari**: Did he tell you what he was doing? **Yáshido**: I was actually surprised myself because you four were missing and I was wondering what he was doing just traveling in the forest in Artea. He kinda-sorta refused to answer me, but he didn't look as if anything bad happened to him. The right thing for me to do at that point was to take him to a Macadamian General and see what they wanted to do with him, but he was gone before I could do anything. **Namari**: I see. Well, I'm sure he wouldn't mind you having this room. **Yáshido**(thts): I'm sure he wouldn't mind either. **Yáshido**: Uhm, before you go, is there a shower here? **Namari**: Yes, but make sure you knock first, it's more of a large bath though. **Yáshido**: That's fine, I'll be taking that first. **Namari**: Do you want some privacy; I know you have to get out of the Dermal to clean yourself. **Yáshido**: Well, I'm sure it'll be fine. **Namari**: Okay. *Namari walks Yáshido to the bath and opens a closet next to the bath* You want spare clothes, right? **Yáshido**: Yes, thank you. **Namari**: No problem. *Namari hands Yáshido a towel and a black robe* **Namari**: This looks so weird. Seeing someone in a Dermal walking into a bath with a towel and robe. **Yáshido**: Hahaha, that is a bit weird. Thanks, do you want me to call you by your first name or last? **Namari**: First names fine. **Yáshido**: Thanks for the introduction, Namari. **Namari**: Thanks for being here, I feel all the more protected. Goodnight. **Yáshido**: Goodnight. *Namari leaves as Yáshido enters the bathroom* **Yáshido**(thts): Woah, this bath is actually huge. Here's where all the space is. *Yáshido walks inside the water* It's perfect. *Yáshido Reverses his Dermal. He sits in the middle of the bath* **Yashi**: Oh yeah~. **Yashi**(thts): It's been almost a week since I've really had a proper bath, that's disappointing. *Yashi starts to bathe himself* Taku's in it for the good all along, just what I needed. I'm surprised though, it's been a couple of days since I fought Korosi and he hasn't made it known to the public yet. Maybe it's benefiting him, he just wants me to make the first move. One word that I'm spotted, and he'll send a barrage of Dicipients at whatever Seira I'm in. Not to mention Dia's not by my side anymore. I can't really rely on a partner who I can perfectly coordinate with, let alone knows my fighting style. Emuna's always a choice, but she's just too busy. What's also surprising is how long Taku says he's been here and somehow hasn't been spotted. *Yashi sighs* **Yashi**: What am I talking about, more than likely they already know he's here and are just spectating. *A few minutes later and someone knocks on the door before it slightly opens* **Otara**(w): Yáshido, are you still here? *Yashi nearly falls forward in the water from hearing Otara's voice. Maintaining his balance, Yashi summons the helmet part of his Dermal* **Yáshido**: Yes. **Otara**: Do you mind splitting it with me, I kind of wanted to take one too. I won't be a bother. **Yáshido**: That's fine. I wouldn't think you'd have to ask for my permission, Otara. *Yashi turns towards the wall away from Otara's way* **Otara**: I would ask no matter who was in here, Hero. Some people like to bathe alone *In the back of his mind knowing who Otara is but not knowing what she is wearing, nor ever being in a situation like this before causes a cold chill to run down his back* **Yáshido**(thts): It's really steamy here anyways. *Yashi looks down* **Yáshido**: Uhm, Otara can I ask you a question? **Otara**: Sure. *A splash of water over in Otara's area, signifying her entrance into the water* **Yáshido**: Why did you want to fight me? *Otara pauses, halfway into entering the large tub, looking at her reflection in the water* **Otara**: Personal reasons. If I was feeling better and we weren't in a bath right now, I would tell you. **Yáshido**: I'll be happy to hear when that time comes. **Otara**: I'll make sure to tell you. *A few seconds later* **Yáshido**: Are you okay? **Otara**(w): What do you mean? **Yáshido**: Like, what happened to you sounds like it was very serious. Not to mention, you weren't able to walk just some minutes ago actually. 'You sure you don't need to go to the hospital possibly? **Otara**: I'm fine. I heal fast. It's just my muscles, they're a little sore. **Yáshido**: Oh, okay. I see why you're taking a bath then. **Otara**: Not the only reason, but okay. *More splashes by Otara. A minute passes* **Yáshido**(thts): I don't have long before the Hero's aura is off me. I'm done anyways. *Yashi climbs his way up the stairs and around trying not to look in Otara's direction* **Yáshido**: Have a good rest, Otara. Hopefully, you feel better in the morning. **Otara**: Thank you for being concerned, goodnight. **Yáshido**: Goodnight. *Yashi puts his towel in the bin. He then walks into a changing room, looking at the set of clothes Namari gave him in the mirror* This doesn't look comfortable at all. At least I'm going to be in my Dermal the whole time. *Yashi puts on the uniform that Namari gave him. With the tunic is a mask that covers his face, and his hair is folded back behind a strip. Yashi then exerts a small amount of Yáshido aura across his body. Yashi exits the bath and walks to his room from before. As he walks around the corner, Savenna is sitting on the balcony where the window is with her back against the frame looking into the sky; One leg is crossed over the edge and the other is lying against the inner wall. As Yashi's footsteps become more apparent, Savenna lays her eyes on Yashi. Yashi stops at his door with his hand on the handle realizing Savenna is looking at him* **Yashi**(thts): At this point, it's just a matter of time before one of them finds out. I wonder how Savenna will feel if she does. I might as well say something before I fall asleep. *Yashi turns towards Savenna after summoning his helmet again* **Yáshido**: Goodnight, Savanna. I look forward 'working with you. *Savenna stands up and walks next to Yashi without turning his way* **Savenna**: It's Savenna, Hero. **Yáshido**: But you said-, **Savenna**: I've passed that now, just remember for next time. **Yáshido**: I will. *Savenna steps back a few steps and looks at Yashi's clothes* **Savenna**: Nice clothes. *Savenna chuckles before walking down the corridor and out the building* **Yáshido**: Nice clothes, hmph. *Yashi opens the door. Walking inside, after closing the door, he immediately lies down in his bed* **Yashi**(thts): Welp, here we go. *Yashi falls asleep*

Chapter 7 – Carnage

Yashi opens his eyes; He is standing in a dark hallway **Yashi**(thts): What, another dream? *Yashi scans his surroundings* This is Korosi's base. ^Yashi senses something thrown at him from the opposite end of the hallway. Yashi holds up his hands to try to catch it, but after realizing what it is he tries to summon a Barre^ **Yashi**: That's right, Magic doesn't work in dreams. ^Yashi puts his back against the left wall as a hammer nearly hits him and smacks the wall that once stood behind him. A trail of steam sticks to the hammer's path^ **Yashi**: That's . . . Dia's hammer. ^Dia's hammer, being forged into the wall, starts to shine behind detaching itself and flying back into the darkness^ **Yashi**: Why would she be attacking me? *Yashi starts to walk down the hall. Yashi continues to walk until he is surrounded by pure darkness* I don't feel her getting any closer, but I feel Korosi instead. No, it's not necessarily Korosi. I feel a bundle of hatred and evil combined. *Suddenly Yashi's amulet starts to glow. He spots a red glow in the distance* That's the Demon King's amulet. *Yashi starts to walk towards it before he feels something from behind him. As Yashi turns around*

-Yashi wakes up-

Yashi: Huh-ah! *Yashi jumps up and looks around him. His heart is beating fast and sweat runs down his face* **Yashi**(thts): Just another dream Yashi . . . nothing else to it. *Yashi stretches his arms, as he tries to stretch his legs something prohibits him from doing so. He looks towards the end of the bed and there is a figure coiled up around his right leg* **Yashi**: What's this? A Familiar? No way I summoned a Familiar while I was sleeping. *Yashi reaches out to the figure and pokes it. It moves slightly* That's definitely not a Familiar. Wait, did I just poke its? Nah~ . . . *The figure leans up as if it was waking up. As it does this, the blankets fall off* Niola?! *Niola yawns* **Niola**: Ahh~. That was a nice nap. *Niola rubs her hair while facing Yashi* Good morning, Yashi. **Yashi**(w): Niola! What are you doing here?! **Niola**(w): What am I doing here? To get to you of course. *Yashi backs up in his bed* **Yashi**(w): Woah-, what do you mean by, 'get to me'? **Niola**: I saw everything . . . after you met Emuna. I've been keeping tabs on you. **Yashi**(w): May I ask why? **Niola**(w): My interests. *Niola moves her legs to the outside of the bed over Yashi's* It seems like you got them good. **Yashi**(w): Wait, you mean you've literally been watching me this entire time? **Niola**(w): Does that question really need to be answered? **Yashi**(w): Yes. It really does. **Niola**(w): Lately, I've been seeking more adventures. As more and more places are being discovered, more adventurers, and societal experiments, it's been too crowded. This seems like a good adventure to me. Something I can feel justified for. Just think of it like you said, I'm your little Familiar. *Niola chuckles and smiles* **Yashi**(m): Please no. **Yashi**(thts): It's like, the way she acts is so contagious. *Sighs* If she already knows what the situation is, I don't see a problem going along with whatever this is. **Yashi**(w): Fine, your name will be Reine, and Kosai will be your main Elilament. *Niola's hair starts shining as it changes from a pink color to a purple color and its formality changes to a different style. The clothes around her also shine a white color before they turn into a standard school uniform* **Yashi**: So, it was your aura who I was feeling. **Reine**: Yup. With the girl in the forest and the Chamber, that was my doing. I have to say though, that was some scene. **Yashi**: Don't remind me. What did you do to her? *Reine looks at the ceiling* **Reine**: Well, I noticed what she was trying to do to you, so I gave her a firm talk. But you know, I guess she is very obsessed with people like us because she nearly captured me too. **Yashi**: She nearly captured you? How? *Reine looks back at Yashi* **Reine**: I don't want to talk about it. I managed to put her unconscious and took her to the school's nurse. **Yashi**: Oh, that was nice of you. **Reine**: You think so? **Yashi**: I'm still not sure why you're doing all of this. **Reine**: The less you know, Yashi. *Someone knocks on the door. With a flash of light, the Hero Dermal appears across Yashi's body. The door opens* **Kamira**: Yáshido, are you awake? *Kamira sees Reine and Yáshido in the bed* **Reine**: You didn't tell me someone would be joining us. *Kamira turns away* **Kamira**: What are you two doing-?! I-, I mean, I never knew the Hero was this indecent. **Yáshido**: What? No, you got it all so wrong. This is my Familiar. **Kamira**: Your Familiar? *Kamira slowly looks back at Reine* So, you finally got your first Familiar? **Yáshido**: Yup, I was surprised too when I woke up and she was just 'here'. *Kamira walks up to them* **Reine**: My master was just soothing me. **Yáshido**(w): Rule of thumb, Reine, I forbid you to call me master. Understand? *Reine looks at Yáshido confused, and nods* **Reine**(m): Okay?~ **Kamira**: Reine. A Type Two Familiar. Nothing less expected from the Hero, but why isn't she fully developed; Reine doesn't have a Dermal. **Yáshido**: Premature. **Kamira**: Oh, I see. *Reine has a mischievous face as Kamira continues to survey her* Well, I'm sure you would like to train with us, right? **Yáshido**: Yeah, that could be entertaining, but it depends, will there be a Barre around us when we do? **Kamira**: You mean like all the time? **Yáshido**: I'm not supposed to be located, so that would be nice. *Reine gets out of the bed* **Reine**: I got you covered. **Yáshido**: Oh, okay. **Kamira**: To be honest, you'll just be watching. **Yáshido**: Oh. **Kamira**: Be ready in 'thirty, okay? **Yáshido**: Okay, thank you, Kamira. **Kamira**: No problem. *Kamira leaves and closes the door behind her* **Reine**: So, what should I call you then? **Yáshido**: What everyone else calls me. **Reine**: I can't say, 'The 7th Generation Hero', every single time I have to call your name. *Yáshido laughs* **Yáshido**: The Hero or Yáshido. **Reine**: Now that you mention it, that makes more sense. *They both laugh* **Yáshido**: That's pretty cool though, how you can imitate your aura to make it seem like you're a Familiar. **Reine**: I think that's an actual Elilament that hasn't been patented yet. *Yáshido jumps, surprised* **Yáshido**: Seriously?

Reine: Yeah, if I get a sample of any aura, I can imitate it. Even yours. *Yáshido*: Why haven't you called it in yourself? *Reine*: I thought about it deeply. If I were to, it'll just cause a lot of problems. At this point, I think I've Aced it. Imagine how bad people will use it. *Yáshido*: What would you call it? *Reine looks at her thighs before looking at Yáshido with a smile* *Reine*: Reinu. *Yáshido*: Really. *Reine*: I like it. You don't? *Yáshido*: It doesn't matter. So, Reinu. *Yáshido*(thts): Ah that's so cringy. *Yáshido*: Is changing your aura, that means if you use the same stage Denryoku, that will mean you can sense the original aura. *Reine*: You have an Aced Denryoku? *Yáshido*: Yes. Do you not remember who I am? *Reine*: That doesn't mean you would have an Aced Denryoku. *They stare at each other* Well? *Yáshido*: I was expecting another remark. *Reine softly laughs. Yáshido activates his Aced Denryoku. The sensation from Reine traces back to the original aura of Niola* *Yáshido*: Cool. It actually works. How much Pure Energy does it take up? *Reine*: As little as Denryoku itself. *Yáshido*: You sure you don't want to Alchemi it? *Reine*: Maybe to mark my name down in those books with those other people. Give the Alchemist something to do. *Yáshido*: I need to get ready for training. Stay here and don't do anything that will draw attention. *Reine*: Me? Drawing attention? I'll try not to for once. *Yáshido*: Thank you. *Yáshido transforms out of his Dermal and washes his face and brushes his teeth. Inside his room. He looks at Reine and she has a plate of food on her lap* *Yashi*: Didn't I tell you not to leave. *Reine*: I didn't, Namari came and dropped this off. She didn't see me though. *Yashi looks at the bedroom door as he closes the bathroom door* *Yashi*: Sorry for blaming you. *Reine*: Don't mind it, as long as I can have some. *Reine looks down at the plate of food* *Yashi*: Sure. *Reine takes a piece of bread. A spark of light appears behind her back* What's that? *Reine*: Oh, this? *Reine takes a plate from behind her and sets each plate on each of her legs* *Yashi*: Did you just make a plate out of Particle Magic? *Reine*: Yes. *Yashi looks at the plate Reine made and it has food on it* *Yashi*(thts): She also made food for some reason. *Yashi*: Can I have my bread back? *Reine*: No. *Yashi*: Why not? *Reine*: Because you said I could have it. *Yashi*: No, I . . . *Reine looks at Yashi* Oh wait, I did. *Reine*: Exactly. *Reine eats the piece of bread in two quick bites* Delicious. *Yashi walks over to Reine and reaches for his plate. Reine slightly moves her legs. Yashi backs away* *Yashi*: May I have my breakfast, please? *Reine*: Sure, here you go. *Reine picks up the plate and hands it to Yashi. Yashi grabs it and sits next to her*

-After they are done eating, they walk towards the dorm's entrance. In front of the dorm door-

Yáshido: I'm already weirded out by this. You'd seem like the type of person I'd run into more often. *Reine*: Will you introduce me when we go out? *Yáshido*: When we go out? *Reine*: Out of the dorm silly. *Yáshido*: I knew what you meant. I'll let them say something about you first. *Yáshido opens the door. Keshio is the only one standing on the porch. He turns to Yáshido* **Keshio**: Good morning, Hero. **Yáshido**: Good morning. *Yáshido and Reine walk outside the building. Keshio notices Reine as they stand next to him* **Keshio**: A Familiar? **Yáshido**: Crazy right? *Keshio scans Reine* **Keshio**: What's your name? **Reine**: Reine. **Keshio**: Nice, my name's Keshio. **Yáshido**: Where is everyone? **Keshio**: They are with Taku. **Yáshido**: You know what they're doing? **Keshio**: Not a clue, but Kamira is already in the training grounds though. *Yáshido looks at the training grounds. Kamira is standing in the middle of the ring spinning in circles. Yáshido then looks at Taku's house to see Laito, Namari, Otara, Savenna, and Taku. Namari and Taku are walking towards them while the others are walking towards Kamira. Once in talking distance* **Taku**: Good morning, Yáshido, Keshio. **Yáshido & Keshio**: Good morning. *Namari stops in front of the stairs* **Taku**: I want to ask you a question, Yáshido. *Taku walks up one stair looking at Yáshido* **Yáshido**: Yes? **Taku**: Yáshido, is it true that Yashi left on his own will? **Yáshido**: Yashi? That's the kid I met in the forest in Artea. Yeah, he left the scene before I could do anything to him. I believe he's still in Macadamia though. **Taku**: You're sure? **Yáshido**: I know he's wanted for good reasons, but he seems like the type who wouldn't get himself caught. **Taku**: Okay, I'll take your word for it then. *Taku looks at Namari and walks back to his house. Namari sighs* **Namari**: Thank you so much. Taku's still kind of scary when he's serious. **Keshio**: He didn't hurt you, did he? **Namari**: There's no way he could with everyone being in there. He realized that Yashi wasn't here and was questioning everyone. And the rest is history. *Namari looks at Reine and gasps* Who's-, who's that? **Yáshido**: My Familiar. *Reine walks down the stairs and stands in front of Namari* **Reine**: My name's Reine, nice to meet you. What's your name? **Namari**: Nice to meet you too. My name is Namari. *Namari scans Reine* You don't even have your Dermal yet. **Reine**: Still working on it, hah. **Savanna**: Excuse me. *They all look at Savanna. She points at the training grounds* They are waiting for you. *While they are walking to the training grounds* **Namari**: Why did you choose a school uniform for her base, Yáshido? **Yáshido**: It was more of her choosing whatever she wanted. *Namari and Keshio jump* **Namari & Keshio**: Wait So You Saw Her Naked?! **Yáshido**: NO, I summoned her during my sleep so she could choose whatever base she wanted. *Namari sighs out of relief* **Namari**: That explains it. *Reine looks at Yáshido* **Reine**: I only choose what I thought would look best from your memories. When you saw me, you looked quite pleased. **Keshio**: Seems like we have another advantage of ours. **Yáshido**: Let's get you guys to Kamira. I don't want you to get in trouble. *After they reach the training ground* **Kamira**: Good morning, all. **Students**: Good morning. *Yáshido looks at Otara* **Yáshido**(thts): She looks completely healed. That's good. *Yáshido focuses his attention back on Kamira* **Kamira**: Today, we will be having our second spar. I have decided that Otara was the winner of the last one. **Laito**(w): Try hard. **Kamira**: Today's spar will be Keshio and Namari. **Keshio**: Namari? *Keshio looks over to Namari. A big smile covers Namari's face as she looks back at him* **Namari**: Sorry, Keshio, I was hoping I wouldn't be your first fight. **Keshio**: Why's that? **Namari**: Because you wouldn't have any chances of winning. **Laito & Yáshido**: Woah. **Kamira**: Wow, Namari, that was so-, so sassy. **Yáshido**(thts): Yet, Namari acts like that in school. **Keshio**: Yeah, when did you get so cocky? **Namari**: It's not that I'm cocky, it's just that I'm confident. I was hoping to fight Otara, to be honest. **Yáshido**(thts): Okay, now that's different. **Yáshido**: Namari, have you ever seen Keshio fight? **Namari**: Once, and that was against Laito. But based on what I know from school, he's still the same Keshio. **Keshio**: The past is the past, Namari. Don't ever let stats fool you. **Namari**: It's a spar, Keshio, that's why I'm so confident. You'll just have to wait and see. **Kamira**: What rivalry, huh? Ok, same principles as last time. You both remember? *Keshio and Namari both nod* Okay, everyone, get out of the way. *Yáshido, Laito, and Otara sit down on the bench* Ready? **Keshio & Namari**: Ready! **Kamira**: Magica! Barre! *The same Barre as before circles Keshio and Namari. On the bench* **Yáshido**: Hm~, already battling each other? **Laito**: More or less. She increases the Konseitsu before we get serious, or someone gets hurt. **Yáshido**: I see, how does that really help though if it can only lower an Ace down about thirty percent? **Laito**: Well, Yáshido, we aren't trying to kill each other so~. **Yáshido**: Yeah, yeah, forgot. **Laito**: You think you might get a spar? **Yáshido**: If there's a chance, maybe, but I'm supposed to be not spotted remember? **Laito**: Oh Yeah~, haha, forgot. **Kamira**: They're starting! *Inside the Barre* **Keshio**: Let's see if you can back up those claims, Katsuni! Emiradosudo! ^Keshio casts a sword. Afterwards, Keshio's entire body shines white before an ocean blue and Dermal appears. Namari maintains her smile. Without saying a word, multiple waves of air spread from her location. After that, a blunt orange Dermal overlaps her entire body. Namari's arm plates turn orange and end in a dark red on her metal gloves. Waves come from Keshio as well^ **Namari**: Stage II Zoka Vision? I don't think that's enough to keep up. **Keshio**: You're using Stage II Zoka Swiftness. **Namari**: Yeah, I think your Uhnyoi is busted. ^Namari slowly starts walking towards Keshio. Keshio takes a defensive stance. Suddenly, Keshio starts running towards Namari with a burst of red aura. Namari stops her movements and crosses her arms around her chest; Still smiling at Keshio^ **Keshio**: Satellite Strike! ^Keshio's red aura gets merged with Zoka Swiftness's blue aura as he jumps above and slams down on Namari. Dusk spreads from the point of contact. The Dusk is so thick that Yáshido can't even see Keshio or Namari's outline through it. Without warning, a wide beam of electricity comes from the top of the Barre and collides at the center of the impact. More dusk spreads away from the center point until it fills the entire hemisphere. Because the Barre is translucent, the sound of the dense electric cylinder escapes outward, blowing Kamira, Laito, and Otara's hair back. The ground and Barre shake until the column of energy disappears. The dust clears in the center first. Keshio stands looking down at a crater which he felt Namari land^ **Keshio**: Yeah! Direct hit! **Voice**:

Are you sure about that? ^Keshio turns around and feels Namari's aura inside of the dust near the edges of the hemisphere. Once it clears, Namari is standing there unharmed, still smiling^ *Namari*: What's the matter, Keshio? Why are you over there? *Keshio*: Heh, you Protojeted, that's the only way. I didn't even feel you move from your spot. *Namari*: Hahaha, I'm telling you, you can't keep up. *Keshio*: You're telling me you've Aced Zoka Swiftness? *Namari*: That's a possibility. *Keshio*: Even with that advantage-, ^Namari dashes at Keshio and he barely blocks her fist with his sword. A wave of wind comes from the impact. Keshio attempts to strike Namari but she jumps up and coils her hands together, aiming them at Keshio^ *Namari*: Battering Ram! ^An orange rectangular prism engulfs Namari and instantly shoots itself at Keshio with a blast of Pure Energy beaming behind it^ *Keshio*: Metal Breaker! ^Keshio's sword turns emerald green as he prepares to strike. Milliseconds later, their attacks crash with Keshio losing. Keshio is tossed toward the wall of the Barre behind him at an alarming rate. Pure Energy explodes off his Dermal before he hits the curved wall. Although taking Keshio's hit dead-on, Namari's momentum maintains its original speed as she smashes against the ground. Namari's Personal Cast goes away as she lays on the ground. Keshio lands on his forearms. The part of the Barre he impacted has a slight crack in it^ *Outside the Barre* *Yáshido*: That was something. *Kamira*: That attack Namari used negated Keshio's Celestial entirely and he got hit directly too. *Laito*: That's obvious. The force of Namari's strength just overpowered Keshio's speed, and she was going pretty fast as well. There was no hope of him not taking a direct hit. *Kamira looks at Laito* *Kamira*: Someone's been learning. *Laito*: Are you trying to call me-? Never mind, I'll take the compliment. *Yáshido*: What about Namari, you think she did a lot of damage to herself as well? *Laito*: Oh, you're talking to me? *Yáshido nods without looking at Laito* I think hitting the ground so hard that it would Reverse your own Personal Cast, yeah. *Inside the Barre* ^Both of them stand up as if nothing happened^ *Keshio*: Not a Familiar either? *Namari*: Nope. No Blazing Lfow here. *Keshio*: What a cast by the way. *Namari*: Well, it seems like your Dermal ate it for you. *Keshio*: Now it's my turn. *Namari*: Wait a second-, not yet! ^At an insane speed, Namari covers the thirty-yard distance nearly hitting Keshio in his stomach. Keshio manages a slash that should knock Namari's fist towards the ground, but instead, Namari's strike repels Keshio's sword up into the air^ *Keshio*: What?! ^The force pushes Keshio all the way to the Barre. Before Keshio can even catch his breath, Namari is already above him preparing a kick. Keshio leans forward before he Protojets to the other side of the Barre. Keshio turns around as he lands on his feet only to see Namari a few feet away about to kick him again^ *Keshio*(Y): Rah!~ ^As Keshio slashes in Namari's direction, a green wave continues to go forward. Namari Atoskitos herself backward. The poison nearly skids the plate covering her nose. Namari lands on the ground in front of Keshio. Keshio charges Namari. Keshio slashes Namari across her chest, then slashes across her legs, then slashes up her helmet in under half a second. With each successful hit, Particles explode off of Namari's Dermal. Before Keshio could land another blow, Namari catches his sword and pulls it towards her. Keshio becomes face-first to Namari and she headbutts him while kneeing him in the stomach. Keshio slides backward against the ground^ **Namari**: Remember what Taku said when he picked us up? We are the strongest four from the school! It's disappointing that you're not representing that right now! ^Namari holds her hands next to her sides and electric shocks appear in her palms^ **Keshio**: Raitosudo! ^Keshio's emerald sword explodes into an electric yellow color. Tiny sparks randomly shooting out. They stare at each other before Namari holds her hands up. The electricity Namari holds in her hand rushes down her fingers, with each one forming an electric-like dagger. Namari puts her hands back to her sides. Keshio takes a step forward holding his sword out in front of him. Namari spreads her arms up like wings and leans down^ **Keshio**: Galvanic Meteors! ^Multiple swords appear around Keshio and fire towards Namari. Namari sprints through the bombard of swords; skillfully dodging each one. As each one of the passing swords hit the ground behind her, they explode into smaller spheres which creates a cloud of electricity. With every foot Namari gets closer, dodging the incoming swords progressively gets harder. When Namari gets within ten feet of Keshio, Keshio lowers the casting of the swords lower to the ground and increases the rate at which the swords come out. Namari takes the chance to rush Keshio directly since there are no swords in this path. However, Keshio summons a sword in front of him in which it immediately gets fired out and flys right past Namari's helmet. Namari decides to jump above instead of fronting directly at the swords, but the swords then aim up at her. Namari is just too fast for them to follow her arc. Right before Namari hits Keshio he summons a Barre. The electricity from Namari's hands fizzles out as she touches the Barre. Right after, each of her blades fizzles out, Namari gets pierced in the back by three of Keshio's swords. The long blades explode while still in Namari's Dermal. Namari feels the electricity move around her body instead of her Dermal. Namari gets stunned from the multiple electric shocks. Keshio Reverses his Barre and beefs up his attack power as much as he can before diagonally slashing Namari from the top right side of her chest to the left side of her waist. Namari flys to the middle of the Barre, but lands on her feet and rolls into a stand. Multiple sparks of electricity flourish around her Dermal. The slash where Keshio hit is seen as a thick line across her Dermal^ **Namari**: That was my fault. I shouldn't have taken the chance that you would have had any Denki Konseitsu on it. **Keshio**: I wouldn't blame you. ^Namari raises her hand and looks at the sparks while looking at Keshio with a mean look^ **Namari**: Nerque! Sekom! ^A dense gray smoke spreads from Namari's Dermal filling the Barre^ **Keshio**: You think it's that easy? HA! ^Keshio's sword turns frosty blue as he shanks it into the ground. The ground quickly starts to freeze over with clear ice. The smoke lifts up off the ground^ **Namari**: Exactly what I wanted! ^Keshio turns around and Namari has her hands on the ice. The sparks from her Dermal enter the ice travels through it contacting Keshio's boots. Realizing it's too late, Keshio lands down after jumping. Keshio's Dermal starts sparkling with the same yellow flash that covers Namari's^ **Keshio**: Hmph, fair play. You can really notice the difference in power from that Aced Konseitsu. Your Dermal should be gone after that. ^A layer of Pure Energy covers Namari's Dermal before the sparks disappear^ **Namari**: Alright. Give it a shot, Keshio. **Keshio**: Ha, Finally! ^Keshio clears the sparks from his Dermal by emitting Pure Energy around his Dermal as well before a glue aura surrounds him. Dashing towards Namari, she activates Zoka Swiftness too. The two of them start exchanging attacks. At the beginning of the strikes, Namari has the advantage in hits and dodging. But as time passes, Keshio's slashes get faster and faster. So fast in fact, that Namari no longer has the time to throw in any punches or kicks and turns completely defensive. Even having to use the back of her forearms to block Keshio's sword. Although being pushed back, Namari blocks or dodges Keshio's strikes relentlessly^ **Keshio**: Who's trying to keep up now! (Y): AAHH!!! ^Namari starts to lose her balance as her feet no longer slides against the ground but deepens in it. Namari takes a blow right on her shoulder from her left. Before being knocked sideways, Namari uses the momentum to circle Keshio with a kick, landing the attack with her lower leg against Keshio's helmet. Keshio lands back first against the ground before Namari hits the ground. Both of them instantly stand back up facing each other^ **Keshio**: I have an idea, why don't you use one of your tournament moves? **Namari**: Name one. **Keshio**: I wouldn't know. Surprise me. **Namari**: Ha, how about this instead. Blazing Lfow! ^Namari Atoskitos herself onto the ground. Her Familiar gets summoned just a few feet in front of Keshio already about to hit him with one of its claws. Keshio angles his sword for protection. Lfow goes right through Keshio before evaporating into the air behind him. The trail of flames surrounds Keshio's Dermal. Suddenly, Namari kicks Keshio in the center of his back from behind. Keshio slams against the ground once more before flipping onto his feet. Namari balls up her hands into fists and slams them together right in front of her while pointing the form at Keshio. Keshio takes a defensive stance^ **Namari**: This will most likely be my last long short-ranged attack. **Keshio**: What do you mean by that? You're not that even that close. **Namari**: Dlof! ^Namari vanishes from that location and starts to rapidly circle around Keshio. This movement only makes it seem like they are clones appearing around Keshio. Keshio looks and blocks in every direction that he feels Namari aura from^ **Namari**: How's Stage I for your Vision! ^Keshio stands still as he starts to figure a pattern in Namari's movements^ **Keshio**: Found you! Galvanic Meteor! ^An electric sword shoots from thin air. Namari appears behind the handle of the sword as it flys four feet away from Keshio^ **Namari**: Single Blow! ^Keshio gets hit in his chest by the massive Pure Energy strike. Keshio's Dermal bursts off of his body as he stands stunned. Keshio falls backward against the ground^ **Namari**: Huh? ^Namari Reverses her Dermal and all of her Zoka Elilaments. Namari takes a step towards Keshio^ **Namari**: Keshio? ^The Barre disappears as Namari runs to Keshio. Keshio's left eye opens as he crouches onto his knee^ **Kamira**: That's it! That's the fight! **Keshio**: Ah~, that hurt, a lot. *Kamira walks up to them. Namari holds Keshio by the shoulder* **Namari**: Are you alright, Keshio? **Keshio**: Yeah, I think you passed that Konseitsu threshold. **Namari**: Hmm~. **Kamira**: I told you, it throws off a lot of what you sense with your Magic, didn't I? *Kamira turns around to the others and points at Namari* Namari is the winner of this spar! Good job to both of you. **Keshio**(m): I almost lost. Next time, I'll have to go full out from the start. *A shadow pauses over Keshio, he looks up and Namari has her hand out* **Namari**: Just a spar, remember? **Keshio**: Yeah, you're right. *Keshio takes Namari's hand and stands. Everyone sits and waits for instructions after Savanna starts talking to Kamira. On the bench, by Yáshido* **Yáshido**(thts): Namari and that smile. I wonder what she said to him, it's like he got a boost from it. *Yáshido looks at Savanna and Kamira* I could be really nosy right now and activate Zoka Hearing and see what they're up to. *Something tugs Yáshido's shirt* **Yáshido**(w): Oh Reine, what is it? *Niola has a frown and an empty emotional look* **Yáshido**(thts): Her hair is back to normal, and she isn't wearing that outfit. **Yáshido**: Niola? *Niola sighs* **Niola**: Come with me. *Niola and Yáshido go into a more private location. In the woods behind the training ground. Yáshido transforms out of the Hero* **Yashi**: What is it? *Niola continues to walk and stops so that her back is facing Yashi* **Niola**: You remember . . . when we first met, and you told me about your fight. When you met Emuna, I heard that Dia went with you, but she was never there when you fell. Nor when you left with Emuna. *Yashi looks at the ground* I couldn't understand how all that correlated until now. It has been bothering me because I knew something wasn't right. **Yashi**(thts): So, it's true that Niola's been watching me. By tone, something bad happened. **Yashi**: What happened, Niola? **Niola**: It's all over-, the news. **Yashi**: What is? *Niola turns to Yashi and looks directly into his eyes. Water appearing in her eyes starts to drip down her cheeks* **Niola**: It's about Dia. *Yashi tenses up* **Yashi**: What happened with Dia? *Niola starts to tear up even more as she turns back around and her Mangole in front of her. Yashi takes a step next to Niola and starts reading the screen over her shoulder. Yashi's eyes widen from the instant interpretation of the postings. Yashi takes a step back looking to his right arm* **Yashi**: No. This, this isn't right. There's no way she could ever. **Niola**: The worst part is, this is ongoing. (m): This will be the first thing anyone will see when they open their Mangole or mTV. *A tear drops down from Yashi's face as he looks back at Niola, who is now facing him. Her face is full of distress and fear* **Yashi**: Niola-, *While reaching out to Niola, before Yashi could finish saying her name, Niola clings to Yashi while gently crying on his chest* **Niola**: What happened, Yashi? Why is . . . why is Dia in Regra killing people? (m): What happened when you fought Lark? *Yashi doesn't respond but closes the hug by wrapping his arms around Niola* **Yashi**(thts): I don't know what to say, they were close friends. *Niola holds on to the back of Yashi's shirt and squeezes the fabric. She looks up at him and speaks with a soft voice* **Niola**: Anything? **Yashi**: Well-, I- . . . I don't know if this is what she meant by 'goal'. *Niola looks back down at Yashi's chest, and with a faint smile, sniffs her nose* **Niola**: What does that even mean? **Yashi**: She told me she had a goal, but then also said she would see me soon. At first glance, it may look horrible but . . . *Yashi remembers that Dicipients were also engaged in the attack* **Yashi**(m): Out of everything we did together, and all of the struggles we stumped, she did this. Even at the castle- . . . I don't know what to do anymore. **Niola**: Em~. *Niola embraces Yashi even more. Yashi starts to sob as the to sit in a morbid ambiance* It really does hurt. *Sniff* I thought the worst had happened when I found out she went with you, Yashi. You were so badly damaged that I could only assume that she was captured by Lark himself, but I never expected her to join him. *More tears fall from Yashi's face* **Yashi**(m): After seeing that, I don't think I can get her back so easily. Rather, I might not have a chance at all until Dia gets what she's after. **Niola**(w): You really want to get her back? **Yashi**(m): I don't think I could live without her. **Niola**(w): Then, I'll, I'll help you. *Yashi leans back from the hug and looks down at Niola. Niola refrains herself from making eye contact, now conscious of the fact she was crying, and her face is still soaked* **Yashi**: Wha-, really? **Niola**: How could I joke about something like this? I want an answer myself. Dia wouldn't go this far for something so little. What is she after that she couldn't already obtain with you? *Niola quietly chuckles. Yashi leans back in the hug and squeezes her tighter* **Yashi**: Thank you, Niola. Thank you so much. This is probably too soon, but you've been a big help. *Niola smiles* **Niola**: I'm glad I have. *After they're both done* **Niola**: At this point, I'm not sure if they know or not. We've been gone for a while. *Yashi walks a couple feet away. Yashi transforms into the Hero. Niola changes back into her Familiar form* **Yáshido**: Let's get going. *They walk back to the training ground, but no one is there. Reine checks the dorm and no one is seen either. They head to Taku's house. Yáshido grabs the doorknob and twists it, it's unlocked. Yáshido opens the door. Laito, Kamira, Keshio, Namari, and Otara are sitting around a table, Taku and Savanna are standing at the end of the table, opposite of the door. There is a paused Mangole in the middle of the table with the news on* **Yáshido**(thts): I'm too late, they've already seen it. *Yáshido looks at Taku and he looks mad, everyone else is staring at Yáshido not knowing if they should say something first or not. Looking at Savanna, she simply grits her teeth and closes her eyes while looking away from Yáshido* **Reine**(w): We all know what's coming, just say something. **Yáshido**: I saw it too . . . *Taku makes an angry smirk* **Taku**: Were you ever going to tell us she's turned?! *The table and Mangole between them vanish into particles, Taku makes his way over to Yáshido* **Yáshido**: Of course I was, when the time was right. **Taku**: So, you would just let yourself and probably Emuna know? Huh! You most likely didn't even tell the Council. Nor tell the person who has made up a plan? You lost Dia! She was a key part of this operation! **Yáshido**: Let me explain. **Taku**: I don't want to hear it, the time you could have explained, she's gone and destroyed nearly a whole Seira! *A noise is heard behind Taku* **Namari**: Savanna, stop! ^Savanna walks in front of Taku with a sword out^ **Savanna**: How could you lose your Trants! *Another tear drops from Yáshido's face inside his Dermal helmet* **Yáshido**(thts): They don't understand, just let me tell you what happened. **Savanna**: To think that all of what I've been through just gets worse and worse! And then I have to put my trust in you! Of all people?! ^Savanna points her sword at Yáshido^ **Savanna**: What do you have to say?! **Otara**: Apara Transa. ^Otara summons her Lance and Dermal. Standing to the right of Savanna, Otara points it at Savanna. Laito, Kamira, and Namari stand and back away^ **Otara**: Step away from the Hero, Savanna. ^Savanna turns her head towards Otara with an annoyed face. Reine stands in front of Yáshido and stretches out her arms to protect Yáshido. Savanna lowers her sword at Reine^ **Savanna**: Hmph! **Reine**: If you're going to strike! Strike! What good will it accomplish?! *Reine looks at Otara, the intention to fight is expressed across her face. Reine looks back at Savanna* Why would you go this far, do all of this, just to turn back on each other? *Savanna slowly puts her sword down* Do you even realize who you are talking to! He has suffered the most out of all of us, and you won't even let him speak! How rude is that? *Savanna backs away next to Taku with her sword fully down* **Savanna**: Tsk. **Taku**: Well miss Familiar, we're still fairly new to this, so keeping our anger under control is a bit difficult. **Reine**: Maybe you should try harder then. *Taku also backs away with a surprised look on his face. Everyone stands silent as Reine lowers her arms* **Kamira**: Just let the Hero tell you what he needs to say. *Savanna quickly turns to Otara. Otara Reverses her Lance and Dermal, eyeing Savanna. Kamira and Reine nod at each other* **Taku**: My apologies, go ahead. *Taku gently taps Savanna on her shoulder. She takes a deep breath then turns back around* **Savanna**: My apologies. **Yáshido**(thts): Really, that easy? *Reine stands next to Yáshido* **Yáshido**: Dia, it wasn't my fault, and she didn't get captured. She . . . she joined up with Korosi herself! *Everyone is shocked* **Kamira, Keshio, Namari, Taku, Savanna**: What?! **Kamira**: No way. **Namari**: Why would she do such a thing? **Keshio**: Not Dia . . . there's no way. **Otara**: That's actually cruel . . . **Reine**(m): So, it's true. *Yáshido turns towards Reine and leans over to her; He whispers in her ear* **Yáshido**(w): Niola, when I was falling, it was because she had pushed me off. You indeed saved my life, and I thank you for that. **Reine**(m): Yashi . . . *Yáshido turns back around to everyone else* **Yáshido**: You see Savanna, she was the one who left me. In the midst of what was happening, there was nothing I could do. *Savanna looks down with mixed emotions. Kamira steps forward with both of her hands together as a shaking gesture* **Kamira**: There we go, everyone is calm, and we fixed the misunderstanding. **Yáshido**: What she told me herself, is that she isn't working for Korosi. **Taku**: Dia's not gonna be a Dicipient, thank God. **Yáshido**: I do in fact want to get her back, but I don't know what she's going to do. *Out of misery, Yáshido turns and punches the wall* **Kamira**(m): Yáshido . . . *A small silence* **Reine**: Don't you all want to get her back too? *Everyone looks at Reine, except for Yáshido* From his memories, I can tell that they were close and that Dia was not at all a bad person. With hope and effort, we can get her back, but Yáshido can't do it all by himself. **Taku**: There is no doubt that if we can, we should. I would want to do that. **Reine**: And you are already working towards that now, right? **Taku**: 'Already'? **Kamira**: Reine's right, Taku. The whole reason for you forming this group is to help defeat the Demon King, right? **Taku**: Right. *Yáshido turns around* **Reine**: Then you just have to keep recruiting and get your group stronger. **Yáshido**(thts): Niola . . . **Keshio**: I like where she's going with this. **Reine**: First you need the authorization to live here. **Taku**: Already accounted for, that's Yáshido's job. **Keshio**: Say if no one wants to join? **Reine**: Obvious, we'll just work with what we have, each other. **Otara**: If we have a treaty, no one can attack us without penalty. What do we do about the ones who decide to? **Reine**: Well . . . **Taku**: In that case, they'll be the ones fined. Once you have a treaty any hate crime will be dealt with by Macadamian officials regardless of the victim. **Namari**: Sounds solid. **Reine**: SO, Taku, how is it? **Taku**: I can roll with this . . . until I tell you guys more info. **Yáshido**(thts): That was smart. She gave them a plan that they can strive for. Nice work. *Taku turns around and walks back to where he was before Yáshido entered* **Taku**: We were just looking at the damage, but we didn't see all of it. I'll start it over from the beginning. *Taku folds his arms and raises one hand up, the table and Mangole slowly appear. Reine, Savanna, Taku, and Yáshido remain standing as the others sit. The Mangole turns onto the news* **Announcer**(M): 4-17, 983, received 15 at 16. Good evening my fellow Macadamians. This is a disturbing yet unsightly report. Right now, in Regra, who we presume to be Dia, the one who we all know to be the companion and Trants of the Hero himself, is demolishing the Seira of Regra. *A picture taken from inside of Regra appears on the screen. Buildings in flames, smoke covering the air, carriages flipped and broken into pieces scattered across the streets. Countless clouds of Doku's green aura are also placed in many places in the image. Another photo taken above the Seira appears in the photo. In some of the shots, you can still even see blasts being fired, or an explosion in the making. The carnage is unbelievable* **Yáshido**(thts): I can't believe it, even a second time. **Announcer**(M): These pictures were taken on the coastline of Glassway, Regra leading all the way to Kedum [Kedum is halfway through Regra from Glassway] with the casualties ranging to almost a quarter million. **Laito**(m): A quarter-million?! **Kamira**(m): That's not good. **Namari**: All those people. **Announcer**(M): Records to eyewitnesses and photos were taken, Dia was not alone on this massacre, and from the pictures we've gathered you can see that. *A picture of three people standing on a horizon in the distance is shown, the picture is zoomed in* **Yáshido**(thts): Dia's the one in the middle. *Dia's right arm has a Dermal around it. All her clothes are black* She has parts of the Dicipient's clothing on?

What's the meaning of that? Is it just for protection? No time to become confused again. The one on the right, that's, Jyokumo. *Jyokumo has two thin stripes coming from above her back* The one on the left. That's . . . *Yáshido squints his eyes. It didn't make a difference, so he uses Stage I Zoka Vision. He scans the outline and measurements of the figure on the left, but nothing comes up* I don't know who that is. I've never seen them before. **Announcer**(M): In the middle, you can clearly make out Dia. Who seems to be wearing partial Dicipient clothes? Sleeves and Stockings. *The brightness of Dia's silhouette increases* **Otara**: Hm~. **Announcer**(M): The one to the left of Dia is Jyokumo. *Jyokumo's silhouette brightens* Understandably, Jyokumo. But for the one to the right of Dia. We came up with the assumption that it is indeed a new Dicipient. *Savanna clenches her fists then folds her arms* **Savanna**: Tsk. *Savanna and Taku make eye contact. Kamira notices the interaction* **Announcer**(M): This unidentified person has Dicipient clothes with the base a Kastopian General. The clothes, matched with their positioning, with the sun and their angle, doesn't side with none of the Dicipients in the database. Nevertheless, whoever this is, is just as dangerous as the others. But these two weren't hostile as if they were specifically protecting Dia. Along with the other Dicipients spotted, none of them let anyone get close to Dia while she and other Dicipients were attacking. Here is an audio clip from a savaged Mangole transmitter, the actual video was corrupted and will take time to recover. (**Savaged Mangole**): ^People are screaming before an explosion is heard in the background. Ice freezes over something outside the building the Mangole is in. Then, a building collapses just outside. Loud footsteps and heavy breathing soon mask the audio, most likely the person who is holding the Mangole* (**Man**): Emi?! *Wall being shot by a blast* (**Emi**): Xa! *More running footsteps* (**Xa**): YOU STAY AWAY FROM HER!!! *The Mangole falls* Peace Savor! ^The sound of a heavy attack being fired, then being knocked away. The blast hits something as a loud crash and the noise of a broken exhaust is heard^ (**Xa**): Emi, come on! (**Emi**): Okay! ^A second pair of footsteps join the first set. The audio becomes distorted for a few seconds until a larger blast of ice hits something again^ (**Xa**): Go!~ ^Not long after, something flys past them and another explosion is heard^ (**Emi & Xa**): Ahh! ^What sounds like flames fill the Mangole's microphone. Laughter is heard^ (**Jyokumo**): Finish them, Dia! **Yáshido**(thts): Jyokumo. (**Dia**): Catatróph! **Yáshido**(thts): Dia. ^The audio becomes extremely distorted for a few seconds^ (**Emi**): No! Stop! Why are you doing this?! (**Dia**): Attack! ^A large number of mCircles are heard shooting something towards them. During the series of multiple clashes^ (**Dia**): I'm coming for you, Yashi! *Namari softly gasps. The Savaged Mangole stops playing after the sound of something smashing it. Yáshido slightly moves* **Savanna**: Is everything alright? Hero? *Yáshido glances at Savanna* **Yáshido**: I'm-, I'm managing. *Savanna clinches more before looking back at the Mangole* **Announcer**(M): Dia's comment at the end of the clip was very . . . saturated. It sounds like her next goal is to pick up Yashi, who we can assume to be one of the four students who were taken by Taku from a recent invasion at Jurono Academy located in Olhy, Macadamia. It is not clear if Dia and Taku planned this out, or if she's coming to rescue him. This would be a little controversial, but we also know there could or has to be a relationship between Dia and Yashi because Dia also attends Jurono. But with all due respect, after this incident, I don't believe she will be attending it anymore. Digona has sent a support for Regra to help stop the charge from the Dicipients and Sablein is already assisting the cause. Currently, that is all the information we have on the topic and will continue when we have more. Here is a list of other spotted Dicipients. *The screen transitions back between the pictures while also showing the names and mugshots of Dicipients* **Yáshido**(thts): Something was different about her, really different, but somehow still the same. Her voice . . . it sounded like she was in her Trants form. And there was a sad but angry tone with it. *Yáshido looks down* I can't believe she . . . she participated in this. By the looks of it, Dia did the most damage to Regra out of all of the Dicipients. How could Regra not even stop them, let alone, try to focus on capturing them? I guess it was a battle even for Regra. **Voice**: That coward! *Everyone looks at Taku* **Taku**: That's why he ran, he knew Dia was coming for'em. It makes so much sense now. What could he have done to make Dia turn to the point where she would kill people?! *Taku swiftly looks at Namari and Keshio* You two! What's their relationship? **Namari**: From what I could tell, they're really close. **Keshio**: It's like they're dating, but they never claim they are. **Namari**: She's one of the few people he talks to. *Taku slams his fist against the table* **Taku**: Blasphemy! **Yáshido**: If he hasn't been found yet, he's probably far gone. **Taku**: That's what I'm thinking too. **Laito**: You're telling me that no one knows where Yashi's vanished to? *Silence* This is hopeless. *Reine steps on her tippy-toes to whisper into Yáshido's ear* **Reine**(w): Maybe he did something while he was out. *Yáshido nods* **Yáshido**: Maybe he did something while he was out? **Laito**: If he was just in Artea, there is no possible way he could travel on foot to Regra. **Namari**: Yeah, cause if he is wanted, Teleporters aren't going to let him travel, and then Regra is its own island. That amount of water is too dangerous for anyone to fly over. *Yáshido makes eye contact with Kamira as she winks at him* **Kamira**: It's only been a couple of days since Taku picked you guys up, what if he did something before then? **Keshio**: Yeah, that would explain it. **Laito**: Did any of you notice anything about them while you were still in Jurono? **Keshio**: Yeah, because Dia is the Hero's second, it gets around fast rather or not if Dia is at school. She hasn't been to school in the past week when I was there. **Namari**: Yashi had been absent too, taking a vacation I believe. *Namari looks at Taku* The day you came was also Yashi's first day back in a week or so. **Taku**: That's a huge coincidence. Where did he go for his vacation? *Keshio shrugs his shoulders. Namari shakes her head left and right* **Namari**: No one really knows. He doesn't really tell anyone where. You probably could find out if you check the records at Jurono. **Savanna**: We are not doing that again. **Taku**: So the boy's presence is still unlocated. **Yáshido**: Hmph. *Taku looks at Yáshido* **Kamira**: He can't be gone forever right? If he isn't taken by any Balancer, he most likely will come back here. For you three, it's dangerous to go out, especially if you want to stay with Taku. We shouldn't just be focusing on one person right now. He'll come back around eventually. *Everyone sighs* **Yáshido**: We'll just have to move past this; It'll only slow us all down. **Taku**: Agreed. Let's stay silent about this unless you find some good information that'll be beneficial. *Taku looks at Yáshido* Sorry about my outburst earlier. **Yáshido**: It's alright. I know you were kind of . . . mad. **Taku**: Ha, yeah, I was. **Laito**: So, does this mean we can leave? **Taku**: Yeah. We're done here. *The Mangole and table disappear. Those who are sitting stand and their chairs disappear as well* **Otara**: Kamira. **Kamira**: Yes? **Otara**: I wanted to ask you directly. I know your schedule is tight, but do you think you could do double lessons? **Kamira**: Double lessons? I'll think about it. *Kamira and Laito walk towards the front door. Kamira turns around as she opens the door* **Kamira**: Stay safe and be ready for some fierce training. **Students**: Yes, ma'am! *Kamira and Laito leave* **Taku**: You all are off for today. *Taku walks towards his room. Savanna walks into the kitchen. Everyone else leaves*

-Later that day in the dorm, Yáshido is walking down to his room. He makes eye contact with Savenna as she is sitting in her spot before. Yáshido stops as she stares at him while getting up and walking towards him-

Yáshido(thts): Why does she look like she's about to kill me? **Yáshido**: Is there a problem? *Savenna stops walking* **Savenna**: Did you do something to Yashi? *Yáshido crosses his arms around his stomach* **Yáshido**: Hahahahaha, what? No, why would I? You understand that being the Hero involves not doing evil stuff, right? **Savenna**: I was only asking it as a general question. So that kind of felt like you were shaming someone I know. **Yáshido**(thts): True. **Yáshido**: I'm sorry. No, the only thing I did to him when I saw him was talking to him. *Savenna walks next to Yáshido without facing him* **Savenna**: You've been looking at me suspiciously since we got you here. Not in a way because of my past, but like you're up to something. Especially whenever Yashi's name has been mentioned. **Yáshido**: So, you've noticed? *Savenna steps back and faces Yáshido in a defensive stance* It was only a joke, and what do you expect? It might just look like that because you can't see my face, but I trust you two. I trust all of you. To be honest, though, you've been quite an eye baller too. **Savenna**: I'm in charge of our safety until we are eligible to live here. If you see me staring, that's just because I'm surveying. **Yáshido**: That makes sense. *Savenna turns back away* **Savenna**: I'm questioning everyone, so don't just think it's you. **Yáshido**: I understand. *A small pause* **Savenna**: Sorry about earlier. **Yáshido**: That? It's no big deal. I know we don't have a good relationship, a friendly relationship, no I don't blame you for acting a little hesitant towards me. **Savenna**: Thank you for understanding. About Yashi, I don't want him to get hurt, he was one of the four original, and if he gets captured or whatever Dia plans to do with him, I at least want to try to protect him. If he ever shows. **Yáshido**: Good, I'll be looking around too. **Savenna**: Goodnight. **Yáshido**: Night. *Yáshido watches Savenna walk to the dorm doors and exit* **Yáshido**(thts): Well then, I guess there won't be any more issues from her. *Yáshido walks into his room*

Chapter 8 - Contention of Kuki Sosa

Yáshido decides to take a bath before entering his room. After the bath, he walks back to his room and walks inside. Closing the door behind him, Reine is laying on his bed. Yáshido walks over to her **Reine**: Oh? Is it that time already? **Yáshido**: If you are referring to sleep, then yes. **Reine**: With if I'm not? **Yáshido**: Can you please stop. **Reine**: What could you possibly be referring to? *Reine pokes Yáshido's chest. Yáshido sits next to her* **Yáshido**: I'm surprised they didn't mention much about you. **Reine**: Yeah, *Yawns* me too. *Reine lays back first on the bed and curls the cover over her* **Yáshido**: Reine, did you just fall asleep? **Reine**(m): Familiars need to rest too. **Yáshido**: But you're taking up the whole bed though. *Reine moves around in the bed so that Yáshido can see her face; she has one eye open* **Reine**: Hm~, you must not mind me sleeping on your legs like last time? **Yáshido**: Well, I personally don't care where you sleep. As long as no one comes in and-, *Yáshido pauses and looks away* **Yáshido**(thts): Wait no, that'll be weird. I keep forgetting it's Niola, not an actual Familiar. **Reine**: Yáshido? **Yáshido**: I prefer you not sleeping on my legs, just don't do anything while I'm sleeping. *Yáshido transforms out of the Hero* **Yashi**: Now, move over. **Reine**: Okay~. *Reine moves towards the wall* **Yashi**: You're not going to stay like that while you're asleep, right? **Reine**: No~ *Yashi lies down. Yashi is facing towards the open while Reine is facing his way. Reine moves the cover so that it's covering both of them* **Yashi**: Goodnight. **Reine**: Goodnight. *Reine quietly laughs*

-In the morning-

Reine: Yashi~, Yashi~~~. *Yashi wakes up slowly* **Yashi**: Hm? *Yashi looks up and Reine is standing in front of him with a Familiar Dermal* Niola? **Reine**: Who's Niola? I mean, I thought my name was Reine? *Yashi leans up* **Yashi**: Reine? *Yashi looks at her Dermal again* Wait, how do you have a Familiar Dermal? **Reine**: Not important at the moment. You were asleep longer than I thought, and I forgot about you. **Yashi**: You forgot about me? How could you do such a thing? **Reine**: You're just someone I know, not Yáshido, he's my master, but don't tell him I called him that. **Yashi**: You're really into this, aren't you? **Reine**: We're wasting time. Kamira is already here and is ready to start, she's brought a guest too. **Yashi**: Okay, okay, move you're blocking me. *Reine moves and Yashi stands up* **Reine**: You literally have a minute. *Yashi takes care of what he needs to do. At the front door of the dorm* **Yáshido**: Today is the third day of me being here. **Reine**: Already? *They walk to the training grounds; everyone is already there* **Yáshido**: Good morning, everyone. **Kamira**: Iah~, good morning, Hero. **Namari**: Good morning. **Keshio**: Good morning. **Otara:** Good morning. **Kamira:** I was getting a little worried that you wouldn't show. **Yáshido:** I wouldn't not show. *Kamira turns to her side and holds her ear as they point up* **Kamira:** Yes, good. Laito's just arrived with the guest. *Taku's door opens, and Laito walks out. A figure stands behind him. Suddenly a line of smoke starts to cross through the grass towards them* **Kamira:** Oh no, not this again. *Kamira summons a Barre in the form of a wall in front of her, but the smoke goes around it and heads straight for her* -Wait, -Kyoka! *Kamira vanishes inside the smoke as it lands on her* **Namari:** Is she alright, should we be worried? **Yáshido**(thts): I know that aura, it's one of her sisters'. *The smoke clears, and someone is hugging Kamira* **Kyoka:** Ooo! My sister wanted me to come help her teach! **Kamira:** Yes, yes, I did. *Kamira hugs Kyoka but then tries to get away. Kyoka hugs tighter her with a stronger grasp* **Kyoka:** This is going to be so much fun! And it's been a couple days since I've seen you. You look like you've gotten taller. *Kyoka starts to rub Kamira's arms, shoulders, and back* **Kamira**(w): Sis, they're watching us please stop. It's kind of embarrassing. **Kyoka**(w): Hm~. *Kyoka lets go of Kamira* **Kamira:** Did you miss me that much? **Kyoka:** Yes, of course, I did! It's so lonely without the two of you. **Kamira:** What about your work? **Kyoka:** It's no fun unless we all suffer through that. *Both of the sisters laugh. Keshio clears his throat. Kamira and Kyoka turn around* **Kyoka:** Oh, I'm so sorry. Ever since the incident at Jurono, while my sisters are attending their schools and having their own jobs to do, I don't see them as often. **Namari:** Really? Your days are so packed. **Laito:** Haha, then she has to deal with you three. Haha. **Kamira:** Excuse me, I have to deal with you too, Laito. *Everyone laughs while Laito holds a straight face with his arms crossed* **Keshio:** I'm just surprised. I've never seen you act this way before. **Kyoka:** Well of course you'd see me act that way in public, but it's not all about formality. Sometimes you have to loosen up. It's kinda annoying that we get treated that way. I just wanted to be a normal Kyoka, but I guess it's nice that my sisters and I are a bit famous in Macadamia and all. **Kamira:** Pretty much. **Namari:** Does Kokoa feel the same way? *Kamira and Kyoka look at each other* **Kyoka:** Indeed, I would say she feels the same way, maybe a little bit less than us, but she prefers to keep the family's name in order. **Namari:** Okay. **Kyoka:** So, how should we start? **Kamira:** Well, because you're new to them, I'll let you pick any two you want to start off with. **Kyoka:** Any two, huh? *Kyoka scans through the choices. She makes eye contact with Yáshido* **Kyoka:** Yáshido? **Yáshido:** Hey. **Kyoka:** I didn't even notice you. Nice meeting you again. **Yáshido:** Ha, I wouldn't notice a motionless person standing next to me in a Dermal either. Nice seeing you're doing well too. *Everyone laughs again. While laughing, Kyoka looks at Reine and gasps whilst doing so* **Kyoka:** A Familiar?! *Kyoka runs up to Reine. Reine stands surprised* Ah~, look at you, you're so cute. *Reine moves back a little smiling* **Reine:** Hehe~, really? **Kyoka:** What's your name? **Reine:** R-, Reine? **Kyoka:** Reine? What a choice. *Kyoka turns to Yáshido* Can I? **Reine:** Can you what? **Yáshido:** Go for it. **Kyoka:** Thank you so much! *Reine backs away a little more. Kyoka turns back to her and swiftly puts her hand on Reine's head and starts to pat and rub her hair* Your hair feels so nice. *Kyoka stops steps back and looks Reine up and down* Ha, you look so similar to someone I saw before. **Reine**: Do I? *Kamira snaps her fingers* **Kamira**: Okay, let's get back to business. **Kyoka**: Yes, right. So, I'll have Otara, Yáshido, and Reine. *Kamira points at the other side of the training ground* **Kamira**: You will have that side. My group will have this end. **Kyoka**: K. *Kamira and Kyoka talk to each other before Kamira's group goes back to their side. On Kyoka's side* **Kyoka**: So, you all know who I am. *Yáshido and Otara nod* And you two are well known of course. Today, my sister wanted me to expand on the Elilament Kuki Sosa. **Yáshido**: Particle Magic, oh~ boy~. **Kyoka**: What's the matter, Hero? You sound like you don't want to do it? **Yáshido**: It's just that, that's one of the Elilaments that I've really tried to get to Ace and have yet to do so. **Kyoka**: I see, that is true. But haha, it took me longer to get to Stage I than Ace. **Yáshido**: Nice. **Kyoka**: So, that means you're still on Stage I, correct? **Yáshido**: Right. **Kyoka**: This is interesting now. I don't know if you've Aced Kuki Sosa, Otara. **Otara**: I have. **Kyoka**: Have you learned how to use Personal Casting with Itilusion? **Otara**: Yes, but I believe that the amount of Pure Energy it takes, makes it a bit of a pointless Personal Cast. **Kyoka**: Now, I guess we'll just practice with you Hero, and if you're lucky, you'll Ace it today. **Yáshido**: How long did it take you to get Ace, Kyoka? **Kyoka**: Hm~ . . . I can't tell you exactly, but I know it was three years ago. **Otara**: So you've had Aced Kuki Sosa for a while? **Kyoka**: Yup. Now, Yáshido, are there any problems you have while training for Ace? **Yáshido**: I don't think so. *Kyoka chuckles* **Kyoka**: I know what your problem is by that answer. **Yáshido**: Elab. **Kyoka**: Learning the next stage of an Elilament always comes down to focus, training, and using it at best efficiency. **Yáshido**(m): Yeah. **Kyoka**: The reason why you're having so much trouble getting to Ace is that you are not confident in Sosa's ability. You're not allowing your mind to accept the fact that Kuki Sosa can almost create anything with enough Pure Energy. With that, you also need to multitask while using it. I found that it helps a lot. **Yáshido**: Yeah, that's something I don't do. **Kyoka**: Before we start your training, we will start with the basics of Particle Magic. Otara, would you mind starting us off? *Otara nods* **Otara**: In Particle Magic Stage III, you can make weak plasmic objects. Those that take up a lot of volume are mostly unstable at this Stage. Like Kyoka said earlier, you can create almost anything with enough Oplitals, but if you don't have a good enough Stage, then it would be impossible for some things. Having enough concentration also determines how well your created object is formed. **Kyoka**: Just talk about the fundamentals of each Stage, I'll talk more in-depth about how Kuki Sosa works. **Otara**: Okay. Uhm, Hero, summon an open barre out of Stage III Particles. **Yáshido**: Gotcha. *Particles surround Yáshido until it forms a barrier* **Otara**: Things that are made from nature are less expensive to make. Muck like a carriage. *Otara looks to her side and Particles start to form a carriage. Otara's body lifts off the ground and she lands inside the driver seat* Kuki Sosa is useful for things like this. Things that aren't permanent or can hold other objects for travel or keep them in place. ^Otara holds up her hand and a flat disk of Particles starts to form; she launches the disk towards Yáshido. It hits his barrier and the Particles crash away without hitting him^ *Otara*: The downside of anything made from Particle Magic is that it will always be weaker than the original; the same can be said when using it to mimic Elilaments. An Aced Raito would be way more dangerous than an Aced Kuki Sosa manipulating Raito. *Otara stomps the carriage with her left boot and the Particles crack before collapsing into thin air. Otara falls and catches herself, standing upright* As you go higher in Stages, things you would normally make in the previous Stage will take less Oplitals. *Kyoka*: Perfect, Stage II. *Otara*: In Stage II of Kuki Sosa, everything you create speeds up significantly. Larger things are more stable, and the denseness of the Particles are overall improved. Kyoka, would you summon a fist from Kuki Sosa Stage III just like mine. *Kyoka*: Ehm. ^Particles appear behind Otara. They get bigger and bigger until they form a giant fist the size of Otara herself. Right after she finishes, Kyoka summons one right behind her as well; equal in proportions to Otara's^ *Otara*: Collide them. ^They make the two fists ram each other with Otara's slightly moving Kyoka's back. As the two fists continue their momentum, cracks start to form around Kyoka's, and Particles drip from it^ *Otara*: The bigger the surface area that is being touched, the harder it is to completely deconstruct its structure in one shot. Okay Kyoka, you can stop. *Kyoka's fist vanishes and Otara's fist flys off into the forest* Make another one. Yáshido, you make a fist made from Kuki Sosa Stage I. *All of them cast another Particle Fist the same size as before* Kyoka and I will unite both of ours together against yours. *Yáshido*: Alright, I'm ready. ^The three fists collide, two against one, creating a loud glass breaking sound. The Stage III fist almost breaks completely on impact, the appearance of Stage II and I fists don't change. The force is slightly equal^ *Otara*: As you can see, Stage I Particles are stronger than both Stage II and III combined. Disperse. ^A wave of wind comes from Otara and all the Particles disappear^ *Otara*: With Stage II, the creation of weapons can be made. *Otara holds her hand out opened and a Particle lance appears in it* Much like everything else made from Particles, this weapon is weaker than my original weapon. Apara Lance. *Another Lance appears in her other hand. Otara holds them next to each other* As you can see, the Particle-Lance looks more plain and undersigned. An exact copy of any Celestial can't be made until I, so are the barriers. *Particles spread around the entire training grounds until it forms a barrier as big as Kamira's* This barrier took way less Pure Energy than a regular one would, but it's still weaker than Kamira's, even if it was made from Ace Particles. *Yáshido*: The jest of what I'm always told is that Kuki Sosa can do everything, but not as good as everything. *Kyoka*: If you want to be very vague and simple about it you could say it like that. *Otara*: You differentiate the Particle barrier and the Elilament by the name. An imitation of a Barre is called a barrier, it's really simple. In Particle Magic Stage I, Magical Circles are now castable. *Two clear white circles appear to each of Otara's sides with a crystal-like sound. Each of them has an exact copy of multiple different bright white lines and formations along with them* Magical Circles are a little more complicated. By itself, it acts as a casting source, but only Particles will be shot from it. Then you have a Magical Circle with teleportation. *Two black circles appear above the white circles with a deep sound constantly coming from them. Instead of white lines, they are purple* Formerly known as a-, **Yáshido & Kyoka**: A tekCircle. **Otara**: Yes, that. Both circles are used for fighting with each having their own benefits. Magical Circles or mCircles don't take much Oplitals because they're always producing Particles. This makes the casting time really fast. Like before, they are weaker than the original weapons or whatever you are deciding to fire. You don't need Tekiration to summon tekCircles, but the number of Oplitals used will be much greater without it. TekCircles, they fire actual weapons or Celestials. In the match with Keshio and Namari, Keshio casted multiple Celestials without a mCircle. The amount of Oplitals he used was a lot, without the Konseitsu being in place, he would lose about thirty-percent of his Oplitals. TekCircles take Pure Energy from the moment something is shot out of them and they take up even more if you force the object out faster. Kyoka, you can catch or redirect these. ^Right after Otara finishes her sentence, blades shoot at Kyoka from the tekCircles. Kyoka's arms and hands turn light blue as she catches the blades or throws them at the ground next to her. A total of fifteen blades came from the tekCircles. Kyoka has three of the blades in her right hand and four in her left. The rest form an elliptical shape around her. Holding her hands across her opposite shoulders Kyoka drops the blades to the ground^ **Yáshido**(thts): She caught all of those without even using Zoka Vision. That's, that's kind of scary. **Otara**: Kyoka wouldn't want to be hit by those if this was a battle. But as talented as she is, she only needed Stage II Zoka Swiftness on her arms. *Kyoka anxiously laughs* **Kyoka**: Otara, why did you Protojet them? I-, I was not expecting that. **Otara**: Oh, sorry. I'm at a point where I always fire objects like that. *Otara's tekCircles disappear* Yáshido, I'll be shooting the same shaped daggers, however, they will be twice as long and twice as many. **Yáshido**(thts): What happened to the celebrity advantage? **Yáshido**: Do you want me to dodge or anything? **Otara**: Sure. **Yáshido**: Wait, the dodging part or? ^One Particle-Spear lands right next to Yáshido's right foot from behind him^ **Yáshido**(thts): There's another one. ^Yáshido turns and prepares to catch the spear. After he catches it^ **Yáshido**(thts): Another one from behind me again? ^Yáshido uses the first spear and launches it in the same motion as the incoming one. He feels multiple auras above him^ **Yáshido**: Ha! ^Yáshido summons a flat barrier above him. Multiple spears stick right in the top of it immediately. Yáshido activates Stage I Zoka Vision and Stage III Zoka Swiftness* **Yáshido**(thts): That's eight. Twenty-two more. ^Yáshido Reverses his barrier. He sees multiple mCircles in the sky above him, they increase in diameter* **Kyoka**: Woah, that's big. *Kyoka jumps back behind Otara* **Yáshido**(thts): That's like fifteen different mCircles. Guess I'll just have to roll with a weapon. **Yáshido**: Argon! ^Yáshido summons a sword. The mCircles start to overlap each other^ **Yáshido**: Uhm, Otara, you never said anything about them being more dangerous! *Yáshido looks over at Otara and she has a slightly angry expression* **Yáshido**(thts): Woah, what did I do to her? *Yáshido looks back up at the mCircles, they are still growing* Hmm . . . how big is she going to make them? ^As Yáshido prepares for the incoming attack, he feels something behind him. Yáshido summons a Barre behind him without turning around. Yáshido feels Particles hitting him on his back and sees some flying past him as his Barre gets hit by multiple objects^ **Otara**: Whew, I was afraid you wouldn't notice. *Yáshido turns around and walks to the side of the Barre* **Yáshido**(thts): All twenty two she shot at me. *Yáshido looks past the Barre and lone mCircle floats stationary* **Kyoka**: You were way too focused on those large mCircles, Hero. Otara had that mCircle back there for a while, charging up and everything, but you didn't notice till she fired. **Yáshido**: Well, I was guessing that she was going to shoot from there. **Otara**: I told you I would only make them longer and cast twice as many. Why would I go back on my word? **Yáshido**: But still, you could have made them smaller in an instant. **Otara**: Hmph, I can't argue with that. **Kyoka**: Just make sure you sense your surroundings every now and then. **Yáshido**: I would just not say anything but come on, you can't just assume things. I'm not going one hundred because Otara was demonstrating something. If this was a spar or something, she wouldn't have a chance. *Otara stares at Yáshido* **Kyoka**: Haha. Now, Otara has talked about Stage III, II, and I. If it's okay with you, Otara, I will be doing Ace. *Otara nods* With Ace, your new ability is a little, how do you say, unique? When Acing Particle Magic, it opens your ability not only to make objects but create space-time as well. **Yáshido**: Yeah, that's what most training rooms are made of. **Kyoka**: Yes, but they can be used in the free world too. *Particles start to spiral upwards around the three of them and as they pass, what's left under them turns into darkness. As they come into complete darkness, a mCircle producing ice glows with a blue color allowing them to see each other* The amount of concentration you need to perform these tasks can get a little outrageous at moments, but if you practice enough you'll be able to create space-time consistently. Now, how you make what you want is entirely up to you. Like instead of thinking of what you want to shoot out of a Magical Circle, think about the general feeling of nature, Seiras, oceans etcetera, to create your own world. Some people refer to it as Dreamworld or World. The distance you want to be physical and what you can only see versus what's in the real world needs to be considered. If I were to make the physical bigger than what is necessary Kamira's group will be inside with us as well. Using Barriers is a good way to start because you can just make the interior of the Barre what is physical. **Yáshido**: Creating space only works because of how dense the Particles are right? **Kyoka**: Ehm.

Creating the physical part is what takes the majority of your Oplitals, but once you've made your own space-time, it will stop taking Oplitals and everything will operate as if you were in Edasia. Observe. *The Particles slowly spiral back down and they are in a forest. Yáshido looks at all the different details in his surroundings* **Yáshido**: Wow, you change the scenery quite a bit. **Kyoka**: Beautiful, right? **Reine**: This looks amazing. I've never seen anything like it. **Kyoka**: You like it, Reine? That's great to hear. I named this place Adenea. As you know, my family has this huge backyard that's at least two square miles. Whenever I want to be at peace, I go back there and create this place. **Yáshido**: From your own energy? **Kyoka**: Yes, our father doesn't want to waste whatever he might use to buy an Energy Dispositor, so in order to come here, I must use my own Pure Energy. **Yáshido**: So not even the Exna's, huh? **Kyoka**: Do you know what this looks like from the outside? **Yáshido**: Yeah, at the end of the physical part, on the outside, there is a thick wave of Pure Energy that is always moving in set directions. **Kyoka**: Good. Otara, do you know what it looks like when Itilusion is involved? **Otara**: There is a thin layer of Pure Energy going around the edges scaling upward. Also being able to see what's going on inside. **Kyoka**: Hm~ . . . This would be a little easier because you two are very skilled already. **Yáshido**: Hey Kyoka, quick question. **Kyoka**: Yes? **Yáshido**: Is it true that you can play back memories? *Yáshido feels Otara's eyes move over him* **Kyoka**: Oh, you've heard that too? Hm~. *Kyoka puts a hand over her chin* I would assume Zoka Vision, Itilusion, and some others would be involved for that time you want to . . . visit? I seriously don't know to be honest. *Kyoka looks at Otara, Otara looks back at Kyoka* Do you know anything about it, Otara? *Otara glances at Yáshido and clenches her fists* **Otara**: Yes, a little. *Kyoka and Reine shiver. A surprised look then goes across Reine's face before she rushes over to Otara* **Reine**: Wait, so you really can?! **Otara**: I-, . . . I can. **Reine**(Talking really fast): How-, is-, it? Can-, you-, interact—, with-, your-, past-, self? How-, much-, Pure-, Energy—, does-, it-, take-, up? Do-, you-, feel-, any-, pain-, when-, you-, do-, it? **Otara**: Well-, **Kyoka**: Woah Reine, calm down. *Yáshido walks up behind Reine and chops her head* **Yáshido**: Really, Reine? Apologize. **Reine**: I'm sorry, haha. *Otara sighs. All of them stand in a circle* **Kyoka**: Are you okay, Reine? I've never seen anyone talk so fast before. **Reine**: I just got very excited that's all. **Otara**(m): Excited? **Reine**: Before I got my form, I looked at my ma-, *Reine looks at Yáshido* Yáshido's memories of his fights, but everything was blurry. Also, I realize that only Type One and Two Familiars can read memories. I got excited because I want to go back and watch some of his fights. **Kyoka**: I would love to do that as well, but I don't think Macadamia's Alchemists will be getting anywhere around that level any time soon. *Reine sadly sighs* Otara, can you read other people's memories? **Otara**: At any moment where they were using Aced Zoka Vision, it will take longer to process it though. **Kyoka**: Good to know, we'll continue that conversation later. Before we start our next procedure, I'm going to change the scenery again.

Particles spiral up around them until they are in darkness once again I couldn't dare to fight in Adenea. I'll make a place more suitable. **Otara**: Do you need any help; I don't want you to use all your Oplitals on making Particle Worlds. **Kyoka**: It's alright, I have some of these. *A bright bubble appears next to Kyoka, she turns it around and two Type X potencies are in the bubble, it disappears* **Yáshido**: So you just have them just in case? **Kyoka**: It's a small object which makes it easily transferable. Father does have a teleport station linked to us. I rarely use it though. **Yáshido**: What are we about to do now? **Kyoka**: Hm-, hm-, hm . . . I'm finishing it up now. Keep an open mind, it might be a little morbid for you, Hero. **Yáshido**(thts): It's going to be Regra, watch. *The darkness slowly comes down. Yáshido looks at the sky and it is covered in smoke with a red tone. As the darkness gets lower, Yáshido feels the presence of heat, he sees skyscrapers and other tall buildings. When the darkness is completely gone, the four of them stand at the intersection of a destroyed city. Reine, Otara, and Yáshido inspect their surroundings* **Kyoka**: Does it look familiar, Hero? **Yáshido**(thts): What does she mean? I do feel some vibe like I've been here before. **Yáshido**: No it doesn't, where are we? *Kyoka walks past Yáshido and stops, looking down one of the roads* **Kyoka**: 1-10, 979, when Mato' Cross was attacked by Lark. **Yáshido**(thts): I remember now. We were issued that same day and Dia, Emuna, and I went out to help. That was going to be our first time fighting him, then we got surrounded by more Dicipients than we could handle. With the power she had left, Emuna teleported us away. In the end, Korosi had damaged the land so badly that the entire island split. *Sighs* **Yáshido**: Yeah, I remember now. **Kyoka**: Is this okay, do you want to stay here, or should I change it? **Yáshido**: It's fine. **Kyoka**: Okay, your training will be incorporating Kuki Sosa into your fighting. **Yáshido**: Fighting? *Kyoka looks at Reine and winks, Reine smiles and walks over to her* Wait, you're not telling me . . . **Kyoka**: That's right, us two verses you two. **Reine**: Yáshido, I'll do my best. **Kyoka**: Wait a minute, there's a catch, only Particle Magic. **Yáshido**: Sounds fair. *Yáshido Reverses his sword* **Reine**: Hey! That isn't fair, Yáshido didn't give me Kuki Sosa. **Kyoka & Otara**: What?! You didn't give her Kuki Sosa?!? **Yáshido**(thts): She just made me look like an idiot. How do I come back from this? **Yáshido**: If I remember correctly, Kuki Sosa was one of the top priorities I was letting off during my sleep. *Reine jumps back a little* **Reine**: Well . . . **Otara**: I see, so it was the Familiar's fault. **Reine**: Haha, I guess you could say that. *Kyoka sighs* **Kyoka**: Well I guess that means I'll take both of you on myself. How 'bout I make it more interesting. *Bluish white lines surround the intersection* This will be our fighting ground, the intersection. **Yáshido**: This is enough room. **Kyoka**: Your goal is to hit me. I'm not the best at these things. Just remember, only Particle-based attacks and weapons. *Kyoka skips backward away from Otara and Yáshido* Oh, and Reine. **Reine**: O-, yes? **Kyoka**: If you see anything unblockable try to call it out for me, also if you see the walls start to disappear, K? **Reine**: K! *Yáshido and Otara walk to the other side of the intersection. By Yáshido* **Kyoka**(Y): We start on you! **Yáshido**(Y): Alright! *Yáshido looks at Otara* **Yáshido**: Any plan you want to do? Or just go for it? **Otara**: Teamwork. **Yáshido**: Teamwork . . . I like it. **Otara**: Hmph. *Otara summons a Particle-Lance* **Yáshido**: Let's get started. *Yáshido summons a Stage I Particle-Sword. He looks up at Kyoka and she has mCircles behind her* **Otara**: To Ace, I recommend you using a lot of barriers. ^Otara starts sprinting towards Kyoka^ **Kyoka**: Not so fast. ^A barrier forms in front of Otara^ **Otara**: Hmph! ^Otara spins before striking the barrier. The increased momentum breaks through it. Otara lands through the disassembled Particles and continues towards Kyoka. Yáshido is running towards Kyoka behind Otara. Right before Otara reaches Kyoka, Kyoka summons an identical lance. They meet with one strong swing of equal power. Yáshido summons Particles that lead into the air above them. Otara backs away from the collision. Kyoka vertically swings, but Otara dashes to her right dodging the attack. Otara starts to dagger at Kyoka as fast as she can, but Kyoka blocks each one with the pole of her lance. In one sway of Otara's lance, Kyoka knocks it to the side leaving Otara wide open. Before Kyoka gets the hit on Otara's side, Yáshido jumps down and his sword collides with the attack, pushing Kyoka back. Kyoka puts more strength into her lance and Yáshido reacts with more strength as well^ **Yáshido**(thts): This is kind of difficult with any Zokas. ^Yáshido sees one of the mCircles light up^ **Otara**: Extilina Xachiet! Yáshido(T)(**Otara**): Move! ^Yáshido rolls to his right as he feels something heavy coming in his direction from behind him. Kyoka jumps back as Yáshido rolls away, noticing the wave coming towards her shortly after. All the mCircles behind her light up and begin to shoot lances at the wave of energy. Yáshido lands on his feet and summons a Particle-Barre in front of him. The wave destroys the incoming lance with ease. Kyoka plants her lance in the ground as the wave hits her. Kyoka's mCircles are destroyed as the wave passes over them. Kyoka smirks after the wave is gone^ **Kyoka**: With your weapon, Otara. **Otara**(m): I know that. **Kyoka**: And I thought I said only Particle Magic. But don't worry, I'll get a pass later too. ^Otara sprints towards Kyoka again, but with a Particle-Barre in front of her. Kyoka lunges towards Yáshido^ **Yáshido**: Hyah! ^Yáshido slashes towards Kyoka, but she quickly summons a small barrier that takes the hit. Yáshido then gets hit in his chest piece by Kyoka's lance and falls onto his back. Kyoka turns to Otara who is already halfway through an attack. Kyoka dodges the incoming attack and charges Otara. Otara summons a Particle-Block between them. Kyoka summons multiple Particle-Lances in the air as she runs into the summoned barrier. Yáshido steps back up^ **Yáshido**(T)(Otara): Knock her back to me. Yáshido(T)(**Otara**): Ok. ^Yáshido holds his sword to his side, pointing it in Kyoka's direction, and leans forward. As Kyoka comes through the other side of the Particle-Block, Otara stabs it, detonating it. The force pushes Kyoka all the way to the outskirts of the intersection^ **Yáshido**(thts): Otara's getting more training in than me. ^As Kyoka comes down on Otara, their lances collide once more. Otara pulls back and nearly hits Kyoka in the chest by charging forward again. Kyoka lands on her feet and swipes horizontally at Otara's legs. Otara falls and Kyoka casts a Particle-Block on top of her. Otara attempts to move it but can't get it off. Kyoka and Otara make eye contact^ **Kyoka**: What? Haha. **Reine**: Behind you! ^Kyoka steps to her side and Yáshido misses his attack. Kyoka then knees Yáshido and diagonally kicks him onto the Particle-Block that sits on Otara. Kyoka throws her lance and it penetrates through Yáshido's sword and continues to go until it hits the wall. Yáshido slides off the Particle-Block as Otara summons a fist which strikes it off of her. Kyoka aims for Yáshido's legs, but during the swing, he steps on it and breaks it. Kyoka attempts to strike Yáshido with her right hand, but he blocks it with his left arm. Yáshido aims a punch at Kyoka's shoulder, but she catches his fist before he lands the hit. Kyoka uses her other hand to punch Yáshido in the chest. However, Yáshido catches it with his other hand. Kyoka starts to lose control and summons a Particle-Barrier in between them. With their arms going through the Particle-Barre; Yáshido's attack is on Kyoka's side, her attack is on his side^ **Kyoka**: You're not going to let go, huh? **Yáshido**: No, you're not going to let go either. Otara's just going to hit you instead. **Kyoka**: But you're supposed to be training as well. ^Kyoka pushes harder but Yáshido's raw strength doesn't budge^ **Kyoka**: Those muscles are coming in handy. **Yáshido**(thts): Maybe if it wasn't for the P.M. only rule this would be easier. ^The Particle-Barre starts to crack on Kyoka's side^ **Yáshido**(thts): Come on Otara. *Otara stands a few feet behind Yáshido not wanting to intervene* I should just take the hit since we are trying to hit her^Right as Yáshido stops trying to land his attack, Kyoka's fist glows with a faded red aura; Particle Magic imitating Zoka Strength. Kyoka's fist continues to go past Yáshido's open hand and she gets a clean hit across his helmet as the Particle-Barre completely breaks. Yáshido feels the part of Dermal cheek that got hit after getting launched back a few feet. A slight dent is felt across his helmet^ **Kyoka**: Oh gosh, are you okay? *Reine is heard laughing in the distance. Yáshido looks over at her and she covers her mouth before putting her hands down and smiling* ^Yáshido quickly summons a spear and tries to prick Kyoka in the abdomen, but she stops the attack with another Particle-Barre. Both of them break on impact^ **Yáshido**: How?! **Kyoka**: Haha, more luck? ^Yáshido summons another Particle sword. Kyoka does the same. They both attack, missing or dodging their blows^ **Yáshido**(thts): She's trying hard not to get hit. ^Suddenly, a lance in between Kyoka and Yáshido, nearly hitting them both. Kyoka steps back as the lance is pulled back. Otara stands to his side^ Yáshido(T)(**Otara**): Hero, Kyoka can easily jungle us, we have to attack together or . . . well yes together. Kyoka's a Resource Manager, not a fighter. Training or not she should have been hit a long time ago. (To Otara): I got you. ^Yáshido looks at Otara and she is staring in Kyoka's direction; he holds on to his sword tighter^ (To Otara): Fine, I'll go one hundred then since I've been kind of slacking. (**Otara**): Good. **Kyoka**: Uhm . . . Hello? You two look like you're frozen.

Yáshido: Sorry about that. Let's keep going. ^Right after Yáshido finished his sentence, multiple diagonally shaped Particle-Blocks that are slightly offset from each other start to form leading up to Kyoka. Kyoka Reverses her sword^ **Yáshido**(T)(To Otara): Now! ^Both Otara and Yáshido sprint in Kyoka's direction. Kyoka summons a Particle-Bow, and arrows appear floating next to it. Otara points her lance forward and a Particle-Barre forms on the tip of it covering Yáshido and herself. Kyoka grabs one of the arrows and aims the bow at them. Yáshido starts to sprint faster than Otara and slides under the Particle-Barre. Kyoka fires at him while he's still sliding, but Yáshido slices the arrow perfectly. After finishing his slide, Yáshido jumps on one of the Particle-Blocks on his left which explodes pushing him to his right. Kyoka creates multiple different bows that are already preloaded and shoots them continuously at Yáshido. Nearly getting hit by several of them, Yáshido fires a blast of Particle-Kosai towards the arrows. Kyoka switches the element surrounding the arrows to Particle-Hydro and those arrows start to go through the flames. Otara imitates Zoka Strength and Zoka Swiftness as she jumps on one of the Particle-Blocks and thrusts it towards Kyoka. Within a second the Particle-Block hits Kyoka. Kyoka and the lance slam against the wall of the physical part of the World. Particles explode from the impact and cover the entire side of the wall. Otara continues to run towards Kyoka. Yáshido has bounced all the way into the air where no one can see him unless they purposely look up^ **Yáshido**(T)(To Otara): I'm way above you, I'm going to create a-, *Yáshido feels something touch his back. Yáshido turns to see Reine standing on the Particle-Block with him* **Yáshido**: Reine, what is it? **Reine**: Don't you think this is kind of cheating? **Yáshido**: I'm not breaking any rules am I? **Reine**: Haha, you are using Dermal Armor. **Yáshido**: Ha, okay, Reine. **Reine**: Hehe~. *Yáshido watches as Reine jumps off and floats back down* ^Otara is standing in front of the wall^ Yáshido(T)(**Otara**): What were you saying? (To Otara): As long as it is a direct hit by our weapon it'll count, right? (**Otara**): Yes. (To Otara): I'm going to surprise her. I need you to jump in and out with your attacks, and when I say go, I want you to purposely overshoot, but if she tries to hit you block it. (**Otara**): You're testing me big time, Hero . . . but, alright. ^Otara and Yáshido spectate the wall for a couple seconds before they start to feel Kyoka's aura beef up a ton. More Particles start to disperse from the wall. Yáshido sees the top of the Particle-Barre and there is a crack leading downward. Yáshido load the Particle-Block he's standing on with more Particles^ **Yáshido**(thts): If she sees me, she'll most likely shoot me down, so I'll have to get under it before then. Whether or not she does . . . if I make contact with her instead of the ground I'll be fine. ^The whole of the barrier becomes clear as fewer Particles are seen around the wall^ **Voice**: Hahahahaha! **Yáshido**(thts): Wait, there's no way. Yáshido(T)(**Otara**): She, she caught it? (To Otara): DIDN'T WE SEE HER HIT THE WALL? (**Otara**): We did see her hit the wall . . . maybe she did it at the last second. Or her luck is off the charts today. ^As all the Particles fade away, Kyoka stands at the bottom with both hands lifting the Particle-Block up. She has a black silky aura around her^ **Yáshido**(T)(To Otara and *Otara*): Pure Energy?! **Kyoka**: I have to say, that was well executed. But hah, no. ^The black aura shoots from Kyoka's body through the barrier and it completely disintegrates into black smoke^ **Otara**: Why use your Pure Energy? *Kyoka sighs* **Kyoka**: You used Personal Casting Otara, I should get one slip, right? **Otara**: Fair point. ^Kyoka summons another lance before scanning around^ **Kyoka**: Where has Yáshido vanished to? *Otara faintly squints her eyes* **Reine**: Kyoka, He's!- ^Otara summons a sound wave proof barrier around herself and Kyoka just before Reine finishes^ **Kyoka**: Iah~, I see. You don't want me to know. **Otara**: No, that's not it. That Familiar is just annoying. **Kyoka**: In general or? **Otara**: You know what I mean. **Kyoka**: Well, Otara, I might just quit because honestly, no offense, you are really scary. **Otara**: I'm not going to hurt you, Kyoka. Maybe he's already behind you. ^Kyoka holds her other hand out and another lance appears^ **Kyoka**: Not foaling for that one. *Both of them smile* **Yáshido**(T)(To Otara): What happened? Why'd you summon a barrier? (*Otara*): Your Familiar. We'll have to change your plan up a bit. (To Otara): We'll just have to go now then, Reine well just tell her as soon as you open the barrier. (*Otara*): That's true, how are you going to get down here that fast? (To Otara): Over filling the Particle-Block. (*Otara*): I don't think that applies to what Kyoka said but . . . that can work. ^Kyoka crosses the lances. Otara stands guard^ **Kyoka**: I get it now, you two have Telepathy. **Otara**: Good job, you've figured it out. I'm willing to share a cookie with you. **Kyoka**: Maybe just a little piece. ^Otara and Kyoka run toward each other. Kyoka uncrosses the lances before Otara hits her and a wave of green aura gushes towards Otara^ **Otara**: Extinlina Jet! ^A duplicate lance intersects right through the green aura and the aura turns into Particles, Kyoka swipes one of the lances up and knocks the lance away. While Kyoka is distracted, Otara runs towards her^ **Otara**: Extinlina! ^Otara's entire body beams towards Kyoka with her lance aimed at her. Otara slightly misses, at the same time the Particle-Barre disappears. Otara is stunned from using a massive amount of energy and missing. Otara stands frozen right next to Kyoka^ **Kyoka**: I should play the lottery today when I go home. **Reine**(Protojet): Above you! Look out! ^Kyoka looks up and sees Yáshido^ **Kyoka**: What are you doing up there? **Yáshido**: Mind your business. **Kyoka**: Mind my business, huh? ^Kyoka summons a bow and arrow and aims at Yáshido^ **Kyoka**: Otara can't fight alone. ^Kyoka fires the arrow^ **Yáshido**(thts): Just what I wanted you to do Kyoka. Three . . . two . . . one . . . ^Otara becomes reactive and turns to hit Kyoka. At the last second, Kyoka blocks the attack. Both of them slide against the ground in the direction of Otara's strike. The arrow hits the Particle-Block after Yáshido jumps off. Kyoka is in a perfect angle for him^ **Kyoka**: Oh no, you got me. **Yáshido**(T)(To Otara): This is it we got her. **Yáshido**: Hyah!!!~ ^Before he hits Kyoka, Yáshido feels Reine approach him swiftly. Yáshido collides with something, being so close to everyone, not knowing who it is^ **Otara**(m): Disperse.

^With a huge gust of wind from Otara's body, the smoke clears. Reine floats just above Kyoka's back with Yáshido's sword against her crossed forearms. A red aura flows around Reine but disappears after she and Yáshido land on the ground. Reine shakes her arms, the plating around her forearms is cracked^ **Reine**: That was Particle Stage I Zoka Strength, and I still almost didn't block it, haha. *Reine looks at Yáshido* That was too strong for Kyoka. She's not wearing a Dermal. **Yáshido**(thts): Stage II Sustain. **Yáshido**: Thanks, Reine. Kyoka would have been alright, but still nice save. *Yáshido Reverses his sword* **Kyoka**: I still didn't want to be hit. If you weren't the Herp, my dad would kill you, haha. You're a lifesaver, Reine. **Otara**: That just makes it worse. *Otara sighs* **Reine**: I was going to call it out, but then Otara attacked and there was no way for you to dodge, Kyoka. *Yáshido walks up to Kyoka* **Yáshido**: You made this really interesting, and this is one of the first times where I really used Kuki Sosa like that. **Kyoka**: Great, it sounds like you learned something. With that said, I think our training is done for today. **Yáshido**: I have to say, you still managed fairly well. **Kyoka**: Hero, you have no idea. My publicity enables me to hide my emotions well. Even though it's a spar, just seeing you lounge at me like that is a nightmare. *Yáshido, Reine, and Kyoka chuckle* We do a little sparring but nothing too serious. Let's see if they are finished. **Otara**: Wait. *Everyone looks at Otara as she stands right behind Kyoka* ^Otara gently taps her lance on Kyoka's shoulder^ There, we got a hit. **Kyoka**: Well. *Everyone laughs but Otara* Okay, I will give you that one. *They are surrounded by the Particles and darkness follows* I hope we didn't do anything we weren't supposed to. **Yáshido**: What, you really think that 'we' will get in trouble? **Kyoka**: The youngest is always the scariest, and now that I think about it more, we probably shouldn't be creating Worlds with Taku trying to stay low. *Yáshido looks at Otara and Otara looks back at him* **Otara**: We all know I'm the youngest in my family, Hero, so I don't know why you looked at me like that. **Yáshido**: Well, it's just that I'm also the youngest in my family. *Kyoka looks at Yáshido and Otara has a surprised look* **Kyoka**: A disclosed Hero, giving such vital information. How insecure. **Otara**: Agreed. **Yáshido**: Ha, whatever you say. *The Particles come back down, and they are back in the training grounds. There is a Barre around them. Yáshido overlooks the Barre and sees Taku staring at him with one of his hands towards the Barre. Once Taku makes eye contact with Yáshido he puts his hand down and the Barre disappears. Otara Reverses her Particle-Lance and so does Kyoka with her bow. Yáshido looks to the bench and everyone is sitting there, including Savanna. Kamira stands and the four of them walk towards her* **Kamira**: How'd it go? **Kyoka**: Fantastic, Otara got the hit as you predicted. **Kamira**: I knew it. That's free lunch. Did you learn anything new, Hero? **Yáshido**: Yeah, there's one thing I learned, using only Particle Magic is a real pain if you don't know what you're doing. **Laito**: That's one thing Dia's always been mentoring you on, haha. *Laito stops laughing and looks at everyone as they're silent* What? **Kamira**: Really, Laito? That's not something you should joke about right now. **Yáshido**: It's alright Kamira, it's true. I remember almost every single time where we needed it and I decided not to use it. She would get so mad. *Kamira, Keshio, and Namari chuckle* Any improvement is a good one. **Kyoka**: That's the goal. How was your group, Kamira? *Kamira sighs* **Kamira**: Don't get me started. **Namari**: I told him I was sorry. **Keshio**: Still hurts, by the way. **Laito**: I can't believe you missed me, and I was like a foot away. *Namari puts her hand on Laito's shoulder and squeezes it. A crunching sound is heard and Laito makes an 'in pain' face* **Namari**: My aim isn't the best today. **Laito**: I mean, not the best today? *Laito puts his hand on Namari's shoulder and squeezes it* **Namari**: Ow . . . **Taku**: I see where this is going, you two cut it out. **Kyoka**: Iah, I forgot you were still here, Taku. Did you have fun holding the Barre for us? **Taku**: Don't start with me, Kyoka. I would have had Savenna to do it, but I don't want her doing everything herself, and this is training for me anyway. **Savanna**: Thirty-three minutes with a Condensed Aced Barre, almost a record. **Namari**: One reason why I was distracted was because of that World you made, Kyoka. It was in the background while I was aiming at Laito. **Kyoka**: Yeah, eyes really don't like looking at a lot of Particle Magic. **Savanna**: Try telling that to Korosi. *Everyone either laughs or smiles* **Taku**: That's messed up, Savenna. **Keshio & Yáshido**: So messed up. **Otara**: Thank you Kyoka, for accepting the request to come teach. **Kyoka**: No Problem. **Kamira**: You all, be ready for tomorrow. **Students**: Yes, ma'am. **Kyoka**: You don't let them call you by your name? **Kamira**: I don't mind what they call me. **Keshio**: Bye, Kamira, Kyoka. I'm beat. **Kyoka**: See you all tomorrow, today was really fun. *Kamira, Kyoka, and Laito start walking away*

Chapter 9 – Partition

Yáshido: Particle Magic is something, isn't it? **Namari**: It's the first thing on the Mentilum[The list of Elilaments]. Even though everyone nearly has it, it's really the most complex out of all Elilaments. **Yáshido**: And that's why I don't necessarily use it. **Keshio**: With that said, I'm going to take a hard nap. *Keshio starts walking towards the dorm* **Namari**: Hero, you mind training with me until it gets a little darker? **Yáshido**: Why not? *Namari looks over at Otara* **Otara**: What is it you want to practice on? **Namari**: The Zokas. Since I didn't go to the tournament, I would still like to use them. **Yáshido**: Exactly what I wanted. I'm in. **Otara**: I'll spectate. *As Otara turns around, a flash of a Protojet goes to her. Namari stands behind Otara about to pat Otara's right shoulder. Otara has caught her wrist with her left hand without even moving* **Namari**(w): The speed. **Otara**: I said I'll spectate, Katsuni. **Namari**: Okay then, sorry, Otara. *Namari notices Reine as Otara lets her wrist go* How about you Reine, you want to practice with me? **Reine**: Practice? Sounds fun. **Yáshido**: Are we going just in general or is there something you want to learn specifically? **Namari**: Nothing specific, just using them is all. **Taku**: Well Savenna, looks like you have to put one over them this time. **Savanna**: You don't think you can go again? **Taku**: I know I can't go again. *Taku starts walking towards his house* See you when you're done, thanks. **Savanna**: Ridiculous. Okay, how big do you want it? **Namari**: We won't be for long so about thirty by thirty. **Savanna**: I want to watch this too, so it's going to be a *sustain*, got it? **Namari & Yáshido**: Got it. *Otara and Savanna stand back. Savanna's raises her hands towards Namari, Reine, and Yáshido* **Savanna**: Alpa Aklematis. *A white Barre overlaps the training ground starting from Savanna until it forms a complete rectangular prism and becomes fully transparent* There. Three minutes. *All of them nod* **Reine**: Can we do a free for all? **Namari**: That was the plan. **Yáshido**: You two will just focus me the entire time. *Both of them smile at Yáshido* **Reine**: No won't. **Namari**: Like come on, Yáshido. *Yáshido sighs* And now I will be focused the whole time. **Yáshido**: How about we activate our Zokas before we start? It'll give everyone a full picture of what they're up against. **Namari**: Wait-. **Yáshido**: Yes? **Namari**: Since you two are already in your Dermals, can I get in mine? **Yáshido**: Yeah, sure, go ahead. **Namari**: Right. I'll be going first then. *Namari stands completely still as a wave of energy bursts from her location. Starting from the tip of her hair, a full suit of armor covers her body. As the Dermal finally overlaps her body, a final burst of energy circles away from her* And now for the Zokas. *More waves of air and energy shoot from Namari's location and a combination of red, and light blue aura emits from her Dermal. The different colors settle a steady glow around her.

With each of their respective glow raising over her head ever so often* **Yáshido**: Pretty intense, Namari. **Yáshido**(thts): Seventy three percent Stage I Zoka Strength. Her Zoka Swiftness is eighty five at Stage I too. Then her Zoka Vision is at seventy Stage I. We just had our check-up at school the week before I left, and she's stronger than then. *Namari's fists glow with a darker red color* **Namari**: I'm all set. **Reine**: My turn. **Yáshido**(thts): Niola. Now that I think about it, I actually don't know what she's capable of. I know being an adventurer of her caliber means she needs the power to go with it, but I'll be seeing her Zokas for the first time. Then again, she's acting like a Familiar so maybe not. *Within a second, Reine lifts off the ground and a spacious red scatters around her, covering her entire body in a sparky, bright, red flame. The pressure of the release of energy causes the Barre to export a buzzing sound. As Reine slowly sets down, the bright flame cools down into a more controlled bright fiery aura around her that reaches a couple feet in radius and a foot or two above her head. The aura constantly brightens and dims* Kosai aura with Zoka Strength and Swiftness, She's got everything at Stage I seventy five efficiency. They are both low but not enough while using Ikkasei? I'm actually nervous, and I haven't even used mine yet. *The aura around Reine starts to spin into two small circles next to her, forming two small red mCircles* **Yáshido**: Good job, Reine. **Namari**: That aura looks amazing. It almost looks like if I touch it, it'll burn me. **Reine**: That's because it will, haha. *Reine lifts her arms, and her aura flows along with it. The heat coming from Reine's Dermal blurs the scenery behind her* **Yáshido**(thts): Considering I know its Nioa, she's tempting me to push her further. The more I look at it, the more intimidated I feel. *Reine looks at Yáshido* **Reine**: Your turn, Hero. **Yáshido**: Hmph, you two ready? *Namari looks at Reine, but Reine's gaze doesn't lift from Yáshido. Namari looks at Yáshido with a smirk* **Namari & Reine**: Ready! **Yáshido**(thts): This is going to be exciting for both of them, hahaha. Nevertheless, I'm not going to push my stamina that much. *Yáshido puts his hands in a thrusting position. A circle of light starts to spin around his feet. Then, multiple circles appear spinning insanely fast around his body. A red aura starts at Yáshido's feet and covers his entire body. Then a light blue aura overlaps the red aura making a magenta color. In his helmet, the part that he sees through sparks with a blue color, the perimeter of the invisible Barre becomes clear. As all of this is happening, the ground under his feet lifts up slightly off, breaking from the rest of the ground. The Barre behind him ricochets the wind of energy back towards Reine and Namari. Yáshido's aura fizzles down across his Dermal. He opens his hands and a silvery sword appears. He grips the sword in front of him. They all stare at each other* **Savanna**: Flashing as always Hero, two minutes. **Yáshido**: On you. ^Namari takes an offensive stance. Reine crosses her arms. Yáshido looks at Reine's eyes. Reine looks back at him and the mCircles next to her start to pulsate. Yáshido slowly looks at Namari and she's already staring at him^ **Yáshido**(thts): They can read where I'm looking with Stage I. Namari's eighty five is a threat. Reine, I have no clue what she'll be using. I should play it safe. Then again, Reine doesn't have any physical weapons. If I get close to her, she can't really do much.^Yáshido slightly tilts his sword and a blast from Reine goes straight for him. Yáshido slashes through the fire and races towards her. Reine fires multiple shots while flying to the top of the Barre. Namari intersects Yáshido's path as she starts going up with a punch. Colliding with his sword, a huge wave of Pure Energy distributes into the air. Namari tries to kick Yáshido, but he blocks it with his sword. Namari uses her other leg for another kick and Yáshido also blocks that one. Namari's combination opens Yáshido into a hard to defend position. While trying to guard, he watches Namari get a job hit in his stomach. A shock blasts him in the air. Yáshido forcefully stops his movements and slashes a thick stream of Hydro at Namari. Namari Protojets up, dodging the hit, but without warning, a dense pocket of flames hits slams against her entire Dermal from above forcing her towards the ground. Reine continues to shoot fireballs at Namari. Hitting the ground with a large thud, Namari begins to punch the blasts while laying back first. Each one evaporating on collision. Yáshido looks at Reine^ **Yáshido**: Momentum Gear! ^Pure Energy surrounds Yáshido as he torpedoes himself towards Reine. Right before he hits her, from his view, the eye that he can see looks at him. In a short time frame, Reine faces Yáshido and lifts her left hand, from both her mCircles and her hand, a wall of fire that impacts Yáshido directly. Yáshido gets pushed back a couple feet as the blast engulfs him^ **Yáshido**(thts): Too bad Kosai doesn't work on me. ^Yáshido's Dermal starts pulsating red brighter through the flame. Yáshido stops being pushed back and Protojets through the fire, with his sword about to hit Reine's Dermal. As they make eye contact again, within a millisecond, Yáshido sees Reine smile, and she dodges his attack. Shocked, Yáshido maintains eye contact as he goes past her^ **Yáshido**(thts): That was Ace just then. ^As Yáshido is about to pass her, Reine places her hand right on his side. Reine creates a ball of fire which takes Yáshido down with it to the ground, and at the same time, Yáshido hits Reine on her side with his sword. Yáshido lands on his feet next to Namari and immediately throws his sword at her. Namari manages to catch the sword and throws it back, but by the time she lets the sword go Yáshido is already in front of her grabbing it. After grabbing the sword, Yáshido elbows Namari. Namari catches Yáshido's elbow, but then gets pierced in the stomach by his sword. Namari stands back and holds on to her contact point. Namari stands up straight as her aura starts to fade into more of a light blue tone. Yáshido feels the Barre's temperature steadily rise. He looks up and there is a disk of fire rotating at the top of the Barre. Both Namari and Yáshido look at the swirling flames^ **Yáshido**(thts): Well played, Niola. No Konseitsu is holding us back, so you decided to lace the air with fire to weaken our attacks. ^Yáshido aims his sword at the disk. His sword freezes over with ice and water starts to revolve around his sword. A chilled smoke comes from Yáshido's sword^ **Yáshido**: Ice Keeper! ^Before Yáshido Casts it, Namari is just a few feet from hitting him in the side. Yáshido summons a Barre around himself just before Namari lands the hit. Namari's powerful hit shatters the Barre, but her momentum isn't halted from the impact. Namari's glowing red fist goes Yáshido. Yáshido blocks Namari's fist with his sword. A heavy wind spreads from the impact following waves of white energy. Yáshido watches a crack form on the back of his sword as he tries to maintain control over Namari^ **Yáshido**: So, you plan to get shot by Reine too? **Namari**: I'm not worried about that. ^Namari and Yáshido lean to the right slightly^ **Yáshido**: If she pulls off her Cast, there's no telling what'll happen. **Namari**: We'll just have to wait and see. ^A burst of energy from Namari's hand glides them both through the dirt. Rocks start to lift up off the ground while creating other large cracks below them. Yáshido notices the crack on the back of his sword extend all the way through the blade^ **Yáshido**(thts): Cheap off-brand swords, she's going to break it. **Yáshido**: Let's see if you're strong enough for this! Solepell! ^Yáshido Protojets a yard back while Namari continues after him. A sphere of energy surrounds them both. Namari suddenly stops with her arms and legs shaking. While the sphere is forming, Namari's posture slowly lowers onto the ground as she tries to fight against the extremely powerful force. Yáshido then shanks his sword into the ground in front of him and Namari immediately slams onto the ground. Namari sits on all fours with her muscles shaking while she pushes against the ground. Large cracks spread on all of the points that Namari's limbs are touching the ground^ **Namari**(m): Aced Atoskito . . . You are incredible, Hero. ^Namari's Dermal begins to make a cracking sound as she is trying even harder to fight against it. Namari's body glows red as she maxes out her Stage I Zoka Strength with Stage I Ikkasei, equalizing the Aced Atoskito just slightly. Namari slowly starts to stand. However, Yáshido slashes Namari on the back, and she falls stomach down to the ground. Yáshido points his offhand at Namari's back. His gauntlet starts to turn snowy white until it is completely changed. **Yáshido**(thts): I don't want to do this, but Namari has to find a way to escape on her own. ^Suddenly, multiple large shards of ice, ranging from three to thirty inches, start to beam out of his hand and pierce Namari in the back of her Dermal. Namari starts to ache in pain verbally from the constant hits. As Yáshido continues, the Barre starts to fill with snow, and Namari deepens in the ground more. Even after Yáshido's vision is obscured, he continues to fire. After Yáshido no longer hears Namari's voice, he stops firing and Reverses his Barre. A heatwave immediately rushes over them melting the snow Particles away. Yáshido sees Namari on her knees in the middle of the seven-foot crater^ **Namari**(m): That, that did it. ^The red aura around Namari begins to intensify as she stands up with her hands balled up to her sides^ **Namari**: I got it, Hero! I can feel it at the tip of the iceberg. (Y): HAA!!! ^Namari starts to scream as the red aura around her expands up, even more, overpassing Yáshido and rising twenty feet in the air. The Barre begins to shake and crack in random places. Yáshido summons a smaller Barre to protect himself. After Namari's episode is over, with a Stage III Ikkasei, the new aura of

Aced Zoka Strength flows around her body. The densely matted red aura shimmers and sparkles around Namari's now red-orange Dermal as she stares at Yáshido^ **Namari**: Guess I don't need this anymore. ^Reversing her Ikkasei, Namari's aura around her bursts up, and disappears above her helmet, but the deathly power still remains. Namari raises a fist up and looks at it^ **Namari**: I can't believe it, two years and I finally achieved Ace. ^With his Barre now gone, Yáshido just spectates Namari^ **Yáshido**: Perfect. Great job, Namari. **Namari**: We're still continuing, right? **Yáshido**: Right. ^Namari slowly lowers her fist to her side^ **Namari**: Then, let's go! ^Namari instantly Protojets toward, while spinning, towards Yáshido with an uppercut. Yáshido holds his sword horizontally, attempting to block, but Namari goes lower while throwing his sword offset with her other hand. Yáshido takes the blow right in the abdomen^ **Yáshido**: Ah-, **Yáshido**(thts): Definitely Ace. ^Yáshido falls to his feet after slightly being tossed above the ground from the blow. Once on his feet, he is still stunned. Namari then follows her attack with a powerful kick. Yáshido takes the hit on the left side of his neck. Propelled to his right and after slamming on the ground a few times, Yáshido manages to land on his feet once more. When he looks up, Namari is already preparing for another punch. Yáshido rolls over to the right barely dodging. Namari's fist hits the spot that Yáshido's feet once were. A heap of land explodes into the air, and a brown smoke covers Namari's location. Yáshido looks up at Reine, and the flames look denser. The rotation of the disk-of-fire is faster than before^ **Yáshido**(thts): Reine's finished, that isn't good. ^Yáshido looks at Namari, and she has a Barre around her also looking at Reine^ **Reine**: Form up on me! ^The disk slowly moves so that it is covering the entire side of the Barre, opposite from Namari and Yáshido, facing diagonally towards them^ **Yáshido**(thts): A Personal Cast won't work anymore, I need to just fire pure Hydro. ^As Yáshido points an open palm at Reine, Reine points at Namari and Yáshido with both of hers^ **Reine**: Scalding Repetition! **Yáshido**: Hyah! ^Hundreds of different fireballs shoot out of the disk while it rotates. Yáshido shoots a large volume of water at the disk. Some of the fireballs hit the dense amount of water without disappearing, and simply explode in the air; Others go through it. One of the slower fireballs heads straight for Yáshido. Yáshido shoots an icicle at it. The icicle penetrates the fireball, and the fireball explodes covering the sky in a large dark cloud. A faster fireball goes through the flame straight for Yáshido again. Yáshido Protojets away, but more fireballs are landing in the direction he is going. With each fireball hitting the ground, it causes an explosion, and the ground breaks apart. Namari summons two plates of Hydro around her arms. Whenever a fireball is about to hit Namari, she knocks it away using the plates. The number of fireballs increases^ **Yáshido**(thts): My Elilament Adapt is taking a while for the Kosai not to damage my Dermal. Not to mention the Type One Zoka Strength on the fireballs. ^One fireball misses Yáshido and hits the Barre behind him^ **Yáshido**(thts): If I'm quick enough, I can get behind her and destroy it that way. ^More and more of the land is in flames or is made into a crater. Namari slowly starts walking towards Reine, still knocking any fireballs that come towards her away^ **Reine**(Y): I'm pretty sure you don't want to get any closer, Namari! **Namari**(Y): Then what am I supposed to do?! **Reine**: Hahaha. ^At the same time, both Namari and Yáshido start running towards Reine with Zoka Swiftness; Either dodging or redirecting the fireballs that come at them. The closer they get the more of the fireballs that they have to account for. About ten feet to Reine's location if she was on the ground, Namari starts to change her angle to intersect Yáshido. Yáshido slashes one of the fireballs towards Namari. Namari ducks as the fireball passes over her. Namari then summons a large wave of Hydro that creates a shield above her covering a path over to Yáshido. Reine aims a finger at Yáshido and shoots a larger fireball at him. When the Hydro shield gets halfway to Yáshido, Namari starts sprinting towards him under it. Once Yáshido sees Namari get extremely close, and he puts an Atoskito under him, stopping him completely. Namari flys right in front of him, missing her strike. The fireball Reine shot hits Namari in the back, and Yáshido follows by slashing Namari on her side as she falls to him. Namari flys to the opposite side of the Barre, and crashes against the ground. Another large fireball lands in between Namari, and Yáshido causing both of them to get pushed back from each other even more. Namari turns the crash into a roll before jumping to her feet. Being right under Reine, Namari Protojets up to her with a metal gauntlet^ **Namari**(Y): Take this! ^Reine catches her catches the gauntlet at the last second with a gauntlet of her own; after the collision both of their gauntlets disappear^ **Namari**: Wha-, how did you see me coming? **Reine**: Maybe not yell? Haha. **Namari**: Oh yeah. ^Namari frowns^ **Namari**: Hmph! ^Namari takes her hand away and comes around with her other fist. Reine moves along with the direction of the swing dodging it. Namari comes with a kick horizontally with her right leg. Reine jumps up in the air avoiding the kick. Namari then uses her left leg to kick up. Reine blocks the kick with her forearms crossed. Namari Protojets in a circle then changes the direction towards Reine with a punch. At the last second, Reine catches her fist, but immediately gets hit in the stomach by Namari's other fist. Reine vomits saliva from the shot^ **Reine**: Ahha, I saw it coming at the last second. **Namari**: Hm. ^Namari raises her right leg over Reine's head, preparing to knock Reine down to the ground. Before Namari pulls it off, the two mCircles next to Reine flash before two blasts shoot Namari. The fireballs explode on Namari arms as she guards and takes her down to the ground. Reine holds onto her stomach while Namari is plummeting to the ground^ **Reine**: That hurts so much. ^While this interaction was happening, Yáshido managed to sneak up behind the disk that had been shooting fireballs at the ground. Yáshido puts his hand on the back of it^ **Yáshido**(m): Disappear out of my sight. ^A blue smoke comes from Yáshido's shoulder down his arm, out of his hand, and into the disk. The spinning disk starts to slow down as it turns blue from the inside out. The fireballs stop shooting out of it. Yáshido sees Reine float up above him from the other side of the disk^ **Reine**: No~! I wasn't able to do it in time. **Savanna**(Y): One Minute. ^Both Reine and Yáshido look at Savanna then at each other. Reine looks at Namari and Namari nods at her. Reine smiles and looks back at Yáshido. The disk explodes and pushes Reine and Yáshido farther apart. The two of them float in midair staring at each other^ **Reine**: I'm going to have my first battle with you. **Yáshido**: About fifty seconds, make it last. ^Yáshido sees a wave of Kosai head straight for him coming from Reine. However, the wave of fire stops before hitting Yáshido. The flame vanishes upwards, and Reine stands directly in front of him with a right pointer finger touching the center of his chest. Yáshido has the edge of his sword on top of Reine's left shoulder^ **Reine**(m.t.l.): I don't want to have only fifty seconds, so I'll just pretend you got a critical on me. **Yáshido**(m.t.l.): I see, that's how you want it to be. I wouldn't want to practice with you in this form either. ^Yáshido feels a burning sensation on his chest. The tip of Reine's finger is covered in a lava-like substance burning^ **Yáshido**: Hmph! ^Yáshido pushes down an Aced Zoka Strength force into his sword on Reine's shoulder. The pressure of the sudden burst of weight knocks her straight down to the ground within a second. A burst of energy comes from Reine's body after she hits the ground. Reine lays motionless on the ground with arms and legs spread out; her Familiar Dermal is gone. Namari looks over at Reine^ **Namari**(Y): Reine! *Namari jumps over to Reine* **Namari**: Are you okay? *Reine opens one of her eyes as she leans up with scratch marks on her limbs and clothes. Reine smiles at Namari* **Reine**: Haha, I'm fine, Namari. Seems like I was too confident. **Namari**: Yeah, that's unlucky. **Reine**: But you don't have a lot of time to win this. **Namari**: Got it. *Namari looks at Yáshido* **Yáshido**: You're next, Namari. ^Both Namari and Yáshido explode within a huge light blue aura as they beam towards each other. Yáshido swings his sword through Namari's side as Namari puts all her strength into one blow and hits Yáshido's side. Both of them hold that position^ **Namari & Yáshido**: Ah-. **Yáshido**(thts): O~, I felt that. That wasn't worth it at all. ^Still in midair after the collision, Yáshido's sword vanishes. Namari's fist still in contact with his side. They both turn for a punch and collide again. Another wave of Pure Energy comes from the impact. The wave is so powerful than ever that it cracks a ring in the same plane in the Barre. Yáshido starts to win over Namari. The blue aura around Namari turns red and their strength turns even. Once again, they punch with their other hand^ **Savanna**(Y): Thirty seconds! ^Yáshido back dashes and Namari falls forward. He blasts her with a wave of fire. She reacts with another wave of fire^ The two flames mix and bursts into a smoke between them. **Yáshido**: You are quite the challenge. **Namari**: Once more! Battering Ram! **Yáshido**(thts): Oh no, not this! ^With Namari suddenly being surrounded by a rectangular prism, her body Protojets towards Yáshido with a loud thud. Yáshido summons five consecutive Barres between him and Namari. Within no time, Namari penetrates through all of them and hits Yáshido in the chest. They continue in a straight trajectory towards the Barre^ **Savanna**: Wait! ^As they hit the Barre, the power of Namari's attack breaks it from the inside and all of the Barre explodes into Particles. The two escape into the forest as Savanna doesn't Cast another Barre fast enough^ **Namari**: Woah, prepare for impact! ^They begin to pierce through multiple trees with Yáshido taking majority of the damage into the rear of his Dermal. After the sixth impact through a tree, the prism around Namari fades away, and they fall to the ground. Yáshido hits the ground first, and Namari lands on top of him. The two of them slide through the ground twenty more yards before being stopped by a rising ground level^ *Namari coughs as she stands up off of Yáshido* **Namari**: Sorry about that. **Yáshido**: It's fine. Are you okay? *Namari steps off to the side* **Namari**: I'm fine, are YOU okay? *Namari reaches her hand out and Yáshido grabs it, pulling him up* **Yáshido**: Once I heard those words, I knew it was over. **Namari**: Sorry if you felt like I was disrespecting you with that attack. I was just in the heat of battle and when Savanna said thirty seconds left, Ram was the only thing I could think of. **Yáshido**: No disrespect taken, you had so much power in it anyways. Those Barres probably took a lot of your momentum away, so it could have been much worse. *They both turn in the direction they came from. Still being able to see the training ground, the six trees they hit have a clear see-through rectangle in them* It wasn't the brightest play, I must admit. *Yáshido activates his Denryoku. Small traces of each of their auras can be seen flooring throughout the forest* As I suspected. *With Namari doing the same thing* **Namari**: Haha, my bad. I was thinking whether or not I should use it with Aced Strength instead of Stage I. Seems like I made a poor choice. *Namari and Yáshido start walking back towards the training ground. Namari 'heals' the land using Patchi Tekiyo while walking, making the forest seem less damaged. They meet Otara and Savanna at the edge of the forest. Savanna gives Namari the look. Namari Reverses her Dermal* **Savanna**: Impressive performance. *Namari gasps* **Namari**: Really?! *Savanna crosses her arms and tilts her head down with her eyes closed* **Savanna**: Yeah, it was, if I take out that fact that you almost completely gave away our location. Other than that, it was entirely entertaining to watch. I could tell you were really trying your hardest. Nothing that would entice the Hero though. *Savanna looks at Yáshido* And I saw that you were putting some of your training into combat. *Yáshido nods* We're about to have dinner, so get ready. *They walk through the training ground. Yáshido scans for Reine but can't find her nor sense her aura. Yáshido stops* **Yáshido**: Where's Reine? **Savanna**: Well, Hero, she barely had any Pure Energy left after you crited her. I was surprised because she didn't naturally Reverse herself. I think she decided to go lay down inside the dorm. **Yáshido**: I see. I'll go and check on her. *Namari, Otara, and Yáshido go inside the dorm* **Namari**: What'd you think, Otara? **Otara**: About your practice match? **Namari**: Yeah, who do you think won? **Otara**: By most damage, Yáshido; by most hits, you. *Namari sighs* **Namari**: Good. **Otara**: Was it a good segment for a tournament match? **Namari**: Much better. Oh, and thank you two for sparing with me. **Yáshido**: No problem, I'll be sure to tell Reine. *Namari smiles. All of them go their separate ways. Yáshido enters his room, Niola is laying down on the bed. She looks over at him* **Niola**: That was fun. *Yáshido closes the door* **Yáshido**: Was it? I was just keeping my fighting skills in check. *Yáshido sits down next to Niola* **Niola**(m): I wonder . . . **Niola**: Are you ever gonna talk business? **Yáshido**: Talk business? **Niola**: I know you've been thinking about all of the Dicipients in Macadamia right now. *Yáshido looks at the ceiling* **Yáshido**: When am I not. *Yáshido raises his hands and clenches his fist* I'm just happy they haven't attacked yet. *Niola leans up* **Niola**: Are you saying they will attack? *Yáshido looks at Niola. He transforms out of the Hero* **Yashi**: Honestly, what we're doing is really dangerous. If we are caught off guard, all of us will be at a disadvantage. For the time I've been the Hero, it would be reasonable to assume that would have attacked by now. They were always so hesitant because it was Dia and I. Counting you, that's only four true fighters. Not to mention Taku has lost a few of his States since he's no longer a Dicipient. **Niola**: Where does that leave us now? *Yashi looks down* **Yashi**: They don't know where I am. **Niola**: Everyone's a little skeptical about what they should do. Whether they should worry or not. **Yashi**: Getting to a General or Macadamia's active Council should be my next serious move. I also want to wait a little longer to see if they do attack. **Niola**: Okay?~ **Yashi**: Also, Namari said thanks for the match by the way. **Niola**: Always glad to help. *Niola lays back down* Not gonna lie, it's been a while since I took such a heavy hit to the gut. **Yashi**: Haha, it has? **Niola**: Whenever I train with other adventurers, we try not to use a lot of uhm . . . Pure Energy cause you never know when a rogue Familiar will pop around the corner. **Yashi**: Yeah, I could see that. *Niola sighs* **Niola**: Namari's really strong. Two years of Stage I, her efficiency on Zoka Strength was 74 at the end of the fight. **Yáshido**: Yeah, I felt the difference immediately after she got it. It doesn't compare to Dicipients, but Namari is getting there. I could see her being a Balancer in the future, maybe even a General. **Niola**: Yup. **Yashi**: Dinner's going to start in a few minutes, are you going to go eat with everyone? **Niola**: I'm already stuffed-, I mean no. *They make eye contact* **Yashi**: Well, I'm going to go eat. **Niola**: Alright, eat well. *Niola turns towards the wall. Yashi stands* **Yashi**(thts): Was there really any point in me getting out of the Dermal? I'm just wasting Oplitals at this point. *Yashi transforms into the Hero*

-Yáshido finds the kitchen in the door. When he gets there, dinner is already being served. Awkwardly, his seat is farther away from everyone else since he is in a Dermal; without the lower part of his Helmet, so he can him to eat. This causes the table to be abnormally quiet as not much of a conversation is happening, and everyone is looking away whenever eye contact is made. After dinner, Yáshido goes back to his room. As he closes the door, Yáshido looks at Niola, who is laying on the bed facing him-

Niola: How was it? **Yáshido**: Delicious. *Yáshido transforms out of the Hero* Oh, today though. **Niola**: You need to find a better way to conserve your Oplitals. You've used so much already. **Yashi**: I know, I know. **Niola**: Seriously, we both know how low you were at Darku. I'm assuming Emuna got you all the way back up in one day. You're in that Dermal more than usual because of your situation. You know what'll happen if you continue. **Yashi**: I'm constantly thinking about it. Yáshido doesn't drain my Pure Energy like other Dermals. **Niola**: Alright~. **Yashi**: And with a bit of sleeping and meditating, it replenishes my Pure Energy just fine. **Niola**: And when was the last time you meditated? *Yashi facepalms* **Yashi**: It's been a couple of days. **Niola**: Ehm . . . *Niola faces the wall. Yashi gets in the bed, facing away from Niola* **Yashi**: Night. **Niola**: Night, night. *A couple minutes pass as Yashi tries to sleep* **Yashi**(thts): Of course I'd have to use the bathroom as soon as I get comfortable. *Yashi slowly gets up, trying not to wake Niola. When he stands, he looks back at her. The small light from a lamp illuminates her figure under the cover* She's out. *Yashi uses the bathroom. He stands in front of the mirror after washing his hands. Yashi splashes some of the water on his face. He turns off the faucet. While doing so, he feels a dark presence soothe in around him. When he looks up, the candles have darkened, and the walls of the small room he's in glow purple* Wha-, what is this feeling? *Yáshido closes his eyes and activates his Denryoku, he feels nothing* **Yashi**: Is someone there? *Someone puts their hands on his shoulders from behind* **Voice**(Girl): Yes, Yashi, someone is here, and she's been trying to talk to you. *Yashi opens his eyes sees Dia in the reflection of the mirror standing behind him* **Yashi**: Dia?! *Yashi quickly turns around putting his back against the sinks. Dia is staring at Yashi while smiling. Her hands are still in the position as if Yashi's shoulders were still there. Dia sets them to her side. Yashi's surroundings completely fade into a purple hue so that he and Dia are the only things visible* **Dia**: Hey, Yashi. *Yashi scans Dia. Dia doesn't have the same black Dicipient clothes she had on when she attacked Regra, but some new clothes he has never seen her in before* **Yashi**: Hey, Dia. *Dia is still smiling, and Yashi's surprised expression is all the more in view* **Dia & Yashi**: So . . . *They pause* **Dia**: Hahaha, what's wrong, Yashi? Why do you look scared? **Yashi**: I'm not scared, I'm frightened. You came out of nowhere. I'm not sure if you're even Dia. **Dia**: It's me. Believe me, I have been trying to reach you two other times, but your conscience . . . wouldn't let me. *Dia stops smiling while looking down* I saw some pretty depressing things while doing so. And . . . I know it's my fault that you think that way about me. **Yashi**(thts): It really is her. *Dia looks at Yashi* **Dia**: I know you want an explanation, but I can't tell you everything. **Yashi**: That's, that's fine. I want to hear what you can say. **Dia**: I can't though, not until you forgive me. **Yashi**: For-, forgive you? **Dia**: Yes, I want to hear you say it. *Dia stares deeply into Yashi's eyes. The moistness of her pupils is noticeable as they shimmer* **Yashi**: I forgive you. **Dia**: Good. *Dia holds and points her hand towards Yáshido. A bundle of Particles starts to form in her hand, stretching all the way to his chest. It's his sword* **Yashi**(thts): Jeshika? No way. *Dia shakes the sword gently* That normally means that she wants me to take it but . . . *As they make eye contact, Dia makes an annoyed face at Yashi. She shakes the sword again* **Dia**: It's only been a week, and you've already forgotten what this means? **Yashi**: No, I-, I remember. *Dia sighs before grabbing Yashi's hands and puts Jeshika in them* **Dia**(m): Dummy . . . *Dia stares at his hands as they touch. Dia then slowly retracts her hands, and she looks away* It's your sword, I found it and wanted to give it back. **Yashi**: Dia . . . *Yashi hugs her from behind* Why did you do it? Please tell me. The world would have been free from Demon King for good, but you attacked me instead? That doesn't make any sense to me. *Dia sees Yashi's arms around her. They fall off as Dia purposely turns around* **Dia**: First and foremost, I want to tell you I'm sorry. For what you might consider as betrayal or treason. It might seem awful from the start, but it's for a good cause. **Yashi**: And I forgave you, we've already passed that. *A couple seconds of silence before Dia takes a deep breath* **Dia**: From the beginning, I planned everything. *Yashi steps back* **Yashi**: Planned? **Dia**: This entire plan I had since I was young. A couple months before I met you. Seeing what the Dark Army was at the time made me feel a way. That I could be one of the ones to stop it for good. I needed to stop it for good. I thought of many ways for me to be able to commence it, but being so young, everything I could hope for was pointless. And even then, my mom wanted me to get a little older before we would do anything serious with my Elilaments. Then, it seemed by fate, I met you months later after being held back. When I heard about the Alma situation and your parents. It truly hurt my core watching someone personally feel the anguish . . . feel the sadness of Korosi's evil. Your spirit, your motivation and determination. I could see a bright path in the future for this journey. I felt as you were my biggest change to get towards Korosi, Yashi. The training we that we did is what I needed for my current succession. You even became the next Hero, the Hero of the 7th Generation. I wasn't jealous or anything. It really only made me happier. Day after day, year after year, you were the person who I was with the majority of my life . . . who understood what we had to do. Who cared for me and enjoyed life with me. We even became Trants partners. Being able to do that with you, really did something to me, Yashi. It's true we never talked much about it, but we both knew how the other felt. And during those years, we had to compress those emotions back to stay focused. Now looking back at all the opportunities I've had in the countless battles of us fighting side by side, I-, I can say I fell in love with you. *Dia looks down as Yashi eyes open* **Yashi**(thts): She said it . . . she really said it. Dia's never told me that before. *A tear drops from Yashi's face* **Dia**: I- . . . it all confused me. I didn't know whether it was okay if I was to just follow you instead of using you. Of course, that would mean we could defeat him together, but that wasn't enough. Not far enough for what I had in mind. *Their eyes cross paths* I could never hold the guilt of killing you, Yashi. The most joy I had ever felt is when we couldn't find you in those Familiars; that meant you were still alive. *Yashi hugs Dia* **Yashi**: I love you too, Dia. *Dia's arms slowly circle around Yashi* **Dia**: That's great to hear. I've been waiting so long for you to say that, Yashi. *Dia's arms completely surround Yashi. After a few seconds of soft hugging, Dia sniffs* The sad part is, after some time I completely forgot about my original idea. When you turned seventeen in fact. Everything was so perfect. Until you told me that our next mission was Korosi, and . . . I thought a lot before deciding to still go along with what I initially planned. *Dia's arms slowly start to come down* That night before, I was prepping myself for what I had to do. *Yashi stops squeezing Dia, he looks down and to see her looking at his chest* The battle was intense against the Demon King. We in fact lasted all the way until the end. During the fight, my mental state was bouncing back from what is right, to what is love, but with every word that came out of Korosi's mouth. All of the pain he's put into people's lives, all those who he ruined. I . . . I just, I just wanted to end that evil more and more. If I didn't do it now, I might not ever get this chance again. When I got that opportunity, I had to take you out, Yashi. *Yashi fully lets go of Dia* **Yashi**: But why me instead of the Demon King? Where does that lead you to next, Dia? *Dia is silent as she continues to avoid eye contact* **Dia**: You wouldn't allow it. **Yashi**(thts): I wouldn't allow it? **Yashi**: It's you, Dia, . . . and me. What could you possibly do that I wouldn't let you? **Dia**: I just can't. *Dia grasps her hair* I didn't answer your call because they would have tracked it, I was also surrounded by a few of them. For your safety and mine, I let it redirect to nothing. **Yashi**: So, you're not working for Korosi? **Dia**: Work for him? I would never . . . but one thing that I do want, is you. *Yashi slightly backs away as Dia pokes him on his chest. Dia stares directly into Yashi's eyes* I want to capture you, for my own purposes. **Yashi**(thts): That-, that can be taken in so many ways. **Dia**: I know what you're thinking. None of that. Just to have you by my side. **Yashi**: Have me by your side? As in imprisonment? **Dia**: Imprisonment is not really what I intended . . . you'd be free to walk around and do things like that. *Yashi face becomes confused* **Yashi**: But, but how will I be able to do my roles as the Hero, Dia? I have to-, **Dia**: Fulfill your duties, right? **Yashi**: Yes, exactly, I can't just let you capture me, Dia. That just doesn't make any sense. We're already a team, why do you have-, **Dia**: I'm sorry Yashi, that's the way it's going to be. **Yashi**: It doesn't have to be this way, why can't you just-, *Suddenly Dia falls on one knee* Dia! *Yashi drops his sword and goes down with her. Dia is holding onto her chest. Small amounts of Pure Energy is leaking from her shoes* **Dia**: It's alright, I'm fine. Ah~. *Dia cries in agony* **Yashi**: What's happening? **Dia**: It takes a lot of Oplitals to communicate with you, and to compensate, I'm putting a lot more strain on my body. This only means I'm running out of time. *Dia looks at Yashi as he moves closer to her making them face to face* Here. *Yashi looks down and Dia has the same knife from before in her hand; stretching it out to him* **Yashi**: No, Dia. I can't do that. **Dia**: Please, Yashi. I don't know the Reverse of this Cast. If I don't get out soon, I won't have any

Oplitals at all. Unless you want to see me . . . *Dia looks down. Yashi slowly takes the knife from Dia's hand* **Yashi**: I'm doing this to help you, not for payback. **Dia**(m): I understand. *Dia clenches her shirt as the pain increases* Hurry. *Dia's body starts to fade starting at her feet* **Yashi**(thts): I-, I really don't want to do this. **Yashi**(w): Ready? **Dia**: Ready. *Yashi gets closer to Dia and partially hugs her. Gently, Yashi pierces the blade through Dia's stomach. Dia smiles before kissing him on his cheek* **Dia**(m): See you soon, Yashi. *Dia's body quickly fades away as Particles. Suddenly, Yashi jumps up in his bed, heart pounding, breathing hard. He scans his surroundings* **Yashi**(thts): What. There's no way that was a dream? *Yashi looks over to his right, and Niola isn't there. Yashi looks down on the blanket and the dull image of a sword sits on his lap* **Yashi**: Jeshika? *He leans up and grabs it. Holding it in front of himself* IT IS. **Yashi**(thts): That wasn't a dream then. *Yashi sits the sword down and rubs his head* What? *Yashi looks around* It must have been a World she made, but without putting any details in it. I know she's had Aced Kuki Sosa but what other Elilament would she have used to contact me over that much of a distance? We don't have a Telepathy between us, maybe a Personal Cast between a forced Telepathy and Tekiration? That would make sense if those other times she couldn't get to me. But when did she learn Tekiration? *Yashi looks at his sword again. With it, he stands. He looks at a cup. Yashi concentrates as he holds his sword up and slashes in its direction. The cup slices in half* It is you!~ *Something knocks at Yashi's door*

Chapter 10 – Serenity

Yashi(thts): Oh crap, I'm not in my Hero form. *Yashi runs to the door and puts his back against it. The door knocks once more* **Namari**: Excuse me, Yáshido, are you awake? **Yashi**: Yes, I'm awake. **Namari**: Sorry to bother you, but Taku wants you to come here for a second. **Yashi**: Okay. Thank you for telling me, I'll be there shortly. **Namari**: No problem. *Yashi listens to the footsteps as they fade away from the door. Yashi sighs* **Yashi**(thts): Namari? *Yashi transforms into the Hero* **Yáshido**(thts): Man, I'm never going to get used to this. *Yáshido walks into the hallway* Wait, she didn't even tell me where to go. *Yáshido starts jogging towards the main door. Before opening it, he looks to his right* Is that music? They must be down there then. *Yáshido walks down the hall following the music. Once around a corner, he sees someone walk into a room with the door closing behind them. Yáshido looks at his sword before Reversing it. Yáshido starts walking up to the room. Inside the room* **Taku**: Good, everything is set. **Namari**: You two can cook so well. **Kamira & Savanna**: Thanks. **Kamira**: I wouldn't say what I made is all that good though. **Keshio**: How could you possibly say that about your cooking? *Keshio points his fork at the many dishes* This looks amazing. **Kyoka**: Well of course it is, I would expect nothing less from my little sister. Kyoka turns to Kamira* **Kyoka**(w): Little do they know you make this all the time back at home. **Kamira**: Yeah, that's probably why it's not as exciting to see it again. **Savanna**: Wait, we have one more. *Savanna comes with one big tray of different meats and garnishes* **Namari**: Woah. **Keshio**: You made that? *Savanna nods* **Taku**: Looks fantastic, Savenna. **Savanna**: Thank you. *Savanna sets the plate down on the table* **Taku**: Moon, would you mind getting the drinks, they're next to the door. **Moon**: K. *Moon starts walking towards the drinks. Outside the room, Yáshido stands behind the door. He looks through the small opening* **Yáshido**(thts): Let's see. *The first person Yáshido sees is Otara with a birthday hat on* OH, it's Otara's birthday? It's 4-18. They even made food though we just at dinner. *Yáshido continues to look around* It really looks like a whole party in there. I don't see anyone who wasn't here before. *Yáshido opens the door, but it stops as if he hits something* **Keshio**: What was that? *Everyone on the inside looks at the door. Silence echoes through the room* **Namari**: Hero? *They look behind the door, Yáshido also leans to look behind the door. Moon is sitting on the floor with spilled cups around the ground and their clothes* **Yáshido**(thts): Sss~ . . . **Moon**: Oh no~ . . . **Namari**: Moon, are you alright? **Moon**: Yes. **Keshio**: Well there goes all the beverages. *Yáshido comes from the doorway and closes it* **Yáshido**: I'm sorry, I didn't see you. **Taku**: Thanks, Yáshido. *Yáshido sticks his hands out. Moon's eyes open as she notices him* **Moon**: It-, it's alright Hero, we all make mistakes. *Moon grabs Yáshido's hand. He pulls her up so much that their faces are nearly touching. Moon turns and looks at both the wet floor and her clothes* I guess it can't be helped. *Moon closes her eyes and starts to glow within a water-like color. The cups move back into the tray, then the liquid on the floor and on her clothes gets shredded through a cloud of smoke before going back in the cup. Moon picks the tray up and sets it on the long table* **Yáshido**(thts): I know she didn't just . . . *When she finishes, Moon turns and looks at everyone with a surprised look* **Moon**: What? Did I miss something? **Yáshido**(T)(**Namari**): She did just take that off the floor, right? (**Keshio**): So I'm not the only one who just saw that. **Taku**: You, you just . . . *Savanna walks over to the tray and grabs it* You moved it from the floor, and your clothes, and put it back inside the cups. **Moon**: Yeah? **Yáshido**(T)(**Taku**): DOES SHE NOT KNOW HOW DISGUSTING THAT IS? **Savanna**: I will be replacing these. **Moon**: Oh. *Moon looks at her clothes again, and at the floor* I cleaned it though, haha. *Savanna comes back with a new set of drinks. Taku looks at Yáshido* **Taku**: I was watching the news, all the things that were happening, and I just so happen to catch that today was Otara's birthday. *Taku looks at Otara* I know it might not be as 'nice' because you're with us and all, but we should still do something for you. *Almost as if not excited at all about her birthday* **Otara**: Don't worry about that, I appreciate this, but you really don't have to do this much for me. **Taku**: This much? That brings me to the next thing. Since everyone is here, we can sing the song. In Nastasian too. *Otara eyes open* **Otara**: No, please. **Namari**: Wha-, why not? *Otara looks at Kamira* **Kamira**: It's only a song, right? **Otara**(m): It's a cringy song. **Otara**: Maybe in Atiro, but not in my native language. **Keshio**: It won't be a real birthday party if we don't sing it. **Taku**: We even got Keshio to learn one word somehow. **Keshio**: Never mind. *An embarrassed face crosses Otara as she looks at her lap* **Otara**: F-, fine. *Savanna Detrantses* **Savenna**: Great. *Savenna walks over to the Mangole that is playing music and turns it off. She then walks over to the light and turns them off. Taku holds out his hand, and a small flame appears in his palm. Savenna comes back with a small cake with two candles spelling seventeen on the top of it. In between the numbers is a small figure of Otara with her Dermal and lance equipped. Small Particles float around her while some of them fall on the top layer of the cake* **Kyoka**: You're so lucky, Otara. That cake looks so good.~ *Taku aims his hand at the candles and two small orbs of fire land on each of the candle tips* **Taku**: Everyone line up. *Everyone lines up in front of Otara* **Savanna**: Three, two, one. **Everyone**: Hasu[Happy in Natasian] Birthday to you~~~. Hasu Birthday to you~~~. Hasu Birthday to Otara~~~ *Keshio coughs* **Keshio**(m): Misugami. *Taku elbows Keshio* **Everyone**: Hasu Birthday to you~~~. *Everyone starts to clap. Otara inhales a whiff of air and gently blows out the candles. The lights turn back on* **Everyone**: HAPPY BIRTHDAY OTARA. **Otara**: Ya~, whew~. Thank you all so much. *Everyone cheerfully laughs while Otara awkwardly holds back a smile. Everyone takes a seat and starts to eat. While eating, they talk about what's happening on the outside of Macadamia, things they would like to do, and their lives. Towards the end of the party, Moon, Namari, and Yáshido sit at the other end of the table away from everyone else* **Yáshido**: So, Moon. **Moon**: Yes? **Yáshido**: How did you find out about us? **Moon**: Well, I knew Taku before, you know, he turned into a Dicipient. *Moon looks over at Taku. He is playing charades in front of the others* **Namari**: What was your relationship? *Moon looks back at Namari and Yáshido* **Moon**: One of the camps I went to. I met him there, and we became good friends. **Namari**: Oh-, I see. **Moon**: He invited me to join his little army. **Yáshido**(thts): Little army? **Yáshido**: What do you mean by 'little army'? *Moon covers her mouth* **Moon**(w): Oops, I wasn't supposed to say, but he said something about this group being made into an army to go against Lark. **Yáshido**(thts): Oh, I thought it'd be something new. **Namari**(w): Woah, so are we actually gonna fight the Dark Army? **Moon**: You still call them the Dark Army? Macadamia doesn't change at all. *Namari rolls her eyes* **Namari**: It's just a name. **Yáshido**: So what's your backstory? **Moon**: Backstory? **Namari**: On why you accepted Taku's invitation? **Moon**: Oh that? Bear with me then. When I was young, I witnessed a lot of bad things head-on. People, getting hurt, invasions, dying, all of that stuff . . . right in front of me, things like that. Our town had it really hard. Then it kind of . . . fell off. Those events made me pretty tough at a young age. I used that toughness to stand up for people who were being mistreated unfairly. I even helped with a couple assaults and captured a few criminals. I've never felt that it was right for innocent people to be hurt in any way. It was really traumatizing to see others suffer, it just 'gets into my emotions, you know? *Yáshido and Namari nod* Townsfolk said that I was there for anyone, and people just started calling me Moon, and I kept it. When I heard about Daphoria, and what they did to Alma. It hurt to see it . . . destroyed. Especially when I just came back from there. **Yáshido**: I feel you. **Moon**: I couldn't just not do anything. I was taking a hiatus from Magic for a while, but now it felt wrong for me to do so. I had to go to Atagu Academy since my original school was destroyed. *Yáshido's heart skips a beat* **Yáshido**: Wait, original school? You're not telling me . . . *Moon looks down* **Moon**: Yeah, I was born in Alma. *Namari sadly gasps, Yáshido also looks down. Namari, sitting next to Moon, puts her hand on Moon's shoulder* **Moon**: They nearly took everything. My mom, my brother, and a sister. *Moon's hand forms a fist on the table* **Moon**(m): My parents wanted to stay, support the war effort, and even though Alma tried its hardest, Lark still won. It's like, I can hear him mocking me. That damned Demon King. *Moon closes her eyes as tears form* **Namari**: It's okay Moon, no need to be upset. *Moon wipes her face before opening her eyes. Realizing what she just did, she chuckles* **Moon**: Sorry 'bout that. *Moon sniffs* **Yáshido**: Sorry for your loss. **Moon**: It's alright, Lark's gonna be the one sorry when I get him. **Yáshido**: Yeah, that's one thing we all got in common. Just leave the finishing blow to me. **Moon**: No worries, I will. *Moon nods gracefully as she takes a bite of her piece of cake. Namari stretches* **Yáshido**: Atagu Academy is? **Moon**: It's in Takamaru, uh, I mean Sablein. Still not used to that name change. **Yáshido**: Right, so how did you get down here so fast? **Moon**: I'll finish then. The Magic at Atagu wasn't really what I wanted to learn, but that's where I met Taku. Anyway, I came here to Macadamia, Zirts Academy. **Yáshido**: Ah, Hydro. **Moon**: Exactly. **Namari**: That explains earlier. *All three of them laugh* **Yáshido**: How long have you been at Zirts? **Moon**: I was a Gamma[5th year]. **Yáshido**: Your Hydro is Stage I. **Moon**: Eighty seven Efficiency. **Yáshido**: That's really good. **Moon**: I told them that I would be resigning. Everyone didn't want me to go; everyone that knew me that is. I am a bit sad that I won't see them for a while. **Yáshido**: Just give me some time, and I'll make sure that you won't be as paranoid as you are now. **Moon**: How did you know I was paranoid? **Yáshido**: Everyone is paranoid. Even me. I know I'll be sorta okay. The idea of having to go through the Council to explain this mess. Especially if Council Maya confronts us. It's not like Macadamia is known for what they do to treasons. **Moon**: Oh, you're right. They could even pressure you into some things. If they wanted to. **Yáshido**: It's a policy for me not to fight back unless Macadamia is corrupted. So, if I get detained, Edasia's going to be at a loss. **Namari**: Oh, just imagining that chaos if the Hero is not trustworthy anymore. That event sounds horrible. **Yáshido**: That's if worst comes to worst. **Moon**: Hm. **Namari**: So Moon, what's your real name? **Moon**: Monaka Ukitima. Moon, Monaka, Ukitima, it's all the same to me. **Yáshido**: Now thinking about it, I have never met anyone who was born in Alma, so I guess I'll need to get used to you calling me-, **Moon**: Kyon. **Yáshido**: Kyon Akima, The Hero of the Sixth Generation. **Moon**: It's so nice, I've only just arrived today, and I feel like I've been here forever. **Yáshido**: That's a good sign. *Kyoka comes over with them* **Kyoka**: 'You three having fun? **Moon**: So much. **Namari**: Yup. **Yáshido**: I'm enjoying myself. **Kyoka**: That's too bad. **Namari**: Why's that? **Kyoka**: Three, two, one. **Taku**: Alright everyone, I think we've reached the downfall. It's getting really late, and we might draw HIGHLY unnecessary attention from any wandering Familiars or Balancers. I hope you had a good time, Otara. *Taku looks over at Otara and she nods* Good, birthday girl doesn't have to clean up. **Keshio**(m): Word. **Taku**: So go ahead and get your rest. **Otara**: Thank you. Yáshido(T)(**Otara**): Have fun. (**Keshio**): Not cool. *Otara leaves the room still having the birthday hat on. After she leaves, Taku takes a bag out from under the table* **Taku**: Let's start. The quicker you move, the faster you can sleep. **Kamira**: Haha, that's our leave because who knows what might happen if we don't get back home. **Kyoka**: Kamira's right, Taku. **Yáshido**: Wait. Why are you two here? **Kamira**: Haha, exactly. *Taku rubs his chin as they walk to the door* **Kyoka**: Bye, everyone. **Kamira**: See you all tomorrow. *They exit the room* **Taku**: Anyone else has any excuses not to clean? *No one says anything* Okay, let's go then.

-Everyone starts to clean up. Once they're done cleaning, Yáshido says goodnight before heading to his room. Inside his room-

Approaching his room, he feels a dull aura of Reine from the inside. After he closes the door **Reine**: It's so late, Yáshido. I was afraid you wouldn't come back. **Yáshido**: And where did you get off to? **Reine**: Nowhere important. How was the party? **Yáshido**: How'd you know? **Reine**: The music, but I saw on the news too. **Yáshido**: Nice. You should have come. **Reine**: I should have? I was across Macadamia when I saw it. **Yáshido**: Ah~, I see. Now you have to tell me. **Reine**: Hehe~, I was called by some fellow adventurers to explore this tunnel they found for more Dermal materials. **Yáshido**: Oh really? Did you find anything? *Reine tries to not laugh but can't suppress it* **Reine**: HAHAHA, DID WE FIND ANYTHING? *Yáshido smiles as Reine falls on her back laughing* **Yáshido**: Sounds like you did. **Reine**: Oh boy, hahaha. Yes, we did. We found a good amount too. **Yáshido**: That's good. **Reine**: We found some for the Hotchkiss and Ferdinand Dermal. **Yáshido**: Two really popular ones. *Reine leans back up* **Reine**: When we got done, we went to a nearby restaurant. That's where I saw that it was Otara's birthday. **Yáshido**: What did they say about it? **Reine**: Just that she won't be able to celebrate it with her family, and all that. That she hasn't been seen in public for a week or two. They tried contacting the Misugamis to see if they were going to help at all but nothing. **Yáshido**: Oh? *Reine leans towards Yáshido with a smile* **Reine**(w): I believe Otara goes and visits them. **Yáshido**(w): I don't see why not. She could teleport to Watashimono just by blinking. **Reine**(w): Yeah . . . **Reine**: Hey, Yáshido, can I ask for a favor? **Yáshido**: Yeah, sure, anything. **Reine**: Before, I had to wait till everyone was asleep before I took a bath. Now because it's already late, I don't really know what's going on out there. **Yáshido**: Okay. **Reine**: Could you like, escort me there? **Yáshido**: Sure, I'll take one right after you. *Reine sighs* **Reine**: Good. *Reine stands. Her Dermal vanishes away from her body with a cloud of Particles. They leave the room, and start walking towards the bath* **Yáshido**: What are you going to wear? **Reine**: I have a cast of clothes on the ready. *As they walk around the corner, Namari walks past them. She turns as they keep walking* **Namari**: Oh-, hey, Reine. *Reine stops and turns around with a smile* **Reine**: Hey, Namari. **Namari**: Where are you two going? **Reine**: I'm going to take a bath. **Namari**: Ta-, take, take a bath? *Namari eyes Yáshido* **Yáshido**: What's up with you, and female Familiars? I'm just guarding the door. **Namari**: Whew, okay. Hey, if you two find a blue, small ribbon, please inform me, and I don't have a problem with that . . . *Namari turns* **Yáshido & Reine**: K. **Namari**: Have a goodnight. *Namari continues to walk* **Reine**: Night. **Yáshido**: Goodnight, Namari. *Yáshido and Reine make their way to the large bath. Yáshido goes over to the closet that Namari took him the first time. He gets a large towel then walks back over to Reine* **Yáshido**: The smaller towels are inside. *Reine takes the towel* **Reine**: Thanks, Yáshido. *Reine puts the towel around her, Yáshido leans up against the wall* **Yáshido**: I don't want to fall asleep waiting for you. **Reine**: I won't take that long. *Reine closes the door. Yáshido feels a small amount of energy as Niola's aura is felt instead of Reine's. After that, Niola's aura is undetectable with Denryoku* **Yáshido**(thts): She must Reversed her Sustain. *A couple seconds later, Yáshido hears a huge splash of water and laughter. Later, he starts to hear humming. Yáshido looks down each end of the hall* Of all the times. Why did she decide to take it here? It's not like she is bound here. I mean, of course, she isn't. Niola probably has a lot of currency too. She could have probably gone to the fanciest shower in Macadamia, but then again Niola doesn't look like the person to-, unless if she really likes this one, hah. *A quarter hour passes before Yáshido faintly feels Niola's aura again. The humming gets closer to the door. The knob twists before opening and Niola walks out. Yáshido eyes Niola's white tank top and jean-like pants that reach past her knees. Niola stops humming and smiles while watching Yáshido survey her clothing* **Niola**: Problem? **Yáshido**: No . . . It's just that. *Yáshido rubs the top of his Dermal* Never mind it. *They make it back to their room after Yáshido takes a bath* **Niola**: That was so refreshing. **Yáshido**: Was it? **Niola**: It's so big for one person, but the water hits the spot. **Yáshido**: So that's your goal. *Yáshido transforms out of the Hero. While Niola is walking towards the bed* **Yashi**: What's up with your hair? **Niola**: What do you mean? **Yashi**: Part of your hair, it's like Reine's. **Niola**: Are you serious? *Niola turns around and Particles form in front of her into a small mirror* Woah, you're right. **Yashi**: Did you do that on purpose? **Niola**: Yeah, I think so. Maybe I goofed up the Reverse on the Dermal. Could you hold my hair back for me? **Yashi**: Wha-, what? **Niola**: Hold my hair while I fix this. **Yashi**: You honestly need me to hold it? **Niola**: Uhm . . . Hero, I thought you were supposed to help those in need? What if it gets infected with a different aura? **Yashi**(thts): We have no clue what this is. **Yashi**: Even though I'm currently not in the Dermal, alright. *Niola holds all her hair except for the purple bang back* **Niola**: Quickly. *Yashi walks up behind her, and gently takes hold of her hair* **Yashi**(thts): Woah~, her hair is soft. *Niola increases the size of the mirror, and moves it up so that it's the same height as her* **Yashi**: Should I put a barrier around us? **Niola**: Yes. *A see-through gray barre surrounds them in an instant* Let's see. *The glass material of the mirror changes to a blue overlay. A Mangole appears on it with Zoka Vision. Yashi looks at the Mangole and sees Niola's face and the purple bang. A stable pink aura surrounds Niola's outline through the Mangole while the purple bang has a pinkish black aura leaking off it* **Yashi**(thts): Void? But why? **Niola**: That's interesting. I don't recall myself using any Void while being Reine. *Both of Niola's hands grip the pink hair as the Mangole and mirror disappear. Niola's Pure Energy comes from her hand and surrounds the purple hair. Within seconds, it slowly starts turning into pink* There we go. *Her hair completely changes back to all pink* **Yashi**: You have Void? **Niola**: No~, I'm trying to think, but I don't remember anything I've done that has to do with Void. *Niola stretches before turning to Yáshido* It couldn't have been the Dicipient from Darku . . . maybe it was the crystals we found. **Yashi**: Elilament crystals. Oh boy, you might want to get that checked out. **Niola**: I didn't touch any directly though. Neither did I use my Magic to obtain them. **Yashi**: Yeah I know, you have excavators for that, but it could have picked up your aura as you were around it. **Niola**: While I was hitting the rocks, huh? That could be it. Do you see something, I don't? *Yashi backs away and scans Niola as much as he can* **Yashi**: No, you look fine. I don't see any aura leaving your body. *Niola vanishes in a speck of Gray Particles right before Yashi makes eye contact with her. Yashi Reverses the barre. He looks at the bed and Niola's under the cover laying on a pillow* **Niola**: Sleep time. **Yashi**: Now this is awkward. **Niola**: Why's that? **Yashi**: Irrelevant. **Niola**: Oh, I get it. *Niola vanishes and reappears with her body laying opposite of the headboard* Less awkward? **Yashi**: Yeah, that's better. *Niola leans up and takes a pillow from the other end and sets it behind her and lies down on top of it. Niola then blows the Gray Particles off of the bed* **Niola**: Even if you're the Hero, it's only awkward if you make it awkward. Even so, I think it's completely normal. **Yashi**: Yeah, normal~. *Yashi runs his hands through his hair. He sits down on the bed. He looks at Niola, and her eyes are already closed. Yashi lays flat as he swings his legs under the cover. Facing outwards he yawns* Hey, Niola. **Niola**(m): Yes? **Yashi**: How long do you think it'll take to get to Korosi? **Niola**(m): I'm not sure . . . but not so long. **Yashi**: Good. Night. **Niola**: Goodnight. *A couple seconds later, Niola slightly chuckles* **Yáshido**: Ha, I just realized as well.

-Yashi falls asleep. While asleep, he feels someone trying to reach him and wakes back up-

Yashi looks at the curtains and it is pitch black. He lays on his back and his Mangole appears above him. Emuna is calling. Yashi turns his Mangole into an earpiece and puts it on **Yashi**(w): Emuna? **Emuna**(M): Hero, how are you? **Yashi**(w): Fine, you? *Emuna sighs* **Emuna**(M): Fine. I have some information you might want to hear. *Yashi sits up* **Yashi**(w): Alright let's hear it. **Emuna**(M): I'll start with the most problematic. Yesterday, there was a sighting of Lethica in Distome. **Yashi**(w): You sure? **Emuna**(M): Yes, I have a full-body shot. I'm sending it to you now. *Yashi's earpiece unfolds back into a Mangole. As this happens, a hologram beams up from it. The picture shows a crowd protesting* Here. *A circle is drawn on a figure in the back. The brightness of the screen increases as multiple auras appear on it. With a variety of colors, the one in the circle has a green tent* **Yashi**(w): Exactly like Lethica's. **Emuna**(M): I'm thinking he wants to be caught. That's the only reason he would still have his Sustain on at all. *Yashi inspects the image more. Lethica is on the opposite side of the street on the sidewalk. His movements seem as if he was walking in a hurry. Yashi makes the Mangole into an earpiece again* **Yashi**(w): Hmph, a possibility; Lethica gets as much done as possible before getting caught. *Yashi looks at the photo some more* When did you get this photo? **Emuna**(M): Today. Along with the Generals. **Yashi**(w): Why did they send it to you? Did they ask anything about me?

Emuna(M): Oh, of course they did. They didn't send it until I told them you would be visiting one of the Council. *Yashi lays back down* *Yashi*(w): Already in a rush, but I guess I do have to. *Emuna*(M): Do you plan on seeking out Lethica in Distome? *Yashi*(w): No, not yet. I know that is problematic but he's not really you know doing anything. I best should tell General Opaine since he's the closest. I'll at least do that first before I try to do anything in public. *Emuna*(M): Okay. *Yashi*(w): What was the second thing? *Emuna*(M): Yes, that. Did Niola already tell you about where she was? *Yashi*(w): No~, I mean yes. She told me what she was doing. Still in Macadamia exploring, right? *Emuna*(M): Yes. I was surprised to even see her there. She told me a funny thing that happened to you while training. *Yashi*(w): Don't want to know. What about the exploration? *Emuna*(M): Well . . . we found more materials for Ferdinand and Hotchkiss Dermals. *Yashi*(w): Mhm. *Emuna*(M): But, alongside them, there are these . . . Amantidite crystals, but instead of Zoka Swiftness, they produce this deadly substance . . . like Doku and Void combined. *Yashi jumps back up* *Yashi*: Really??? *Yashi looks at Niola from his accidental outburst* *Emuna*(M): Ye-, yeah. Did something happen to Niola? *Yashi*(w): Yes. When she got back from taking a bath, part of her hair was like this purplish color. *Emuna*(M): Like her Reine Dermal or different? *Yashi*(w): Wait, how'd you know about Reine? *Emuna*(M): She showed me while she was here. No one else saw so don't worry. *Yashi*(w): Come to think of it. It was darker than Reine's purple hair. *Emuna*(M): Has she removed it? *Yashi*(w): Yeah, like right after I told her about it. *Emuna*(M): We tested the substance on some other crystals, Dermals, and everyday things. With every object, it would start turning it into a purple color. It only spreads so far though. If the object has any Pure Energy, it-, the substance removes it. Lowering the maximum amount of Oplitals in total. *Yashi*(w): You mean, it can lower the amount of Pure Energy one can hold? *Emuna*(M): I'd rather you say Oplitals, but, precisely. *Yashi sighs as he looks at Niola's sleeping body again* *Yashi*(w): When she was fixing it, through a Zoka'd mirror, we saw a darkened version of her aura coming off that piece of hair. *Emuna*(M): That's what it looks like. Either Pure Energy or Patchi Tekiyo will reverse the effects. One drop of it can cause problems, but one small dose of either of those Elilaments will fix it. *Yashi*(w): About that, you said that it's Doku and Void, right? *Emuna*(M): An Aced of both. *Yashi*(w): Both Aced? Well, I thought if Void made any contact with Pure Energy, an explosion would occur? *Emuna*(M): I'm not sure about that either. Until we conduct more research, the best guess I have is that the Doku negates it in some way. *Yashi*(w): Another thing, there's no way this hasn't happened before. Haven't you tested it in a Personal Cast? *Emuna*(M): That's the difference, it's in an Amantidite crystal. *Yashi*(w): Yeah. That would change some properties. *Emuna*(M): There's only been one known way to forcefully penetrate one with a Personal Cast, and unfortunately that took the lives of many Alchemists. *Yashi*(w): Was there anyone else who was hurt by the material? *Emuna*(M): Niola is the first case of a human I'm hearing this on. We might have to conduct experiments if she's okay with that. **Yashi**(w): I have a couple questions. **Emuna**(M): Okay. **Yashi**(w): How does it necessarily get onto an object? **Emuna**(w): Via by an aura or direct contact. Tomorrow we should have a name for it other than Amantidite, but it has its own aura. It's similar to Void as in physical nature, but the difference is they don't read the same codes from a UZVT Scanner. The amount that makes contact doesn't determine the rate of Pure Energy lost by the object. The longer it stays in contact with the object, the more that it takes away over time. **Yashi**(w): I understand. So in Alchemy terms, it could start taking away one Oplital when it starts and an hour later, ten Oplitals? **Emuna**(M): Yes, exactly like that. Unless someone could tell you that your energy is being drained or sees that purple texture on your body, you would never know. **Yashi**(w): Macadamian borders have DZVT Scanners, do they not sense the Amantidite stuff at all? **Emuna**(M): Yes, it does sense it, but because it's new, the scanners aren't registered to trigger it if sensed. **Yashi**(w): You've already sent an issue out on that right? **Emuna**(M): Yes. **Yashi**(w): What happens when an object gets all of its energy wiped? **Emuna**(M): Well that's . . . One of the Raw Dermals we tested, once all its Pure Energy was gone, it acted like a normal piece of armor. When tested on an Eta Familiar, the Familiar could no longer use Magic. Neither did it have a Sustain. It became its own entity. **Yashi**(w): As in you could no longer Reverse it? **Emuna**(M): Remember me telling you about a force summon a couple years back? That may be the only way. Besides that, no. The interesting part is that, because the Familiar doesn't have any more Pure Energy left to support it from Magic, if it receives a powerful enough blow, it will disintegrate into Particles. **Yashi**(w): That's a bit strange. **Emuna**(M): A lot more tests must be conducted. **Yashi**(w): Hey Emuna, in the photo, that is a protest or riot, right? **Emuna**(M): I suppose you wouldn't have a TV there. They were demanding to know what's happening between the Hero and Dia. One stated, 'Dia has taken apart in an assault with other Dicipients. Yet the Hero himself hasn't even been seen in a week. Does that mean Dia has converted, and the Hero is dead?' End quote. **Yashi**(w): It's much more difficult than that, Emuna. I wish it was easy. It's nothing like what happened to Kyon, but I hate to see it tremble down this way. **Emuna**(M): Right now, this has been the only one in Macadamia. The most has been five, of course in Regra. **Yashi**(w): Should I send an apology letter? **Emuna**(M): What? Really? **Yashi**(w): It was a joke, but uhm I'll just have to go to General Opaine. **Emuna**(M): That's the plan. Before you go, how are your Oplital levels? **Yashi**(w): Would you be mad if I told you I was already half-empty? **Emuna**(M): No . . . you'd just have to come all the way back so I can refill you. **Yashi**(w): If that's the case, I'm half full. **Emuna**(M): Just stay safe. Hopefully, you only run into one or two on your way. **Yashi**(w): I'm glad we think on the same plane. I'll have Reine to go with me. **Emuna**(M): I doubt Niola would let you go without her. **Yashi**(w): Now that you mention it, that's probably true. Alright Emuna, I'll speak to you soon. **Emuna**(M): Bye, Yashi. Oh and sorry for calling you so early in the morning. **Yashi**(w): No, it's fine.

Emuna(M): You sure? I know you have a tendency to not go back to sleep if you wake up like this. *Yashi*(m): I'll be okay. *Emuna*(M): Hm, alright, bye. *Yashi's Mangole disappears* *Yashi*(thts): I have a lot of things to do. *Yashi looks at Niola again before laying back over*

-A couple hours pass before Yashi wakes back up. With the same routine as the day before, they all meet in the training grounds-

Kamira & Kyoka: Good morning, everyone. **Students**: Good morning. *Kamira*: Unfortunately, our lessons will be cut short today, but it's going to be simple. The group that was with Kyoka will be my group and vice versa. Also, from now on after today, I will be helping in live practice battles. *Kyoka*: And I will be helping you learn and perfect your Elilaments. *Keshio*: Sounds good. *Kamira*: Alright, get in your groups from last time. *Otara and Yáshido line up next to each other, and Keshio and Namari line up opposite them. Moon and Laito remain next to Kamira* Laito and Moon, you two can choose the group that you want to be in. *Laito*: You can go and pick first, Moon. Doesn't really matter to me. *Moon*: Okay. *Moon looks between the groups* Namari's group looks the funnest, but I think Kyon and Otara would be more of a challenge. *Laito*: Whatever you say, Moon. *Kamira*: Good, Otara's group will be with me, and Namari's will be with Kyoka. We don't have long so let's go. *The two groups go to their own side. By Kamira* *Kamira*: Today, we will be working with patching, especially when it comes to fighting. *Everyone stands completely still* What's wrong? Do you all not know what patching is? *Kamira looks at Otara, and she shakes her head* What about you, Hero? I know you've done it with Dia before. *Yáshido*: I really have no idea what you mean by this 'patching'. *Kamira*: Well you're about to learn it. I'm positive when I show you, you'll realize what it is. You three spread out a bit. *Moon, Otara, and Yáshido spread out, forming a triangle* *Yáshido*: Now what? *Kamira points at Yáshido* *Kamira*: I'm going to start off by injuring you. *Yáshido*: O-, kay~. *Kamira*: No jokes intended, you need to take damage for us to proceed, and it's not like you'll be able to dodge it. *Yáshido*: Kamira, I'm starting to think everyone is a little bit too confident in their abilities but, go ahead then. *Moon*: Wait, by Patching do you mean Patchi Tekiyo? *As soon as Moon finishes her sentence, Yáshido feels something from behind and gets hit by it, pushing him forward and causing dirt smoke to rise as he slides across it. He lands on one knee before standing. Yáshido looks back at his recent position, and two flares float before rushing towards and circling Kamira* *Yáshido*(thts): I was not expecting that. *Kamira*: Alright, and now you are damaged. To start the patching process, you need to start off a flow of energy between you three. The more people sharing the energy, the faster the main target will be healed. *Otara*: Kamira, why did you stop using Alchemy terms? *Kamira*: I thought it was obvious that patching would be Patchi Tekiyo, but I guess it's just me, and the flare was on its way before Moon even answered me. Go ahead and do the energy flow. *Yáshido*: It's settled that we know what it is. *Kamira*: Just do it. *Moon and Otara focus on Yáshido* Patching increases body stamina slightly, heals some physical injuries, and can just block away general pain. The only way to see a patch in progress is with Denryoku. If you use Ikkasei, you can see the different energy sources moving throughout the air. *Yáshido activates Ikkasei and a mixture of Otara's gray aura and Moon's canary aura appears around him* **Moon**: This feels weird because Otara is using Ace. *Otara looks at Moon* **Kamira**: I'm glad you brought that up. If everyone is using the same Stage Patchi Tekiyo, then the process will move along quicker. I'm going to hit you two as well. **Otara**: I do not approve. **Kamira**: What? **Otara**: I understand what you say, which is true, but in a case where the receiver is conscious, if they accept the side that has a higher value than the other connections then they heal faster. **Yáshido**(thts): That is also true. **Kamira**: Really? *Otara nods* Well Yáshido, try to accept Otara's Patchi more than Moon's. **Yáshido**: The sad part is that I only feel Otara. **Kamira**: You only feel Otara? *Everyone looks at Moon. Moon has a worried expression across her face as she puts both of her hands towards Yáshido* Moon, is Stage III really your highest? *Moon sighs before frowning* **Moon**: Yes. **Otara**: Hmph. *Otara raises both of her hands towards Yáshido too. Yáshido feels Otara's flow die down so much that he feels an equal amount of her and Moon's energy* **Kamira**: See, was that so hard, Otara? **Otara**: Considering I'm using ten percent, yes, it was. **Kamira**: Now, I have to hit all three of you. ^Sparks of Particles appear above Kamira before multiple flares burst towards the three of them. Each one of them taking at least two blows^ **Yáshido**(thts): On the inside, she's probably having a blast. *After the smoke clears, Kamira has her hand over her mouth before taking a deep breath and putting her hands behind her back* **Kamira**: Good. Now the fastest way to heal all of you would be? **Yáshido**: Stage III. **Kamira**: True but not entirely. There are two ways. All of you making direct paths to each other, or one path that flows through all of you. **Moon**: Wait, could you say that again? *Kamira looks at Moon* **Kamira**: So, what you two were doing was making a direct path to the Hero, correct? **Moon**: Yeah. **Kamira**: Now, because all of you are a bit damaged, you could heal the second way. Instead of everyone making their own direct paths to each other, you can connect the flows. Oh-, wait. *Kamira rubs her hair* You can't do the second way because you don't have Stage II. **Moon**: Really? I'm sorry. **Kamira**: No, it's okay. Otara can make a flow for you since she has Ace. So in this case, Moon, you just have to stay relaxed, and everyone will get healed. *Otara lifts a hand towards Moon and Yáshido* **Moon**: What do you mean by 'stay relaxed'? **Yáshido**: When you first make contact, it feels like your stamina is being drained and a heavy fatigued sensation takes control over your body. *Moon jumps back with her eyes open* **Moon**: That sounds scary. **Otara**: It only lasts for a couple seconds; You should be able to handle it. *Yáshido raises a hand at Moon and Otara* **Yáshido**: Ready? *Moon nods. Moon's body starts to glow pink* **Moon**: Woah~. **Kamira**: You okay? **Moon**: I've never felt anything like this. A-, and my body, I think I literally almost fainted. **Kamira & Yáshido**:

Haha. **Moon**: But I'm okay now. *A few seconds later* **Kamira**: Okay, you can stop. *Yáshido and Otara put their hands down. The pinkish aura between them disappears* **Yáshido**: Whew. **Kamira**: You three think you got it? *All of them nod* Nice, let's see if my sister is done. **Yáshido**: Wait, that's it? **Kamira**: I told you it would be simple. *They turn towards Kyoka's group and they have a Barre around them. Taku stands to the right of the Barre. He turns towards them and motions them towards him. The four of them all walk towards him. Once they are a few yards from Taku* **Taku**: Morning you two. **Moon & Otara**: Good morning. *Taku scans Moon* **Taku**: You fit so well already, Moon. **Moon**: I do? *Taku nods* **Taku**: Yáshido, Exna. **Yáshido & Kamira**: Good morning. **Taku**: I've been thinking about the Dicipients here, Yáshido. I have yet to fight any of them and can sense then with my Denryoku fairly easily. I can tell you now that Lethica is close, but I'm not sure if he is headed our way. **Yáshido**: Lethica? The Dicipient one? *Taku nods* How accurate? **Taku**: Dead on. **Moon**: Wait, wait, wait, we're going to be invaded by Dicipients? **Kamira**: That's not what he's saying, Moon. *Taku holds out his hand and a Mangole appears. It's a map of the location around them. **Yáshido**: This is? **Taku**: A Personal Cast I learned before I left the Demon King. It's a copy and paste of all the auras I can feel. The blue one is Lethica. Not sure about the others. *Kamira stands next to Yáshido* **Kamira**: I have so many questions. How exactly can you inject the auras you know into a visible field? **Taku**: The Alchemists in Darku are pretty wild. They do countless experiments and tests that are insane. After a prototype version, I was able to sneak me one of the final products. *Taku flips the Mangole. This side has a lot of gray dots surrounding one black dot showing a five hundred yard radius* **Taku**: The field is not live because I'd constantly have to be inserting it with Oplitals. It's much easier to document if I can get a direct contact, like if I shake your hand, or hit someone, I take the smallest amount of aura and instantly seal it within a Tekiration. You would never notice it. *Yáshido looks at the map and there are six gray dots by one black dot* **Otara**: I'm guessing you're the black dot? **Taku**: Yeah. **Yáshido**: Why are there only six? **Taku**: Well, I have you and Savenna on another sheet. And, I haven't . . . gotten a sample of Otara's aura. *Taku looks at Otara who is still looking on the map. Otara makes eye contact with Taku before she steps back behind Yáshido* **Kamira**: Why are you just now showing us this? **Taku**: Don't know to be honest. It may be useful later though. I never really used it like that. It only came up during a conversation I had with Savenna. Plus, it takes up a lot of Pure Energy. *The map and Mangole disappear into Particles* **Kamira**: He's not lying, his Opitals just decreased a significant amount. **Taku**: Why would I have to lie for? **Yáshido**: Is it a handoff? **Taku**: If only it was that simple. *Everyone looks at Yáshido* **Yáshido**: What? **Kamira**: None of us are even compatible. **Yáshido**: Neither am I. Yeah I know that. It would help Macadamia is what I'm saying, especially if they had a larger one. Then we could strategically take all of them down. *A loud noise happens to the side of them. They all turn to see Kyoka's group standing inside where the Barre once stood. Namari is sitting down while the others are standing. Taku Reverses his Barre, they look over at them before talking amongst themselves* *Taku*: We'll talk more about this later, you two have to go, right? *Kamira*: Yes, yes, I completely forgot. *Kamira starts to jog towards Kyoka's group. By Kyoka's group* *Kyoka*: How was it? *Keshio*: Hate to admit, this might actually be a tough one to Ace. *Laito*: Namari, you were trying so hard. *Namari laughs* *Namari*: I know right. *Deep breath* I think I might have overdone it a little. *Laito*: And what do you mean by a tough one, Keshio? *Keshio*: I'm just saying Laito, I really don't push myself to learn Elilaments. It just happens while I'm practicing how to use them effectively. *Laito*: Alright, so what Elilaments have you Aced so far? *Kyoka*: One second you, two. *Kamira arrives* *Kamira*: Sis, finished? *Kyoka*: Ehm. *Kamira*: What did you three learn? *Keshio*: Particle Magic is a pain. *Namari*: That's only if you don't know what you're doing. *Namari stands* *Laito*: Creativity is key. *Keshio*: Well said. *Kamira*: Good. Anything you want to tell them while we're here? *Kyoka looks at Namari and Keshio, then looks behind Kamira at everyone else* *Kyoka*: Nope. *Kamira*: Okay, training is over for today. We'll see you all tomorrow. *Keshio*: Really? That's it? I thought you were just messing with us? *Kyoka*: Sorry to say, but we really do have to leave early today. *Namari*: Bye Kamira, Kyoka, Laito. *Laito*: See ya. *Laito's body disappears after swiftly being surrounded in a gray outline* *Kamira*: Bye you two. *Kyoka*: Bye little ones. *Kamira and Kyoka start walking away. By Yáshido. They see Kamira and Kyoka wave at them as they start walking towards the exit. Taku, Moon, and Yáshido wave back. Namari and Keshio start walking towards them* *Yáshido*: That was quick. *Taku*: Family business. Probably wants to know what they've been up to. *Moon*: Wait, they don't have permission to be here? *Taku*: Not by a long shot-, I thought I told you this before you even got here? *Moon*: I was a bit in a rush, so I probably forgot. *Taku*: I told them if they think they need to stop coming, they can. So if they don't show up, you all know why. *Keshio*: 'Know why', what? *Taku turns and both Keshio and Namari are just now getting to them* *Taku*: Kamira and Kyoka, they must make time to get here. I don't know exactly what they do when they're not here, but they probably want to keep it under family guidelines, or something like that I don't know. *Yáshido*: So what have you been working on? *Taku*: We have other members they want to join; Moon was easier because she was closer, but these other members are going to take a while. *Yáshido*: Backgrounds? *Taku*: It's sad because everyone that is joining is literally all my friends that I had before, you know, being a Dicipient. *Yáshido*: Oh-, I see. *Keshio*: Sounds ironic. *Taku slightly chuckles* *Taku*: You think so too, huh? *Namari*: How many? *Taku*: There's two coming from Catalyst, and three more from Zenni. *Yáshido*: Yeah, crossing over from Catalyst is especially going to be hard. *Keshio yawns* *Keshio*: New members, I don't think our dorm can handle five more people. *Taku*: Savenna's got that covered. *Keshio*: Well never mind then. *Yáshido*: What is she going to do? *Taku*: More P.M. How else would she make the dorm bigger? *Namari*: You must have used Solitary Kuki Sosa then. Where's that going to come from? *Taku*: She's been carefully doing her best to make her own. Speaking about that, she's probably done with a batch now. Yáshido, Keshio, want to come help and bring them out? *Yáshido*: Why not. *Namari*: Excuse me, Yáshido. *Yáshido turns to Namari* *Yáshido*: Yes? *Namari*: Where's Reine? I wanted to do some more training. *Yáshido*(thts): That's a good question, I haven't seen her either. *Otara*: She's in the kitchen, that's the last place I saw her. *Namari*: Kitchen? *Keshio*: She couldn't be . . . *Keshio's body turns light blue before he's already inside of it* *Namari*: What's he about to do? *Namari's body turns light blue as she also dashes inside of the dorm as well* *Taku*: You all seriously don't care if we are caught, I see that now. Otara, you care to help? *Otara*: Sure.

Chapter 11 - Implausible Ambuscades

-Taku leads Otara and Yáshido into his house, up the stairs to a door far back. He gently knocks on the door-

Taku: Savenna, I'm coming in. *Taku slowly opens the door and quietly walks in. Savenna is sitting down legs folded facing a radiant blue Particle-Block in front of her. To the right are two others, but with Magic bounds around them* **Savenna**: This last one shouldn't take long. **Taku**: No need to rush. *After Otara and Yáshido walk in, Taku slowly closes the door behind them and leans on the wall next to it. Yáshido and Otara stand behind Savenna as she focuses on the Particle-Block* **Yáshido**(thts): That's some immense concentration. Haven't made one of those things since I was in Anzen. *Taku and Yáshido watch Otara walk on the opposite side of the Particle-Block and sit facing Savenna. Savenna looks at Otara* **Savenna**: Yes? **Otara**: I'm just watching. *Savenna smiles* **Savenna**: You want to help, don't you? *Taku and Yáshido look at Otara. She glances at Taku and Yáshido before looking at Savenna* **Otara**: If you would let me. **Savenna**: Join in. Carefully. *Otara turns towards the block and points her hands at it* **Taku**: Can we go ahead and get the other two? **Savenna**: Yeah. **Taku**: Let's go. *Taku and Yáshido walk towards the other two Magic bound blocks. Taku's hands surround in Particles before he picks up one of the blocks* **Taku**: We're taking them to the dorm. *Taku steps aside as Yáshido's hands become wrapped in a dense amount of Particles as well. Yáshido picks up the block. They walk back towards the door. It opens by itself and they start walking towards the dorm. Outside the dorm, another seal surrounds Taku's block and vanishes. Yáshido hands him the one he's holding and Taku vanishes that one in a seal as well* Thanks. **Yáshido**: It wasn't that hard. **Taku**: Yeah. I'll see you later, Yáshido. **Yáshido**: Alright. *Taku starts walking back to his house. Yáshido walks inside of the dorm. He walks to a room next to the bath and opens the door. Keshio is sitting on a bench without a shirt on while drinking a bottle of water. Keshio notices Yáshido walking in as he puts down the bottle* **Keshio**: Hero. **Yáshido**: Uh-, Denki Master, what are you up to? **Keshio**: We found your Familiar. Other than that, about to take a steam. **Yáshido**: Oh, what are they doing? **Keshio**: Namari and Reine are talking about things. Wasn't too interesting to me. *Yáshido sits on the bench next to Keshio. Yáshido yawns* **Yáshido**: Ah man, being taught again is a little tough. **Keshio**: Haha, you think so? Must have been fun making your own strategies and lesson plans, huh? **Yáshido**: If only. *Keshio drinks more of his water* What all have we learned here anyways. **Keshio**: Before you came, we summoned some Familiars, we did Kuki Sosa, and we fought a lot. Not much when you say it out loud though. **Yáshido**: The fighting is to know what you all specialize in. **Keshio**: To be honest, I feel like the real training starts now. **Yáshido**: Yeah? **Keshio**: I mean yeah, now it's just collecting more members. **Yáshido**: I guess you could say that, but I still have to register Taku. **Keshio**: Oh~, that's what I'm forgetting. We are screwed anyway if you can't do that. **Yáshido**: Don't say that. It sounds like you don't have any confidence in me. **Keshio**: Sorry, didn't mean it like that. **Yáshido**(thts): Did I just hear Keshio say sorry? **Keshio**: Who are you going to speak to? The way I was thinking is that you would speak to a General in Macadamia, but then they'll have to tell the Council to get their approval. **Yáshido**: Of course there's going to be some tension, but I have to try. 'Only thing they really need is evidence that he's changed. **Keshio**: Who are you going to tell. **Yáshido**: Hmm~. There're so many to choose from. **Keshio**: You haven't even thought about it yet? **Yáshido**: Maya might be the highest hope. **Keshio**: Maya . . . that could work. She's converted some pretty bad people herself. **Yáshido**: Sadly, I'm not going to her though. **Keshio**: You're-, you're not? **Yáshido**: Don't think the Council will care about something like this. Being in Macadamia, General Opaine would be the best option; knowing that I could get to him the soonest. *Keshio starts drinking more water as he takes a towel from the rack behind him* So, Jurono, how do you think they're doing? **Keshio**: Not sure. I've been going so long to where I don't really care. I mean, I have learned some things, but I would probably switch Academies if I was to go back to one. **Yáshido**: So that's how you feel? **Keshio**: Don't get me wrong, it's a great school, students can be annoying at times, but I just want to focus on what I'm best at. **Yáshido**: Reasonable. **Keshio**: Here, I can go out right now and start electrocuting whatever I want, when you register Taku of course. I guess it just feels like this was the best situation, and, I have to admit, it's pretty cool for you to be here. **Yáshido**: About that. *Keshio looks over at Yáshido as he takes another sip of his water* **Keshio**: What? **Yáshido**: I can't stay like this forever. *Keshio turns away and looks down* **Keshio**: Yeah, I can tell. Since you joined, I've been seeing your Oplitals fade away. **Yáshido**: Oh, so you've noticed. **Keshio**: I'm sure I'm not the only one who's noticed. **Yáshido**: I'll be letting Taku know before I go. Really, I can register for Taku and get a Flag Treaty if I go to General Opaine. **Keshio**: Woah, you think we'll be able to fight alongside the Macadamian Army? **Yáshido**: Of course. *Yáshido stands* **Keshio**: Still hurts to know that we might eventually have to fight Dia. I've known her in Jurono for a while and I just don't see her doing what she did. She and you are just so powerful, it sucks to see her dip to the other side. Sorry you have to go through this, Yáshido. **Yáshido**: Thank you, I needed that. *Keshio stands* **Keshio**: Alright that should be enough water. **Yáshido**: I might need one of these too, see you around, Keshio. **Keshio**: See you, Yáshido. *Yáshido leaves the room and walks to the kitchen. Namari and Reine aren't there, so he walks back to his room. Walking down the hall, he notices someone standing in front of his room staring inside* **Yáshido**(w): Moon, is that you? *Moon looks at him* **Moon**(w): Oh-, hey, Kyon. **Yáshido**(w):

Hey, what are you looking at? **Moon**(w): That's your Familiar right? *Yáshido looks through the slightly opened door and sees Reine leaning across a dresser looking out of a window. Yáshido backs away from the door* **Yáshido**(w): Yes-, **Moon**(w): I thought it wasn't healthy for Familiar to be out for so long? **Yáshido**: I know, it's just that she prefers to stay summoned. **Moon**(w): I guess that's good that you take your Familiar's feelings over your own. **Voice**: Wha'cha two talking about? *Both Moon and Yáshido turn to the sudden voice. Reine stands at the door. Moon gets startled and squills onto Yáshido. Holding onto the left side of his chest and arm* **Yáshido & Reine**: Hm? *Yáshido and Reine look at Moon* **Yáshido**: M-, Moon? *Moon looks at Yáshido's arm as she continues holding on to it. After realizing what's going on, Moon lets go of Yáshido* Are you okay? **Moon**: Ha~, haha. Uhm~. *Rubs the back of her head* Sorry 'bout that. She scared me. **Reine**: Oh, I'm sorry. *Yáshido looks at Reine* **Yáshido**: Moon was just asking some questions about you, Reine. **Reine**: Oh~, okay. *Reine folds her arms while looking at Moon* **Moon**: Hi there . . . **Reine**: Hi. *Moon awkwardly laughs* **Moon**: I don't know what to say, I've never been in a situation like this before. *Yáshido stands in front of Reine* **Yáshido**: Let's start over then. **Moon**: Right. *Moon turns around and takes a couple of breaths. Yáshido stands behind Reine. When Moon turns around with a big smile* **Moon**: Hey Kyon's Familiar, my name is Moon, what's yours? *Reine unfolds her arms and smiles back* **Reine**: Hey Moon, my name's Reine. **Moon**: Oh~, so you were who I heard Namari talking to. **Reine**: Yup. *Moon scans Reine* **Moon**: Did you choose your Dermal yourself? **Reine**: Ehm~, you like it? **Moon**: Yeah, could you step into the hall; I want to get a better view of it. **Reine**: Okay. *Reine steps into the hall. Standing in front of Moon and then slowly spins in a circle* **Moon**: What a Familiar, Hero. **Yáshido**: Thank you. *Reine stops twirling* **Moon**: Not making a pun here, but she looks strangely familiar to that popular adventurer, Akimora. Niola Akimora I think her full name is. *Reine and Yáshido look at each other for a split second* **Reine**: You're the second to say that. **Yáshido**: Niola, huh? *Reine turns in Yáshido's direction standing next to Moon* **Reine**: What do you say, Hero, do I look like this Niola girl? **Yáshido**(thts): It's almost like Reine is Niola. **Yáshido**: Yeah, I do see a resemblance in the face. *Reine laughs* **Moon**: Right? **Yáshido**: It must bother you that she looks similar to Niola? **Moon**: No, I just wanted to share what I thought. **Reine**: Now, I want to see Niola, and see if she actually looks like me. **Moon**: I wish you luck on that. She seems like a very busy person. Although, since the Hero's your master, you might have a better shot. *Moon looks at Yáshido* You do have her Mangole information, right? **Yáshido**: Now why would I have that? **Moon**: Yeah, I realized you're not the type to have a full contact list, staying disclosed, and everything. That would mean Emuna would have her then, right? **Yáshido**: On point. If only Dia was here, she has over a hundred different contacts. *Moon's eyes open* **Moon**: Dia. *Moon looks at the wall. Yáshido notices her fists are balled* **Yáshido &**

Reine: Moon? *Already standing next to Moon, Reine bends down to look at her face. Moon. Reine stands back up and steps a foot back* *Reine*: She's upset. *Yáshido*(thts): It has something to deal with Regra. *Yáshido*: What's the matter, Mo-, *Moon quickly looks at Yáshido* *Moon*: Isn't it obvious! *Moon swiftly turns away and starts running towards the exit* *Reine*: It'd be better if we stay with her. *Yáshido*: Yeah. *Yáshido and Reine run after Moon. Moon continues to run to the training ground. After realizing that Yáshido and Reine weren't going to stop chasing her, Moon slows her pace and comes to a stop. In the middle of the training ground* *Yáshido*: What happened in Regra? *Moon's fists tighten* *Moon*: The thought of it all, makes me feel terrible. *Yáshido*: Moon, I understand what Dia may have done to you, just tell me what happened. *Moon wipes her face* *Moon*: Well, I told you about what happened to my family in Alma, and most of my past up until now. But there's a second side to the reason why I'm joining. *Moon looks over her shoulder at Yáshido* What happened to her that would make her do such a thing? *Yáshido*: Moon. *Moon*: Well?! *Yáshido*: The truth is, I know as little as you do. *Moon looks back, straight in front of her* *Moon*: That just makes it even worse. *Moon turns completely around and looks at Yáshido. Tears are dripping down Moon's face* You fought him, didn't you? You did, you fought the Demon King and lost. *Yáshido clenches his fists. Reine looks between Yáshido and Moon* Is that the reason why she left you? You were too weak? I would never expect Dia to convert just because her allies were too weak. That's not like her at all. *Yáshido*: Let me stop you there. One thing and for one thing is sure, Dia did not convert. *Moon*: She didn't convert? Then what do you call (Y): DESTROYING A WHOLE SEIRA WITH OTHER DICIPIENTS!!! *Yáshido*: I . . . I can't explain that, but I'm sure that it was-, *Moon*: You are the freaking Hero and-, still you don't see that she has converted?! You know how insecure that makes you look! She killed hundreds of thousands of people with her hands, Kyon! There's an entire recording of her doing it! She's even seen in a photo with other Dicipients wearing their uniform!!! What information you could possibly have to say that she isn't gonna become a Dicipient?! How can you not tell that this girl you have been with since you were little kids is joining Daphoria! *Yáshido*: She told me herself that she isn't joining the Dark Army. *Moon*: That she isn't fighting for Lark? *Yáshido*: Yeah. *Moon*: And you believe her? *Yáshido*: Of course I do. *Moon*: Even though she tried to kill you?! *A gust of wind spreads from Moon as she takes a step forward towards Yáshido* *Yáshido*: The only thing I can do at this point is believe. Believe in what she says. As you said, I've known her since we were little, and she's been my partner for as long as I can remember. I can't deny that she tried to kill me, but I . . . I'm not just going to give up on her. I can't. *Moon's eyes open* *Moon*: You're not telling me you're trying to get her back? *Yáshido*: That's part of why I'm here. *Moon looks down again. Yáshido can see the pressure of Moon's Elilaments increase with a split second of Uhnyoi* *Moon*: I see . . . you're not going to change your mind. *Yáshido*: Moon, fighting is not going to go well for anyone. **Moon**: I wish you would have told that to Dia before she attacked Regra. *Yáshido slightly jerks* The Demon King was all this was supposed to be about. Helping to get rid of that evil presence. *Moon looks back up at Yáshido. Moon's eyes are now light blue* **Yáshido**: And that's still the goal. **Moon**: Ha, is that so. *Moon takes a step towards Yáshido and opens her right hand, keeping it next to her waist. Reine steps in front of Yáshido with flames surrounding her hands* **Yáshido**(m): Reine. *Yáshido looks at Moon and she is still staring at him* **Yáshido**: And getting Dia back is my own personal goal. **Moon**: I'm the last one, Hero. **Yáshido**: Last one? **Moon**: Yup~, the last in my family~. My uncle and younger sister. The recording they aired, was them being killed. *Reine and Yáshido's stand sickened. The flames from around Reine's hands dim* **Reine**(m): What. **Yáshido**(m): You . . . Dia killed them . . . **Moon**: I looked up to her. She was an inspiration to all the girls who wanted to be strong. Strong enough to change the world. And-, that same person who I admired, turned right back around and killed my family in cold blood. *Long tears start to form rapidly flow down Moon's face* Makes me want to kill her myself! *From inside the helmet of his Dermal, Yáshido feels a tear come from his face into his chest plate* **Moon**: It might look like I'm crazy, it may not, but these feelings are logical. The Demon King, Dia, and you trusting her . . . I CAN'T TAKE IT ANYMORE!!! ^Within a blink, Moon casts a blade of Hydro, sharp enough to slice through any material, and appears right in front of Reine and Yáshido preparing for a slash. Her body is surrounded by the constant threshold of Aced Zoka Swiftness, and Aced Zoka Strength alongside Ikkasei^ **Yáshido**: Reine! **Reine**: Woah-, ^Yáshido quickly pulses Reine to his right and holds up his arms to defend himself from Moon's attack. Yáshido summons a Barre around himself and Moon right before her weapon collides with him. When they impact, Yáshido gets knocked to the wall of the small pyramid Barre as Moon's thin water blade pierces through his arms Dermal and against his chest and head. A yellow spark spreads from the impact and shocks all around the Barre. The blow and smash against the Dermal causes Yáshido to fall unconscious. His Barre vanishes into Particles as he falls down chest-first onto the ground. Moon stands above him. The aftershock of the blow creates a ring around them, and also hitting Reine in the back^ **Reine**(m): A critical? **Moon**(m): There. *Reine turns around to see Yáshido lying completely still on the ground. Reine doesn't feel Yáshido's aura* **Moon**: Stand, Hero. **Reine**: Yáshido?! *Moon wipes her face after looking from Reine back to Yáshido's body* **Moon**: Kyon? *Reine runs to Yáshido and sits next to him. Reine puts her ear near Yáshido's mouth and her hand on his chest* **Reine**(m): He's breathing but unconscious. *Reine looks at Moon* **Reine**: I understand how you feel, but you shouldn't have taken your anger out on the Hero! *Reine notices that Moon has started to cry again. Moon falls down on her knees next to Yáshido and covers her face* **Moon**: I'm sorry-, I'm sorry-, I'm sorry-, I'm so sorry. I didn't mean to, I really didn't! I was mad and couldn't control my actions~. *Moon starts to sad fully moan. Reine looks at Yáshido and grabs his hands;

Interlocking hers in his* **Reine**: As long as you feel regretful, it's fine. **Moon**: I'm sorry, Reine, you had to see me like that. I feel ashamed of myself. I can't believe I attacked the Hero. **Reine**: You're right, Moon. *Moon stops crying as she looks up at Reine who's staring down at Yáshido* I don't know much, but from what you've told me, I would feel devastated. You lost something you can't get back. Because he's my master, I must follow him and do what he says. So, I personally believe in Dia too. *Reine's hands glow pinkish-red around Yáshido* **Moon**: This is hard for me to decide. I'm not a bad person, but yet I still came here with benevolent intent. Should I just leave, Reine? *Reine looks at Moon* **Reine**: No, you can't. Not now. You have to stay. *Reine looks back at Yáshido* I don't believe that Yáshido could fight Dia if he tried, and if he did, many people would already be hurt beforehand. *Reine looks back at Moon* It's only right for you to fight her. Everyone else has some type of emotion bound with her it seems, but it looks like she broke yours by what she did to your family, so it'll be easier for you to fight her at full potential. I don't know how strong she is, but if she was Yáshido's partner, she had to be strong. Do you even think you could beat her? **Moon**: I'm just as strong as she is. **Reine**: Hmph, but if you need it, I'll help you. **Moon**(m): Really? **Reine**: Only if Dia has really converted, *Reine once again looks at Yáshido* But until then, stay positive. I don't want this to happen again. Nor do I want you to make Taku feel some type of way by leaving. Try to keep those emotions back, do you think you could do that for me? **Moon**: Yes. I promise I won't do it again. *Reine closes her eyes* **Reine**(w): Because then I'll have to fight you . . . **Moon**: Huh? What was that? *Reine looks back at Moon* **Reine**: Could you come to help me heal him back up? **Moon**: I only have Stage III, I can't bring him back from unconsciousness. **Reine**: Well, do you have Psychokinesis? **Moon**: Yes, Stage II. **Reine**: Take him back to our room. If anyone asks, we'll just say he's sleeping. *Moon wipes her face then opens the palms of her hands and the water on her face floats into a ball above them. The ball then vaporizes. Moon crawls to Yáshido's body. Reine stands. Moon stares at Yáshido's body and it slowly levitates a couple feet off the ground as she stands up. Once Yáshido is completely horizontal, they start walking towards Yáshido and Reine's room. They make it to the room without being noticed by anyone. Inside the room, Moon sets him down on the bed. Reine sighs* **Reine**: Thank you. **Moon**: No, thank you. If you weren't here, who knows what would have happened. **Reine**: It's . . . no problem. *Moon hugs Reine from behind* **Moon**: I'm serious. **Moon**(w): When this is all over, I won't-, *Moon lets go of Reine. Reine turns around and Moon is smiling wiping her eyes again* **Moon**: I'll do as you said. I won't think about it. **Reine**: Good. *Reine sits next to Yáshido* I have it from here. **Moon**: Are you sure? **Reine**: Think about it. The last thing he saw was protecting me from you. Plus, I don't know how long he will be out for. **Moon**: Yeah, you're right. *Moon watches Reine as she fixes Yáshido's position over her lap* **Reine**: See you in a bit, Moon. **Moon**: Okay. *Moon leaves the room, the door slowly closing behind her. Reine looks down at Yáshido* **Reine**: I didn't expect this to happen. *A small amount of Pure Energy comes off Reine as she Reverses her Dermal* **Niola**(w): The one time you needed to be smart, you didn't. *Niola sighs* Haha, you have invincibility, but you decided to push me away instead. I guess I should be thanking you . . . I probably wouldn't survive a hit like that. Now I have to wait until you wake. *Niola sighs again*

-A couple of hours past-

Yáshido starts moving **Yáshido**(thts): Oh man. What happened? *Yáshido rubs his head, he leans up and scans his surroundings. Niola is sitting in front of him* **Niola**: Good afternoon, Yáshido. **Yáshido**: Uh-, good afternoon, what's going on? I thought we were. *Yáshido looks down* Moon. What happened to Moon? **Niola**: What do you mean what happened to Moon? **Yáshido**: We were talking about Dia, right? With her. I-, I don't remember. **Niola**: Yeah,~ we were. Then you collapsed suddenly. **Yáshido**: I did? *Niola watches Yáshido as he looks at his Dermal and notices a small scratch on his forearm plates and across his chestplate. Yáshido looks back at Niola* Care to explain? **Niola**: I'd rather not. **Yáshido**: Seriously though, what happened? **Niola**: Alright you asked for it. *Clears throat* You fell. That's what happened. **Yáshido**(thts): I fell? **Yáshido**: Is that the truth? **Niola**: Hey, I wasn't facing your way, so the only thing I can say is that you were on the ground when I turned around. **Yáshido**: And why were you not watching? **Niola**: Because you pushed me. **Yáshido**: I pushed you? **Niola**: Yes. I should push you back right now if I'm being honest. *Yáshido looks at the curtains* **Yáshido**: Why would I push Niola for? That doesn't sound like me at all. I guess if I did fall, I got what I deserved. **Niola**: You really don't remember what happened? **Yáshido**: Nope. 'Last thing I remember is talking to Moon about Dia, and I don't even remember exactly what we were talking about. *Niola stands* **Niola**: That solves a lot of future problems. *Yáshido looks back to Niola* **Yáshido**: Did we get attacked? *Niola turns around* **Niola**: If we got attacked, I don't think you'd be in the dorm right now if you did fall unconscious. You can't deal with the fact that you fell, can't you? **Yáshido**: No. You would too if you literally can't remember what happened that felt like a second ago. *Yáshido stands* **Yáshido**(thts): Fine, I'll just presume that nothing bad happened. **Yáshido**: Can I see my Familiar for a second? *Niola glows within a white aura until her hair is back to Reine's style and is wearing a school uniform* **Reine**: Yes, Yáshido? **Yáshido**: I was going to tell Taku about leaving for a bit, so I can refresh my Oplitals. **Reine**: Have you thought about everything? **Yáshido**: Yeah, I just don't want to leave without saying anything. I want you to go as well. **Reine**: Of course, you didn't have to tell me. **Yáshido**: I'm just confirming your suspicions. Come on let's go to Taku's house. *Yáshido and Reine walk out of the room. As he turns, Moon is walking down the corridor slowly as if she is trying to sneak away* **Yáshido**: Moon? *Moon turns around* **Moon**(m):

Yes? *Yáshido walks up to her* **Yáshido**: What happened earlier today? **Moon**: Uh-, you fell, and I Psycho'd you to your room. **Yáshido**(thts): She was standing outside the door listening to us I bet. **Yáshido**: So, what you two are basically saying is that I fell on flat land? Just out of nowhere? **Moon & Reine**: Yes. **Yáshido**: Hmph, Okay. See you later, Moon, we'll be back in a few days. **Moon**: Okay. *As they walk pass Moon, Reine and Moon make eye contact. Yáshido and Reine make their way to Taku's house. In front of his door, Yáshido slightly opens it* **Yáshido**: Taku, you in here? **Taku**: Yeah, come on in. *Yáshido and Reine enter. Taku and Savenna are sitting around a table eating something. Reine closes the door behind them* What's up? **Yáshido**: I was planning on leaving. *Taku is eating some ramen after he finishes his current bite with a slurp* **Taku**: Leaving, huh? *The four of them stare at each other for a couple of seconds* Sure, go ahead. I'm sure you have other things you need to do. You are the Hero, so I guess you have that going for you. *Taku takes another bite of his ramen* When are you leaving? **Yáshido**: Now. *Savenna, with a full mouth tries to talk but chokes. Savenna coughs a few times* **Savenna**: Now?~ **Yáshido**: Yeah, now. **Savenna**: You want some ramen before you go? **Yáshido**: No, I'm good. **Savenna**: Do you want some, Reine? **Reine**: I would love some ramen. *Reine starts walking towards Savenna* **Savenna**: Here. *A container flys from the kitchen to Reine, before landing in her hands* There's already a fork inside. **Reine**: K-, thanks. *Yáshido opens the door and Reine walks out. Before Yáshido walks out* **Savenna**: Make sure you stay safe. **Yáshido**: I will. Keep this place under control. *Taku and Savenna nod. Yáshido and Reine leave. Walking through the forest* **Reine**: What are we doing first? **Yáshido**: Well first, I have three thousand *ca*. I need you to buy me something to cover up. **Reine**: Where? **Yáshido**: Dreium's Second Gate. Oh-, and you can buy yourself something too, but we need at least a thousand left, so we'll have a place to sleep. **Reine**: Got you. Anything else? **Yáshido**: At the moment no. Oh, let's change back now. *Yáshido summons a Barre around them and they each transform back to their normal form* **Yashi**: Alright, let's get on the road to Dreium.

-An hour passes from walking through the forest until they notice others walking along a path. The darkness allows them to join in without being noticed. The lights on Dreium's gate wall are not that far from where they stand. Right before they enter-

Yashi(w): So, do you know any clothing shops? **Niola**(w): Yeah, our safest bet is to go to the one after the Tai River. **Yashi**(w): Hopefully, the Balancers aren't very aggressive. **Niola**(w): Hopefully we're even able to get in. **Voice**: Woah, watch out! *Suddenly an aura of a Familiar is felt in front of the line. One of the carriages turns right off-road and another completely Reverses into Particles. There is a group of four Delta wolves in the middle of the passage blocking them from continuing. There are seven other people in front of Yashi and Niola, and two behind them. Two fall from the Reversed carriage and jump back aligning with Yashi and Niola* **Niola**: What's going on? **Wagoner**: Wild Familiars I suppose. They just came out of nowhere. *Three others come from the parked carriage and run to everyone else* **Voice**(From Behind): Hmph, Rita, let's take care of this! **Rita**(From Behind): Right! *Everyone turns around to the voices. Two individuals stand, they each have Balancer Dermals on each equipped with a sword, but with the lack of helmets. The two Balancers run towards them. Rita, Balancer 374, and Aran, Balancer 348* You all get back. We'll deal with this. *Niola looks at Yashi and he nods. They run to the left side of the path, four others run behind the two Balancers, and the other three run to the right side of the path. The Balancers pause in front of the four wolves. Each of the wolves has a dark red aura illuminating from their eyes. They begin to growl* You ready, Aran? **Aran**: Yeah, let's do this. *Rita and Aran point their weapons towards the wolves. One of the wolves moves forward* Quick question, we are sealing them, right? **Rita**: What do we normally do? **Aran**: Ha, I thought so. ^For a split second, a burst of light blue surrounds both Balancers, right after one of the wolves' full-throttle jumps towards them preparing for an attack towards Rita. Before it even gets close to her, Aran slashes it from the side and it launches towards one of the carriages. On collision, the carriage explodes into Particles^ **Voice**(From the Right): MY CARRIAGE. **Aran**: Don't worry, I'll get you another one. ^Rita's sword starts glowing red while she lifts it above her shoulder. The wolf from before joins the other three and they all slowly walk towards the Balancers* These ones are weird. They aren't doing much, but they're Deltas. **Rita**: They must be up to something. ^Two of the wolves charge Aran. He blocks both of their strikes simultaneously. One of the wolves lands on its hind legs and charges back, this time with a blue wave surrounding the front of it. Aran and the Delta collide, with Aran being pushed back slightly^ **Aran**: I see, you want to play, huh? Hyah! ^A red aura surrounds Aran, and the Delta starts to lose. Then the Delta roars and a red aura surrounds it, the strength between them turns equal^ **Aran**: That's only Stage II. Take Ace!!! ^The power from Aran increases to its max and he hits the Delta clean on. The wolf hits the ground multiple times after getting knocked back once more wailing in pain. Rita is surrounded by the other three wolves^ **Aran**: You need some help? **Rita**: Just watch my six, this seems like it'd be fun. ^One of the wolves snares at Rita as it takes another step towards her. The other wolves follow^ *By Yashi. He turns towards the forest behind him as he feels multiple auras* **Yashi**(thts): Feels like more of them. *Yashi looks at Niola and she has a smirk on her face still watching Rita. It then goes away for a second as also glances behind her* **Yashi**(w): You feel that too? **Niola**(w): This seems very shady, but then again, it could just be a large pack of wolves that are hungry or something. *By Rita* **Rita**: I'll go ahead and clean this up. ^The wolves start barking as they are all surrounded by a red aura^ **Rita**: Hahaha, do you Familiars really think that that will save you? ^Rita sword starts changing between a blue and red color^ **Rita**: Everyone down! ^The wolves all jump at Rita at the same time. Before they even get off the ground, Rita spins her sword in a circle. It causes a massive wave of energy to spiral upwards bringing any debris and the wolves with it. Some of the wave of energy clips the top of nearby trees^ Rita: And down you go! ^Rita slams her sword into the ground. The wave of energy turns into an arrow towards the ground slamming against it. Two of the wolves Sustains blasts off and the other two are immobilized as they fly off into the forest; still visible^ *Yashi and Niola feel the auras behind them get closer. Aran and Rita look at each side of the forest* Rita: What's that? Aran: I don't know, but it seems like a lot of them. (Y): Everyone come to the center! *Everyone runs and gets in between Aran and Rita* Rita: Who's confident in their Elilaments? *Niola and one other raise their hands* That's it? Seriously? Aran: Well have to make do. *A barrier surrounds all of them* Rita: Alright, you two, what are your names? Nitori: Nitori. Niola: Niola. Rita: Niola? Aran: Heh, wouldn't expect you to be here. Rita: Well I guess she makes count for all the others that are here. Civilian: Woah, that's a lot of Familiars. Wagoner: I knew today wasn't going to be a good day. Rita: Quit your whining and stay quiet. *The Wagoner puts his hands up* Wagoner(m): Someone's grumpy. *Rita turns towards Niola and Nitori* Niola: I count ten on each side. Nitori: Are we going to intersect them? Aran: Just wait for Rita's command. *Rita looks at everyone inside the barrier* Wagoner: Hey, can't you wait till they surround us and do that move again? Rita: Ssshhh!!! *Everyone is quiet* Rita(w): Do you hear that? *Rita turns back around away from everyone* Aran(w): I'm using Ace, and I don't hear anything, Rita. *Complete silence for a couple of seconds. Yashi then hears a faint siren in the distance. He looks at Niola and she is just now hearing it* Wagoner(w): Okay, maybe I do hear something. Civilian(2): I don't think those are Familiars. Rita(w): Stay inside. Aran: You know you shouldn't go out alone, Rita. *Rita turns around* Rita(w): It's an ambush obviously. Think about it. The wolves are distractions, we are far enough from the gate that they can't sense it. Whoever it is, I don't want them to get away, so I'll be the bait. Yashi(thts): This is even more of a bad spot. Civilian(3)(w): 'You saying a Dicipent could be attacking? Rita(w): Yeah. *Rita turns back towards the barrier* Niola: I'll be the bait then. *Everyone looks at Niola* Wagoner(w): You? Be the bait? Hahahaha. Civilian(2)(w): The auras are getting closer. Rita(w): It's my job, just watch my six, Akimora. All of you. Aran, be on the ready. *Part of the Barrier opens as Rita walks out of it and closes right as she's completely out. The Barrier becomes transparent from the inside view. Rita slowly walks away from them with her guard up. Aran holds his right hand to his ear. The speaker loud enough for everyone to hear* Rita(M): I'm getting false readings, but someone is definitely out there. Aran(w): Where exactly? Rita(M): There is one to my right that has a constant-, ^Rita looks to her right and summons a Barre that looks like a shield as an orange stream of energy comes from the right side of the forest. The blast forces the shield against her and pushes her to the opposite side of the forest. Rita collides with a tree before the stream stops^ Aran: One of you seven, summon a barrier. Nitori and Niola, let's go! *The

Barrier quickly vanishes as the three fighters jump out of the barrier. Another tan Barre overlaps the remaining seven. The three fighters land next to Rita* **Rita**: You should have waited a little longer. **Aran**: The blast was orange, which means it's Saramaenous. **Voice**: You'd be correct! Here's another one! ^The four of them turn to see someone with their hands in a firing position at them. A spiraling orange energy instantly forms and rushes towards them. Both Rita and Niola hold up their hands with an ice shield. The blast ricochets off, but while they are doing so Saramae appears above them with two more orange energy spirals. All four of them take the hit and catch themselves in the forest^ **Aran**: Rita, I don't think he's worth the effort for capturing. **Rita**: You don't think us four can take 'em? **Niola**: He's coming! *Saramae lands in front of the four* **Saramaenous**: Let's see here. *Saramae scans the four* **Saramaenous**: Two Balancers, a random and-, *Saramae smiles as he looks at Niola* **Saramaenous**: Oh~, a bit of a famous adventurer. This shouldn't be too hard. **Rita**: I wouldn't say that. You're actually kinda 'outta luck. **Saramaenous**: Oh? And why is that when I have these! ^Saramae spreads his hands out like wings and multiple wolves jump from the forest and land to his sides. Each with an enormous power^ **Saramaenous**: Earlier was a test. Deltas? How about these Charlies! **Niola**: Charlies won't be enough to deal with us. **Saramaenous**: You think so? Attack the pink-haired girl! ^Two of the wolves jump towards Niola, but she jumps back with a darkened scythes. The wolves stretch their claws as they impact Niola. She slashes right through them, however, Saramaenous appears floating right in front of her. Niola attempts to slash Saramae with her weapons, but he catches her wrist. A red aura surrounds his arms. Saramae swings Niola, but then a white light surrounds both of their wrists. Saramae stops his swing^ **Saramaenous**: I see, you're no joke after all. ^Saramae turns to see Rita and Aran about to hit him^ **Saramaenous**: Woah! ^Saramae tries to let go of Niola, but Niola grabs the upper part of his arms and pulls them towards herself. The two swords explode on impact. As all the spectators are waiting for the smoke to clear, another blast happens in the center of it. Aran, Niola, Nitori, and Rita all fly away from the explosion towards the ground at an insane speed. Nitori slams first face and slides against the ground, Aran hits a tree that gets decapitated, Rita and Niola manage to land on a knee. Saramae floats in the air with a shield of Pure Energy around him. Saramae chuckles as the white sphere fades into Particles^ **Saramaenous**: Maybe in another time, that pathetic attack would work against me. ^Saramae looks at Rita, at the same time, Nitori and Aran are getting back to their feet* Well, Rita, since you believe that Balancers can rival Dicipients, bring it on! Saramae Protojets towards Rita while shooting orange laser beams at her. Rita isn't hesitant to Protojet towards Saramae for one moment. Although the beams pierce her Dermal, Rita prepares for a strong slash. A wolf jumps in between the two and takes the slash from Rita. Saramae then gets multiple jabs off. Rita takes the hits, although being pushed towards the ground, she notices that the shots didn't really hurt, as she tries to raise her sword, her arms are not moving^ **Saramaenous**: Noxetal! ^A giant head of a wolf gets summoned just in front of Rita. The creature looks down at her with its large, sharp, and many teeth^ **Rita**: Guys!? ^Aran comes from behind Rita right after she says that, preparing to slash to Familiar. Saramae moves out of the way and opens his hands to Cast something else, but he feels a fast object coming from behind him. Turning around, Niola is there with her shadowed scythe about to slash him. Niola gets a hit into his abdomen, then slashes him on his left, then from under across his chest. Niola then charges a ball of fire in her hands^ **Saramaenous**: Clafxetal! ^Niola launches the fireball at Saramae and it explodes on impact. However, two large claws come from above Niola and hit her. The claws slam against the ground with Niola under it. Then, the claws start to slash Niola's entire body at a quarter of a second intervals. Niola, not being able to move, continuously takes the blows. Niola Personal Casts more of her shadowed scythes above the Familiar. The weapons stagger the claws, and Rita comes from over Niola with two ice balls. The claws freeze over before falling to the ground and exploding. Rita lands in front of Niola, guarding her against Saramae who is just now standing up^ **Rita**: Akimora, you alright? **Niola**: Yeah. *As Niola stands, Aran picks her up from under her arms. Surprised, Niola turns around* **Aran**: There you go. *The three of them surround Saramae as he is finally on his feet. Red embers are patched around his clothes. Saramae uses his hands to pat all of them out, annoyed while doing so^ **Rita**: Awh~, what's wrong, does someone not have Hydro to put the tiny flames out? *Saramae looks at Rita and chuckles^ **Saramaenous**: You should watch your tone. **Rita**: Niola, I assume you know how to chain, right? **Niola**: Yeah, I know how. **Rita**: Perfect. Aran and I will start off, don't let him out of the chain. **Niola**: Right. **Rita**: Come on, Aran. **Saramaenous**: Lowering your numbers, not a smart play. *Both Rita and Aran start walking towards Saramae. Saramae holds his guard. Suddenly, Rita takes a knee and Aran gets behind her^ **Rita**: Ultimate formation, protocol B. **Aran**: Engaging. *Aran climbs onto Rita's shoulders, and sits around her neck* **Everyone**: What? **Niola**: Wha-, what are you two doing? *Rita stands with Aran still around her neck. Rita tilts her head to look at Niola* **Rita**: We're about to fight, just stay ready. ^Aran points his sword at Saramae, and Rita starts walking towards Saramae. Saramae drops his guard and immediately starts laughing^ **Saramaenous**: What is that?! Hahahaha, what type of cruel joke are you trying to play on me? *While still walking, Rita smirks^ **Rita**: What's wrong, Saramaenous, scared of our unbreakable formation? *Once again laughing, Saramae looks up again, this time his eyes are light blue* **Saramaenous**: Toying with a Dicipient will get you killed! **Aran**: Back up those words then. ^About fifteen feet away from Saramae, Saramae holds up his hands towards them^ **Saramaenous**(Y): Maxetal! ^Without warning, a giant claw, the size of a skyscraper, shoots out of Saramae's hands. Rita and Aran look up at the hand almost taunting it. Aran even fires a lightning strike at it, but it simply just whiffs into Particles, not doing any damage. Niola smiles after seeing this, holding up her shadowed weapon. Rita takes a step back^ **Rita:** Wait, Aran, that looks quite dangerous. **Aran:** You think so? **Saramaenous**(Y): Decimate Them! ^A red overlay of Zoka Strength surrounds the claw. As Rita tries to lift her foot to walk backward, it gets forcefully pulled down. An Atoskito is under them. Before they could even try to retaliate in some way, the claw comes down on them. The multiple fang-like nails penetrate through both of their Dermals as they fall flat onto the ground. A loud boom follows as they are covered by the claw. Then, Saramae feels a large aura charging him from the rear. Saramae blocks a shot from Rita and quickly summons a claw that slashes her chestplate. Rita takes the hit as she Protojets a stab which turns Saramae around. Rita then gets a perfect stab into his back with her sword. Aran follows it up with a Protojet kick, kicking Saramae straight towards Niola. Niola takes the opportunity to slash him back to them. The large claw on the ground fade away into Particles as Saramae flys on them. Rita jumps into the air^ **Aran & Rita**(Y): Intersection Dismantling! ^Both Aran and Rita slash toward Saramae. Aran's is light blue and horizontal, while Rita's is red and vertical. Saramae makes contact with the two attacks at the same time. A shock of energy spreads outward and follows a loud and bright purple cloud obscuring everyone's vision. The purple cloud soon turns brown. After the smoke clears seconds, Aran and Rita stand next to Niola, and Saramae is nowhere to be found. **Aran:** What? **Niola:** No . . . ^They turn back around and Saramae is behind Nitori with a giant claw covering his waist^ **Saramaenous:** Hahaha, it's too easy. I didn't even notice when you made that Dreamworld out of Particles, but that combined Cast just wasn't enough to put me down permanently. *Rita scoffs* **Rita:** Let him go. **Saramaenous:** And why is that? ^Another set of wolves have formed around them^ **Rita:** As I said before, you're out of luck. **Saramaenous:** You're surrounded. Not me. What'd you do? Call more Balancers? I thought saving lives was more important than taking down a Dicipient? ^The nails dent into Nitori's stomach. Nitori is trembling in fear^ **Nitori:** Someone, please get him off me. **Saramaenous:** What's the matter? ^Saramae lifts the claw closer to Nitori's chest^ **Saramaenous:** Don't like rough play? **Nitori:** I don't like to play at all. **Saramaenous:** That's unfortunate. **Rita:** How about I show you why. **Saramaenous:** Go ahead, amuse me. **Rita:** Number one, you're in Macadamia. After all the crap that's happened here, you honestly believe that we haven't prepared for something like this? **Saramaenous:** I'm just as prepared, you all are in as much threat as me. All of you are gonna take some hits. I may even kill a few. **Rita:** Aran. **Aran:** You see Saramaenous, due to us having the second-largest tech advantage in Edasia, we can do stuff like . . . lets say, know that you've been trying to ambush us for a couple of days now. *Saramae quivers* **Saramaenous:** Hahaha, sounds like you're just as much of a stalker like me, but that doesn't explain my unluckiness. **Rita:** Secondly, we shouldn't be telling you, but since we know you'd be dumb enough to stay after listening to number one, we lured you into a Konseitsu on Ancestrials zone. So. ^Rita lifts her fists and squeezes them. The wolf to the right of Saramae starts to cough before falling to its side and fading into Particles. The remainder of the wolves slowly start to fall one by one vanishing into dust. Some are heard in the distant forest weeping. Many Particles are seen going into the sky^ **Saramaenous**: Hmph, that doesn't change much. I'm strong enough that I can take you on, plus the other seven. **Rita**: Aran. **Aran**: And, we've also collected data from you, so we know you have a Stage II Sustain. **Rita**: Ten good shots and you're done or just 'one' could be enough. ^Saramae steps back^ **Saramaenous**: That's a bit worrisome. You know my Elilaments. **Rita**: Thirdly, you may think that person you're holding is a hostage . . . but it's actually a bomb. ^Saramae steps back leaning Nitori with him^ **Saramaenous**: Wait, a-, ^A mass explosion comes from Nitori's body before Saramae says another word. Aran immediately summons a Barre around himself and Rita as the wave rushes over them. The radius expands enough that everyone in a hundred-yard radius takes some form of damage even if they are inside of a Barrier. Yashi's group gets nudged against the ground as their Barre gets destroyed. A few of them slide back against the ground, moving backward with the fierce wind. Although big, the explosion quickly ends. The top portion of the trees are gone with a crater in the ignited site. Saramaenous is lying on the ground. Part of his blackish clothes is ripped and his Dermal is gone. Rita and Aran walk up to the motionless Saramae^ **Rita**: How does it feel to be outplayed? **Aran**: Twice. **Saramaenous**: Teehee. *Aran and Rita throws Dicipients' Whips around Saramae that prevents him from using any Magic* **Rita**: You made this too easy for us. You're going to love the new interrogation room. *Rita laughs as she and Aran walk towards Saramae. Then Rita feels something wet hit her leg of her Dermal. She looks down and there is a small clump of saliva sliding down the metal plate over her right thigh. Rita looks at Saramae with a mean look* **Saramaenous**: Hahahaha, not so funny now is it? ^Rita's arms glow red as she swiftly picks up Saramae by his neck^ **Rita**(w): So disrespectful, you're lucky I didn't find you around Catalyst. ^Rita throws him back down onto the ground. His face squinches from the pain as the ground shakes* Aran, call a mCarrier while I watch him^ **Aran**: On it. *Rita throws a speck of something out of thin air, and it forms a cell around Saramae. Aran summons a Mangole and requests a mCarrier. Niola starts to walk away* Thanks for the help, Akimora. *Niola puts a peace sign up* **Niola**: Don't mention it. *The six onlookers walk over to Aran while Niola walks over to Yashi. By Yashi* **Yashi**: So, they knew the whole time. **Niola**: Oh~, so you heard. **Yashi**: Zoka Hearing. *More travelers start showing up. Aran redirects them to continue along the path. While walking, Yashi and Niola pass a mCarrier with four other Balancers on it heading towards Saramae. They continue walking to Dreium. The path becomes more modern and electrical lights run along the path. One side. walking to Dreium, and the opposite side walking away from Dreium* **Niola**(w): Balancers up ahead. **Yashi**(w): I see. **Niola**(w): Do you just want to walk past them? **Yashi**(w): What other choice do we have? *Forty feet from the Balancers* **Niola**(w): That's right, I have a bracelet to use in the consoled parts of Macadamia. **Yashi**(w): How would you use it? There are people here who'd notice and say something. **Niola**(w): Let's pull over to the side. *Niola and Yashi try to go right into the forest, but a long carriage blocks them. Yashi nearly collides with the carriage and stops. Someone bumps into him from behind* **Civilian**: Excuse me. *They quickly lift Yashi back up and continue to walk, as does Niola and Yashi. Thirty feet from the Balancers, Yashi notices that they have small scanners, quietly scanning everyone who passes them* **Yashi**(w): They have scanners, Niola. **Niola**(w): Uhm~, *Niola grabs Yashi's hand* **Yashi**(w): Wha-, what are you about to do? **Niola**(w): It's risky, but hey-. *Twenty feet from the Balancers, Yashi slightly looks up and makes direct eye contact with one of the Balancers as they are turning towards his direction* **Niola**(w): Here we go. *About ten feet away, Niola turns to the left into the opposite traffic and starts going away from the Balancers* **Yashi**(thts): No she didn't-, **Voice**(From Behind): Hey! Why'd you two turn around! *Niola stops a bit before walking faster* Hey! I'm talking to you, stop! **Niola**(w): Don't hate me for this! *Niola starts sprinting, bringing Yashi with her. Both of them feel at least two Balancers chasing them. Some of the travelers stop and move out of the way or look at them. Niola accurately dodges multiple people, going around, under, and above many people and carriages. Yashi turns his head slightly so that he can see behind them. The Balancers have Dicipients' Whips in their hands, preparing to throw it. Yashi turns back around* **Yashi**(w): Seal!-, Seal!-, Seal!-, Seal! **Balancer**: Ha!~ *Suddenly, Niola stops, gets behind Yashi, and locks her arms under Yashi's. Niola uses her Flight ability and Fukashi taking them both go up into the air with Gray Particles surrounding them. The bound nearly touches Niola's shoe* **Niola**: Disable your Sustain. *A small covering of Pure Energy comes from Yashi as he manually disables his Sustain. *About twenty-five feet in the air, they look down to see the Balancers looking for them* **Balancer**(A): Where'd they go? **Balancer**(B): Looked like they flew up and Fukashi'd. **Niola**(m): That's not good. Don't move a lot, I only have Stage II on Flight. *They begin to fly towards the gate. *After three minutes of slowly flying over the forest, Niola hovers them a couple yards from the Dreium's West Gate Wall. Niola and Yashi are about fifty feet in the air now. The Energy Dispositor of Dreium fills the sky with mystical blue and purple shade. The Barre that surrounds Dreium sparkles every now and then* **Yashi**(thts): Oh~, this is so beautiful. Even though Dreium's not that well, uh, organized I suppose, it looks amazing from above. *Niola stops going towards the gate* **Niola**: Man you're heavy. **Yashi**: Oh, Really? Shall I use Atoskito? Would that make it better? **Niola**: Haha, you can't even use Magic right now. Good try though. **Yashi**: Hmph. Besides that, how are we going to get in? I think I'm going to have to transform into the Hero anyway? **Niola**: Yeah, the only entrance is through the DZVT Scanners, they instantly tell who passed through it no matter what, even with Fukashi~ . . . *Yashi tilts his head to look at Niola's face. He can't see much but can tell she's smiling* **Yashi**: What? **Niola**: I just thought of something crazy. **Yashi**: Oh no, what is it? **Niola**: Okay, remember Reinu, right? **Yashi**: Yeah? **Niola**: If I Personal Cast it, and because you have no Sustain, if I were to use my aura as a Kemuri around you, would it register us both as me when we go through? **Yashi**: Wow, that's actually a pretty good idea. Try it. **Niola**: Stay still. *A white smoke surrounds Yashi, the smoke then turns into a pink color* Haha, now what? **Yashi**: Make an Energy compacted Barre around the Kemuri with Fukashi. **Niola**: Wouldn't that hurt? **Yashi**: If you hurry through the scanner after you do it, I won't feel a thing. **Niola**: Either that or I accidentally drop you. **Yashi**: You say that like you want to drop me. **Niola**: I couldn't possibly drop you even if I tried.

-Inside the capsule on the gate wall-

Balancer(377): Dreium is always so active. **Balancer**(B): More now than previously. Stay sharp. **Balancer**(342): You two feel that? **Balance**(B): It's moving fast. *All three of the Balancers look at the Mangole Map that is centered in the room. A blue dot appears to be moving towards the gate entrance at a fast rate* Whoever it is, is registered. *Balancer A and 342 move to the list of personal registered IDs* **Balancer**(A): 377, tell me when this person is passing through. **Balancer**(377): On it. *377 stares at the map intensely as the fast-blue circle is about to past the border* Now! *The numbers and transcript of a new entity show up on the screen that sits in front of the other two Balancers right as 377 finishes his sentence. As the ID tag gets completed, Balancer 342 taps it. Both Balancer A and 342 sigh out of relief. Balancer 342 rolls his chair so that he is facing 377* Who was it? **Balancer**(342): It's just Akimora. **Balancer**(377): Adventurer or one of the other two? *Balancer A stands, staring at Niola's cross information with a mean look* **Balancer**(B): Niola Akimora. *377 leans back in her chair* **Balancer**(377): Oh, then we're good. **Balancer**(A): Not quite. Some's off. *Balancer 342 turns his chair back around* **Balancer**(342): What do you mean? **Balancer**(A): 342, come look at these attributes. *342 scoots his chair closer to the screen to get a better look. Balancer A swipes the screen so that it compares the last dated entry with the current one* **Balancer**(342): Woah, that's weird. Some of her stats are different. **Balancer**(A): Right? And look at the personal bio check, density is a little over double than last time. Basically, double than any recorded density check ever. **Balancer**(377): Meaning? **Balancer**(342): Someone went through with her, or she's gotten really fat. *Balancer A smiles for a second and 377 laughs uncontrollably* **Balancer**(377): That's just mean, but you think she brought someone through the gate with her? **Balancer**(A): Think about what you're saying. If someone went through the scanner with her, we would see them as a separate log. **Balancer**(342): You're right. How'd she do that? **Balancer**(377): Now that I think about it, how did she do that? **Balancer**(A): Strange. **Balancer**(342): Hah, it's Niola of all people. Isn't she like one of the kindest people in the world? **Balancer**(A): You said the same thing about Dia, but you only claimed her top five. If Dia turned to the way she is now, Niola would be much worse. We'll just check the thermals, and if something's weird, we're going to have to question her. **Balancer**(342)(377): Affirmative.

Chapter 12 – Shrive

-After the wall is a series of shops and markets. The area is really crowded until they reach the Tai River. Niola slowly goes back down, still high enough that she is above the people walking-

Niola: I can't use the bracelet beyond this point, so you'll just have to be cheeky. **Yashi**: Cheeky? Really? **Niola**: Once we pass here, if we take a right, then a left, there should be a clothing store right in the middle of the block. **Yashi**: Perfect. **Niola**: Or~, you see that building with the purple light. **Yashi**: Yeah? **Niola**: There's an alley we could walk through and come right out by the store. **Yashi**: Sure, why not. *Niola waits until more people pass so they have room to land. Once there is an opportunity she lands and disables her Fukashi* **Niola**: Too bad you're taller than me. **Yashi**: I don't know if that is an insult or not. **Niola**: It wasn't. *Niola and Yashi start walking over the bridge. Yashi faces the opposite way as people walk past. Once at the alleyway, they wait till no one is looking and enter. Yashi follows Niola through the alley. Before the clothing store* **Yashi**: Do you-. **Yashi**(thts): Well, I can't do that when I have money on me. **Niola**: Do I? **Yashi**: Don't worry about it. Wait, do you remember what I told you to get? **Niola**: Something to cover you up, right? **Yashi**: Good, and if you find something you like, you can buy it too. **Niola**: Really? **Yashi**: Yes but leave some so we can spend a night somewhere. **Niola**: Haha, okay, see you in a bit. *Niola starts walking out of the alley* **Yashi**: I'm serious. **Niola**: I know, that's why I laughed. *Niola walks around the corner. Yashi leans up against the wall* **Voice**: Psh~. *Yashi looks back over at the exit and sees Niola with a cap* **Niola**(w): There's a 'no soliciting sign'. *Yashi sighs* **Yashi**(thts): They can't make it easy can they. **Yashi**: Give me the hat. *Yashi walks to Niola and she gives him the hat. They stand in front of the store* Please don't take long. **Niola**: I won't. *Niola turns around and enters the store. Yashi leans against the glass and crosses his arms *Inside the shop* **Niola**(m): Something to cover up the Hero. What could do such an action? *Niola notices someone watching her in her peripheral vision and the two make eye contact* **Employee**: Good afternoon, Miss. **Niola**: Good afternoon. **Employee**: Do you need any help finding anything? **Niola**: Yes, thanks for asking. Do you still have Hidden Ware products? **Employee**: Emhm, we sure do. Actually just got a brand-new shipment earlier today. Right this way. *The employee takes Niola halfway down the small building to the new shipment of clothes* They're right here. *Niola stops walking. The employee turns to see Niola's hands on her jaws and mouth open* **Niola**: These look awesome~. *Niola charges towards the clothes looking through the various styles* **Employee**: Fan of Hidden Ware? **Niola**: Yes! I've been collecting their products since the Z1 Overlay Jacket. **Employee**: Hahaha. *Niola stops searching and looks at the employee* **Niola**: Speaking of fans, does Ozumi Yasimae still work here? **Employee**: Yup, she's here actually. **Niola**: Really? Can I see her for a moment? **Employee**: You're already looking at her. *Niola scans the girl again* **Niola**: Ozumi? *Ozumi takes off her employee hat and her pocket of light blue hair and the rest of her black hair falls* Ozumi! *Niola pounces on Ozumi with a hug. Ozumi hugs her back* **Ozumi**: How've you been, Niola? **Niola**: Great, you? *Niola backs away from the hug* **Ozumi**: I've been hanging on. **Niola**: I can't believe you still work here. **Ozumi**: Haha, yeah. Almost my five-year anniversary. **Niola**: Geez, time flys by so fast. **Ozumi**: I heard you, Huko, and Vandel got another jackpot recently. **Niola**: We sure did. **Ozumi**: Man, I remember when we first started, and you'd be so excited when we found the smallest of gems. **Niola**: Hahaha, and I still am. *Niola turns back around and starts looking through the clothes from Hidden Ware. Ozumi notices that Niola has a slight frown on her face* **Ozumi**: Niola. **Niola**: Yes, Ozumi? *Ozumi holds on to Niola by her shoulders* **Ozumi**: You have that face again. **Niola**: How could I not? **Ozumi**: I feel like you come here just to make me cry. **Niola**: You're still my friend, seeing you every now and then lets me remember those memories. It's just that, I can't believe it happened to you, of all possibilities. **Ozumi**: I wish it was different too, Niola, but life just had a different route for me. I've been living a good life without . . . being able to use Magic. It feels normal now, you know? My sister keeps saying it's just living without ever using your Sustain. **Niola**: Heh-, we've had this conversation so many times. *Ozumi turns Niola around and bops her shoulder while aggressively smiling* **Ozumi**: That's because silly you keeps on bringing it up. I can tell that I'm not the only thing that has you acting strange. *Niola stops searching through the clothes and turns around to Ozumi* **Niola**: I'm acting strange? **Ozumi**: You seem stressed. **Niola**: Just a lot of emotional activities lately. That's all. **Ozumi**: Like? **Niola**: The usu. *Ozumi smiles and grabs Niola by the hands* **Ozumi**: You found a man, didn't you, Niola? **Niola**(m): A man? **Ozumi**(w): Caught you, usually you'd say, 'A man for what?', or 'That's a good joke', neither did you deny me, Niola, hahaha. **Niola**(w): That was a good joke, Ozumi, but if I was to happen to have one, you'd be the first to know. *Niola raises their hands to their chest level. **Ozumi**(w): I better be. *Both of them giggle. Outside the shop* **Yashi**(thts): Everything seems the same. *Yashi looks at a restaurant across the street* Ooo~, what's that over there? Delicious steak and pork dish only 250 *ca*. Maybe I should have gotten those noodles after all. *Yashi looks back down as a group of people are walking past him. Two legs stop and turn in his direction* **Yashi**(thts): Oh, no. **Teen**(Boy): You good? **Yashi**: Yeah, I'm just relaxing. **Teen**(Boy): Relaxing, huh? **Yashi**: Yup, just waiting for a friend. *Yashi tilts the front of his cap down a little* **Teen**(Boy): Well, I'm sorry to disturb your 'relaxation', but you probably didn't see the no leaning on glass symbol. *Yashi jumps away

146

from the glass and looks at it* **Yashi**: Really? *Yashi scans the glass left to right trying to find the symbol* **Teen**(Boy): Hahahaha, just kidding, just kidding. *Yashi sighs* **Yashi**: Oh~, man you shouldn't joke about things like that. You know how much those fines cost. **Teen**(Boy): Ha, yeah, that's why I said it. *Yashi looks at the glass again and swipes his finger across it* **Yashi**(thts): This glass doesn't even get stained. *Before Yashi leans back on the glass he gets a slight glance and the person* Gadgets, lightweight clothes, must be . . . an Expisimist? Or maybe an adventurer? Niola's took away my whole sense of recognizing people's occupations. *The teen also leans on the glass next to Yashi* **Teen**(Boy): Iah~, I'm also waiting for a couple friends. Just trying to stay awake. **Yashi**: What are they doing? *The teen points across the street* **Teen**(Boy): They're across the street, getting measurements so they can buy some castable Dermals. **Yashi**: Sounds cool. **Teen**(Boy): I noticed you didn't have your Sustain active. Is there a reason why? **Yashi**: No~, no reason in particular. *Silence for a couple of seconds* **Teen**(Boy): What's on the ground that has your attention so grabbed? Please don't tell me it's the Diorite. **Yashi**: It's something in the Diorite that has my attention. *The teen moves closer to Yashi so he can get a look* **Teen**(Boy): What? **Yashi**: See that. *Yashi points at a tiny root that is sprouting from in between the tiles* **Teen**(Boy): Yeah? **Yashi**: If this continues to grow, this whole store might completely collapse. **Teen**(Boy): I'd love to see that. *Yashi cracks a slight chuckle* **Yashi**: It'd never happen because of monthly inspections. **Teen**(Boy): Oh~, well. *Inside the shop* **Niola**: Hm~. **Niola**(m): I could use my own money to buy these because they just look awesome, or, I can get these, and we'd be matching. *Niola looks between the two choices and sighs* Maybe I should ask Ozumi. *Niola turns around and steps on her tippy toes to look over the rackets. Ozumi is at the counter with another customer* **Ozumi**: And here you go. *Ozumi hands the customer a bag* **Customer**: Thanks. *The customer starts walking towards the door* **Ozumi**: Come again! *The customer waves as they walk out the door* **Customer**: I will! *Right as the door closes, Ozumi notices Niola looking at her but doesn't say anything and indirectly starts to make her way over. Niola lands on her feet as Ozumi walks in her section* **Ozumi**: Do you need help with something, Niola? **Niola**: Yeah, actually. *Niola hands Ozumi one of the sets of clothes* **Ozumi**: Expensive Hidden Ware products. **Niola**: But it's worth it. **Ozumi**(w): I can give you a friendly discount depending on how much you have. **Niola**: I can-, **Ozumi**: On second thought, don't answer that question because I know you have the money for it. *Ozumi holds the two half-equal clothes in her palm then smiles* Oh~, I get it. It's for your man, isn't it? **Niola**(w): Stop 'false claiming me, Ozumi. **Ozumi**: K, I'll stop . . . for now. So what's the problem? **Niola**: The set your holding is one of the brand-new, top quality, most expensive ever in the world, majestic, awesome, most ever cool looking overlay hoodie ever. **Ozumi**: Right~. **Niola**: As you can see, they aren't the same. **Ozumi**: But the ones you're holding are. **Niola**: Yeah. **Ozumi**: Interesting choices, but between me and you. (w):

I'd go with the matching ones. **Niola**: Then I would like to buy these. *Ozumi hangs up the other set Niola gave her. They walk to the register. Outside the Shop* **Yashi**(thts): I knew I would be out here for more than ten minutes. You're just buying clothes, and I didn't even give you that much money. **Yashi**: I see what you mean about not falling asleep. **Teen**(Boy): I know right, but I've been out here for an hour or two. **Yashi**: Is this their first time? **Teen**(Boy): Yup. **Yashi**: Two hours is normal. **Teen**(Boy): The manager there said it would only take thirty minutes. **Yashi**: They told me the same thing, and before I realized it'd been two hours. *They both laugh. Something knocks on the glass behind Yashi in slow intervals. Yashi turns around to see a bit of Niola's hair. She raises a bag up* **Yashi**: Oh, my friend's done. **Teen**(Boy): Alright, see you around. *Yashi holds his hat down as he walks past the Teen and into the store* Okay, then. *The teen stops leaning on the glass and continues to walk around the block. Inside the store. Niola moves Yashi to the side* **Niola**(w): My friend's a~, uhm . . . lets 'say a bit suspicious of us, so try not to make any type of contact with her, okay? **Yashi**(w): I'll try. *Niola takes Yashi in front of a changing room* **Niola**: I hope you like it. *Niola hands Yashi a bag as he walks inside the changing room. Inside of Yashi's* **Yashi**(thts): Let's see what she got me. *Yashi opens the bag and takes out the clothing. He unfolds it and spreads it out* A Hidden Ware permeable cloak. Not half bad. *Yashi puts on the cloak and hoodie that goes with it. The Hidden Ware logo flickers once he is completely in it* **Cloak**: No source of Oplitals found, permeable feature not available. **Yashi**(thts): To think I was going to be able to turn invisible without an assist, hahaha. *Yashi pushes the emblem to make it stop flashing* Now I'll be the world's first Hero Assassin . . . wait no Sacrumed kind of did that. **Niola**: Are you done? **Yashi**: Yeah, coming out now. *Yashi steps out of the changing room. Niola is standing a couple feet from him* You got the same one? **Niola**: Ehm, how do I look? *Niola spins around to show off her cloak* **Yashi**: It fits you fine. **Niola**: This one has a shadow display so you can't see our faces, but anything lower than our noses you can see. **Yashi**: That explains why I'm getting a creepy vibe from you now. **Niola**: You can increase the lengths of the cape and sleeves without a Sustain. **Yashi**: Too complicated, I don't want to imagine how technology can even get that far, but still, show me. **Niola**: Ha, okay. Raise your right arm. *Yashi raises his right arm* Push down on your forearm region. *Yashi pushes down on his forearm region. A couple seconds later his emblem sparks a faint white color* Now, move your finger down your arm to make it longer and up your arm to make it shorter. **Yashi**: Is there a way to make it tighter? **Niola**: Yeah, grab your forearm and squeeze, depending on how many fingers you squeeze with will determine how tight it is. **Yashi**: Cool, I'll customize it tomorrow. *Yashi looks to the right of Niola and sees an employee coming towards them. Niola turns around towards Ozumi. **Ozumi**: Is it okay, Niola? **Niola**: Yeah, it's perfect. Thanks, Ozumi, for your help. **Ozumi**: Don't mention it. *Niola walks to Ozumi and gives her a hug* **Niola**: I'll see you soon, Ozumi! **Ozumi**: Ssshhh, I know you will. *Niola continues walking towards the door. As Yashi passes Ozumi, she taps him on her shoulder. Yashi turns to see her smiling with a mischievous look and winks* **Ozumi**(w): T. K. O. H. *Yashi turns back around* **Yashi**(thts): T. K. O. H.? What does that mean? Why did she look at me with that face? *Outside the shop* **Yashi**: How much do I have left? **Niola**: Seven hundred. **Yashi**: Good, that's enough for at least one night. **Niola**: Hahahaha. **Yashi**: What? I'm being really serious when I say that. **Niola**: That's why it's funny.

Chapter 13 - Allocated Information

Yashi: Now, do you know where an Inn is? **Niola:** An Inn. I know of two, but personally, I think the best one would be Mitsu. **Yashi:** Okay, take us there. *Niola turns to the right and starts walking down the sidewalk. Yashi follows. As they pass people, a few every now and then stare at them and whisper to each other. They reach an intersection and wait until the vehicles pass through. After crossing the street* **Niola:** Let's speed up, we're almost there. *Niola starts to skip along the path* **Yashi**(thts): She's really doing this right now. *Yashi jogs to keep up with Niola. After several corners, Niola comes to a stop in front of a building* **Niola:** We're here. *Yashi scans the tall building* **Yashi:** Seems welcoming for no sign. **Niola:** Last time they had the name of the hotel on the outside, it was vandalized. *Niola walks in front of the entrance* You can see the name on the inside from here. *Yashi walks next to Niola and looks inside the building. A flashy sign reads *Mitsuku Hotel* above an empty long desk* **Yashi:** Did they change the name? I could have sworn it was Misittiku. **Niola:** So you're an original, nice. Yeah, they changed the name. **Yashi:** I wouldn't say I'm an original customer. I slept here once after an expedition. **Niola:** Sounds like original customer material to me. **Yashi:** Hah, yeah. *After entering the store, a receptionist stands behind the desk looking down at something. When the door closes, a small ding echoes through the room. They continue walking towards the employee* **Yashi**(thts): The glass itself is its own World? That must be expensive. It's amazing what Macadamians will do for satisfying others. **Yashi:** Hahaha. *The receptionist looks at them as they are halfway to her* **Receptionist:** Oh, sorry I didn't hear you enter. Welcome to Mitsuku Hotel! **Niola & Yashi:** Pleasure to be here. *Niola and Yashi turn their heads towards each other* **Receptionist:** Ooo~, nice to see some original members. *Yashi pats the back of his head as the receptionist opens a Mangole* **Yashi:** Didn't know that would happen. **Receptionist:** Room for two? **Yashi:** Yes. **Receptionist:** Okay. *Taps buttons* Together or separate? *Yashi looks at Niola* **Yashi**(w): What does she mean by that? *Niola raises one hand with two fingers and her other with one finger* **Niola**(w): Do you want to have two 'beds' or one 'beds'. *As Yashi turns towards the receptionist Niola puts her arm around his shoulder* **Yashi:** Uhm . . . Separate. **Receptionist:** Alrighty, give me one moment. *Niola takes her arm off of Yashi's shoulder and pouts before crossing them around her chest* **Yashi**(w): What? YOU know how weird that would be for me, and we're not forced to do it. *Niola opens one eye and looks at Yashi. She looks to his right as both of them open, then puts one of her fingers under her lip and smiles* **Niola:** Oh, you're right. I was even thinking on that level. I was only trying to save you *Ca*, hahahaha.

Yashi(w): Did you have to say it out loud though? *Niola turns all the way around to Yashi* **Niola**: It's okay, we can still-, **Yashi**: No~, no~, no~, no-, none of that. **Niola**(m): Practice Particle Magic. **Niola**: We can't, why not? **Yashi**: Wha-, why that of all things? **Receptionist**: Particle Magic? That should be the least of your worries. *Yashi turns to the receptionist* You must haven't been here in a while, ori. About a year ago, our CEO bought out new technology-enhanced walls for all his establishments. 'Alchemy Saturn Metal' I believe the name was. It makes the entire building Magic resistant, and the Alchemists have been improving it since then. Now the whole building could take an entire wave of Aced Hydro for ten seconds or something crazy like that, and then it'll have to get through the next wall, hahaha. It's really, REALLY strong, but if you follow our guidelines, then you can use as much Magic as you want. **Niola**: See, no harm in that right? Plus you're not draining your Oplitals. I don't see a problem. **Yashi**: Niola it is . . . **Receptionist**: Eleven o-clock. **Yashi**: Eleven o-clock, I want some sleep. **Receptionist**: Also, if I must mention, if you read the guidelines there should be a way to split your rooms with another Magic proof Barre, and did I also mention that each room is soundproof? **Yashi**: You guys really went all out. **Receptionist**: Ehm. **Yashi**: So what's the cost? **Receptionist**: Let's see, for your set up . . . *The Receptionist taps a few more buttons on her Mangole* 500*ca*. **Yashi**: Perfect. Surprisingly not expensive. **Receptionist**: We offer only the best for our customers. *Yashi looks at Niola* **Yashi**: May I have the rest? **Niola**: The rest of what? **Yashi**: The rest of my money. **Niola**: I thought I gave it to you. *Niola checks her cloak pockets and pats her legging pockets through her cloak. **Yashi**(m): What. *Yashi digs into both of his pockets* **Yashi**: There's nothing there. *Yashi awkwardly looks at the Receptionist* **Niola**: I'm only kidding, here you go. *Niola takes out 500*ca* from her pockets and gives it to the Receptionist. **Yashi**: Oh man, *Yashi sighs* Please don't do that again. **Niola**: The look on your face hahaha, I won't. *Niola gives the remaining 200*ca* to Yashi as the receptionist puts the currency inside of the register* **Receptionist**: Alright here's your room key. 2B3L; Second floor, Corridor B, the third room on the left. *Niola takes the room key* **Niola & Yashi**: Thanks. **Receptionist**: You're welcome. If you want to take the stairs, they're behind me on my left, and the elevators are over there. *They look in the direction where she points. The elevators are on the farthest wall* You two have a good night's rest. *Niola and Yashi enter the elevator* **Yashi**: All of this just to get some sleep. **Niola**: Ha-, it was your idea to leave during the night. *Niola pushes the 'Floor Two' button* **Yashi**: I know, I know. *The elevator moves up, and a few seconds later opens* Corridor B. **Niola**: Over there. *They walk down Corridor B* **Yashi**: And finally the door three on the left. *Yashi walks and looks down the doors* No numbers. *Niola walks to the side of Yashi* **Niola**: Just listen to what she said. *Niola walks to the third door down the hall. She holds up the key to the door and multiple white lines come from the top of the door to the bottom* **Yashi**: Did it open? **Niola**: Not sure. Seems like they've upgraded their door scanners since

I last came. *Niola reaches for the door to push it, but her hand goes through it. A second display appears next to Niola's hand. It reads 'Would you like to identify yourself' with a 'Yes' or 'No' box under it. Niola pushes yes and the display changes to a shot of Niola doing a pose of her smiling with her right eye closed and her hands as peace symbols in front of her face with short shorts, and a half shirt with an undid jacket. Above the picture reads 'Niola Akimora'. She Niola instantly moves in front of the picture to block Yashi's view* Hehehehe~. **Yashi**: What was that? A picture of you? *Niola starts to swipe the display randomly* **Niola**: It's just that particular one you don't need to see. *The picture vanishes as Niola falls forward through the door. Yashi enters behind her* [A door is on the left, the bathroom. Across from the entering door is a window that stretches across the middle to the right side of the wall. Two beds lay perpendicular to the wall on the right with a small dresser in between them.] *Niola jogs and jumps into the bed by the window* **Niola**: Iah! It's so comfy! **Yashi**: You would get the one next to the window. *Niola smuggles herself in the blankets* **Niola**: Yup! It's all mine. *Yashi walks to the jacket hangar* **Yashi**: Are you going to sleep with that cloak on? *Yashi takes off his cloak and hangs it on the rack. Niola turns her head towards him, still stomach down in the bed* **Niola**: No~, I'm going to take a shower, eat those noodles Savenna gave me, then I will sleep with the cloak on. *Silence* **Yashi**: Really. *Niola laughs as Yashi lies down in his bed. Once Niola is done laughing, she sits up in her bed* **Niola**: You're not falling asleep now, are you? **Yashi**: No, I'm not . . . maybe . . . Yes, yes I am. **Niola**: No fun. **Yashi**: Please, what was the reason for me getting an Inn in the first place, to sleep. **Niola**: Boy, you could have slept in the morning. *Yashi sits up in his bed with a determined look* **Yashi**: Girl, I did that so it would be easier for me to hide. **Niola**: Boy, you could have asked someone to buy you some clothin

g. **Yashi**: Girl, I'm not the type of person to ask someone to walk two hours back and forth for me just for some clothing. **Niola**: Boy, that's basically what I'm doing now. **Yashi**: Girl, you said you were going to come anyway. **Niola**: Boy, you still would have asked me to come. **Yashi**: Girl, I came with you. **Niola**: Boy, who did all the shopping? *Yashi rests his head back down* **Yashi**: I give up. **Niola**: Ha. *Niola lays back down* Goodnight, Ya~shi~do~. **Yashi**: Please don't combine those names, that sounds horrible. **Niola**: It doesn't sound that bad. **Yashi**: Yes it does, and you know it. **Niola**: Haha, yeah it does sound pretty bad. *Niola stands back up* I'll be right back. *Yashi hears the bathroom door Yáshido open and quietly close. A few minutes later the sound of shower water starts to hit a tile floor* **Yashi**(thts): It all happens tomorrow. He's either going to give Taku the treaty or arrest him. This is probably what Taku was saying, about a wider audience, or an announcement. The information he could tell is vital. We might get a real upper hand. Niola gave them a perspective, but what Taku says and does is on him. I don't expect him to rat out Korosi's future plans to the entire world, but what else could there be for him to say. *Yashi turns towards the wall* And Dia, I have no idea what what's going through her head. Could it be a double cross? She won't tell me nor isn't she working for the Demon King. She didn't even mention Regra. Maybe she really has been using me this whole time. I've never been without her for so long. *Yashi feels his hands turn into fists under the blankets* All those people's lives Dia, and for what reason? *More minutes pass before the water stops and Niola walks out shortly after. After the door closes, Niola lays in her bed towards Yashi* **Niola**(w): Yashi~? Are you still awake? **Yashi**(w): I am now. **Niola**(w): You're gonna be so tired in the morning. **Yashi**(w): You would think my body would realize that, but it never does. **Niola**(w): Haha. Goodnight, Yashi. **Yashi**: Night.

-In the morning-

Yashi(thts): Hmm~ . . . day already. Couldn't be. **Yashi**: Ehm~ *Yashi opens his eyes and they start to burn from a bright white light* Oh man, too bright. *Yashi tries to stretch, but after moving his legs so far out of the bed, something silky blocks him from going further. Not knowing what it is, he jumps up against the wall out of the blanket* **System**: Barre Separation currently active, if wish to disable please use the control Mangole. *Yashi wipes his face* **Yashi**: Ooh, it's just a Barrier. Why is it up in the first place? *Yashi looks through the Barrier with more purpose and notices a thin red light that spreads on the left side of the Barrier* What's this? **Yashi**(thts): It doesn't look good whatever it is. *Yashi looks to the left of his bed at the Mangole. The Mangole is a smaller version than yesterday. Yashi stands from his bed taking the blanket with him and takes a knee looking at all the options* Split rooms. *Yashi pushes the button and finds the disable feature. Looking at the Barre next to him once more, he pushes this one* ^Instantly the Barre dissipates into nothing and the room fills with a sparkling red light. A loud constant crashing-like glass sound is heard. Yashi looks over to where the red light seems to be coming from. Niola is wearing her Familiar Dermal staring at what seems to be a dummy. Both of her hands pointed at it with two swirling flames just inches away from her hands. With a focused look on her face, Reine's mouth opens^ **Reine**: Solar Combustion! **Yashi**(m): Niola? **Reine**: Hu?! ^Reine instantly turns towards Yashi, slightly moving her aim downwards^ **Reine**(m): Yashi? ^Right after she moves her arms, the spirals dramatically increase in size. A ring of flames burst from Reine. After seeing the wave form, Yashi raises his hands to block and ducks on the bed as the air pressure forces the blanket across his head. The sound of the attack reaches Yashi's ears before the actual Cast, causing a loud ringing sound in his ears. Although preparing to take damage, the noise stops, and nothing makes contact with him. Slowly moving the blanket off one of his eyes, Yashi sees a blue Barrier At a couple inches from his face. Multiple cracks line around the equator of the Barrier in the same plane as the ring of fire shot out of Reine^ **Yashi**(thts): Barrier? *The Barre just slightly covers him, a part of the bed and a bit of floor. The ringing in his ears gets worse as he attempts to get out of bed. In response, Yashi plummets back under the blanket covering his ears. After a while, the ringing stops* Oh~, man, what was that all about? *Yashi feels as though a gust of air spreads out from his location* **A Faint Voice**: Yashi? Yashi, you're okay, right? **Yashi**(m): And now I'm hallucinating again. **A Faint Voice**(m): Hallucinating? **A Faint Voice**: What, I'm not a hallucinate voice. It's me, your Familiar, Reine. I can't believe I managed to summon a Barre that quickly. Get those covers off your head. **Yashi**: Reine? *Yashi takes the blanket off and Reine is standing next to him rubbing her head. All the walls are beeping red* **Reine**: Are you okay? Not hurt or anything? **Yashi**: No, the Barre you made formed in time. **Reine**: Whew~, that was a close one. You kinda distracted me though. *Reine looks at the dummy. Everything above its knees has been completely removed. The small foil behind the dummy is also scorched* The Cast wasn't even supposed to do that much damage. It was really a straight shot, I just put the split room up just in case it backfired. Why would you even open it up if it told you I was doing Magic? **Yashi**: Where'd it say that at? **Reine**: You undid it as soon as you got out of bed, didn't you? **Yashi**: Yup, why? **Reine**: Nothing. *Reine walks back in front of the dummy* **Yashi**: The fact that the first things I encountered when I wokc up were a bright light and an explosion. Today's going to be a great day. **Reine**: I wish all my days started out like that, but I was only practicing. **Yashi**: Yeah, I saw. **Reine**: And maybe just testing how strong the Barriers were. *Yashi swings his legs around to the outside of the bed* **Yashi**: What if you somehow got through? *Reine looks at Yashi* **Reine**: Then the next Barrier would stop it. **Yashi**: Okay, Reine. *Yashi stands* I'm taking my shower now. Make sure you're ready to go when I'm out. **Reine**: K! **Yashi**(m): So loud. *Yashi walks inside the bathroom while stretching some more. Reine walks over to the Control Mangole* **Reine**: No point in using the dummy anymore. *Reine deselects the dummy option. Before exiting the settings she runs across a Mangole Television mode* **Reine**: MTV? *Reine pushes the button and it takes her to a separate channel* **Reine**(m): Four by three, ten by seven, or sixteen by nine. *Each option has a small and large sub-option. Reine pushes sixteen by nine large. Behind her, a large screen unfolds from the ceiling and flattens on the window. Reine watches as it sets up* **Reine**: Neat. Before they only had one option. **System**: Please stand out of the displacement zone. *A red rectangle appears around Reine. She quickly stands and moves out of the rectangle. The Control Mangole, and the dresser it sat on, completely disappear and Reine's bed automatically starts sliding towards Yashi's. The sound of flowing water starts coming from the bathroom. Once the two beds are connected, the Control Mangole reappears facing the same way the mTV is, positioned in the corner. A welcome animation appears on the mTV before switching to the news* (mTV)**Announcer**: Recorded by 4-20, 983, at 9. *Reine gracefully lays across her newly made double bed. The host of the news is sitting alone on a long table* Good morning, afternoon, or evening my fellow Macadamians and all. Today, a Council Tsuno will be bringing explaining information they have collected on these unfortunate events that have passed in the last week up until now. Come and have a seat, Council Tsuno. *A gentleman in a set of formal clothes comes from the right side of the screen and sits next to the Announcer* And how are you today, Council Tsuno? **Tsuno**: I'm alright, Mr. Flech. How about yourself? **Flech**: Couldn't be better. *The host looks down at a sheet of paper* We'll start off with the supposed Dicipient attack at Jurono Academy. This attack happened six days ago and lasted a short period of seven minutes before the Balancers arrived. I will now read the collected information that has been obtained through eyewitnesses and mCameras scattered throughout the Academy. Taku was first spotted with his Trants, Savanna, walking along the main entrance. Two witnesses claim they did not have the formal Dicipient clothes on, nor any of the alternatives. The mCameras confirmed this. *A picture of Savanna and Taku appears on the screen* Macadamian style clothing indeed. *The picture shrinks to the bottom left of the screen* Upon entering the Academy, they went straight to the main desk. Arylia Jade, a six-year assistant, was at the desk at this time. Here is an audio sample she managed to capture. *Flech and Tsuno both lean against the table with their eyes closed. A display forms in the middle of them, showing audio waves. The camera zooms in on the waves* (Audio)(**Taku**): Well, are you going to call their names? (**Arylia**): You, you really are Taku. (**Taku**): Hmph, of course, who else could I be? I came here for a simple task. Listen, I don't want to cause any trouble, at least it won't go that way if you cooperate with me. (**Arylia**): If by, you wanting to be detained, then that's the only way I'll listen. *A hand lightly thumbs the top of a table* (**Taku**): That can't happen, and I'm not here to let that happen. Nam-, (**Arylia**): You think it's going to be that easy to trust someone like you? All of my people that you've killed. The Balancers are going to be on they're-, (**Taku**): Don't. That'll only-, ^A Cast is heard^ (**Arylia**): Hyah! ^The sound of two metal objects colliding^ (**Savanna**): Watch what you're doing! (**Arylia**): I don't care even if you are a Fallen Dicipient! That's not going to happen! ^The sharp metal sound happens again^ (**Savanna**): We know what they look like, Taku. I can activate the Fukashi, and we find them ourselves! **Flech**: The person who is about to enter is Elilament Dec'crador, Hamsley Rans. (Audio): ^A door is forced open^ (**Hamsley**): Arylia, move! ^A gunshot flys past the recording device^ (**Savanna**): Syah! (**Taku**)(Y): No, Sava-! ^The sound of a sword slicing through a thin object before an explosion masks the audio for a few seconds. Large chunks of brick are heard slamming against the ground. Arylia is coughing next to the recording device^ (**Hamsley**): Alert the school now! (**Arylia**): Right! ^Arylia is heard standing and opening a cabinet. Beeping noises come from the inputs she types in. A long morse code note is heard^ (**Arylia**): This is a Code 4 Halo! This is a Code 4 Halo! All classified personnel please prepare for battle! The target is-, (**Voice**): No! ^A loud fast-moving object gets extremely close to the recording device and explodes on what sounds like the wall next to it. The single morse code stops shortly after. Arylia and the recording device hit the ground away from the explosion. Another set of running footsteps is heard coming towards Arylia^ (**Hamsley**): Arylia. Arylia! Tsk! Damnit! (**Taku**): I just wanted the four kids. What I didn't want was to hurt anyone. (**Hamsley**): Explain your intentions with that Cast just now?! And NO one, And I Mean NO ONE will just simply hand over four students to a Dicipient! ^A grip of a gun is heard^ (**Taku**): Doesn't matter now. The Balancers are already on their way here. Savanna. ^Instantly a set of footsteps hit the ground close to Hamsley. A sweep of a gun like Hamsley is heard turning and multiple gunshots are heard inconsistently. Ricochets off of metal and shots piercing sheets of paper are heard before another clack of a gun being hit by a sword. The gun flys into the distance and hits a wall^ (**Hamsley**)(m): I hope you two get what's coming for you. (**Savanna**)(w): I'm sorry. (**Taku**): Ha! ^Hamsley gasps and a loud thump is heard hitting the ground^ (**Taku**): Looks like you were right. (**Savanna**): I knew I was right as soon as I told you. (**Taku**): We have to get a move on and find those four before the Balancers get here. (**Savanna**): Mhm. Let's go then. ^Both of them run out of the room^ *The camera zooms back out to fit Flech and Tsuno in the shot* **Flech**: Unfortunately, Jurono has not yet received the Pure Energy Use Enhancer. The blast that hit the telecon hit several other services that disabled some other the mCameras alongside many recording devices. The good news is that one out of the five remaining still caught something which could be highly convenient and useful. Although the audio is a little corrupted, you can still make out what is being said. *The wall behind them turns into a display. Flech and Tsuno turn to look at it. On the screen, the camera is watching from a corner view. The entrance is a single door on the left wall from the camera's perspective. About twenty feet directly in front of the door stands Savanna. A student is between her and Taku. Taku is sitting in one of the loose school chairs with his legs crossed* (Display)(**Taku**): Rosken, Max's son. Luckily I found you here. (**Rosken**): My father wasn't lying when he said he knew you but . . . Wha-, what is it that you want from me? (**Taku**): Listen, I'm not going to hurt you. Max would probably kill me if I laid a finger on you. (**Rosken**): Just ge-, get to the point! (**Taku**): I am going to show you a picture of these four students I need. Be a hundred percent honest if you know them or not. (**Rosken**): Okay. *Taku raises up something to Rosken* (**Taku**): Namari Katsuni. (**Rosken**): Yes, I know her. (**Taku**): Can you bring her here? You of all should know not to do anything that could end badly. (**Rosken**): Yes. I know, I'll bring her as soon as possible. *Ro steps back but bumps into Savanna. Ro quickly turns around as Savanna is covering the handle of her sword as if protecting him. Savanna's sword is in a brown pouch on her leg* S-, sorry. *Rosken turns back around and walks out of the door. Savanna is seen turning towards his direction as he walks out of the room. The door closing causes the screen to glitch, but it returns soon after* (**Savanna**): You never told me Max had a son. (**Taku**): Well now you know. *Savanna turns towards Taku* (**Savanna**): Do you think he would really bring them here? (**Taku**): It's either him or us. How's the Kuki

Sosa World doing? (*Savanna*): I can hold it for a couple more minutes if need be. Those Academy bracelets are making it a bit easier for me to contain them. Some of them can't even use Magic as you said. (*Taku*): Hmph, I'm just happy you were even able to properly use that Personal Cast to single out everyone loose in the Academy. *Savanna looks at her sword and many auras start to glow around it* (*Savanna*): And you said getting Ace would be useless. (*Taku*): Heh, you got me. *Both of them look at the door* (*Taku*): That was quick. Come stand next to me so we can properly meet our guests. *Savanna takes out her sword from her pouch and holds it down to her side as she stands next to Taku. The door opens. A girl enters first and Rosken behind her* Namari Katsuni, take a seat. *Namari hesitantly pauses but continues her approach* (*Namari*): Taku and Savanna. What's this about? (*Taku*): Just take a seat. I'll say once everyone is here, but just so you're less frightened of me, -Unidentified words-. *Namari takes a seat at the first desk to the right, about five feet from Taku* **Reine**: Wait, so that means Yashi's going to be in here. *A slight chuckle* I want to see what he did. (Display): *Taku holds up another picture* (*Taku*): Keshio Revalorese. (*Rosken*): Keshio? *Sighs* Yeah, I know where to find him. *Rosken exits the room once more* (*Taku*): So how has your day been going so far, Katsuni? (*Namari*): What happened to all the people that tried to fight you? The halls are surprisingly empty. (*Taku*): Empty space. (*Namari*): How do you even have permission to use Magic in this area? All Magic is off-limits, literally. (*Taku*): Everyone that has attempted to capture me is fine. For the most part. (*Namari*): For the most part? What are you even trying to do right-, *The door opens again. Namari looks at the door* (*Taku*): Keshio Revalorese, welcome. (*Keshio*): Taku's the Dicipient that attacked? No way, I never thought you'd actually be capable of making all those people disappear. Not only that but thanks for seriously messing up my schedule. (*Taku*): I expect nothing less from someone like you. (*Keshio*): Spare me. *A fireball appears floating a foot away from Taku's face* (*Taku*): I chose you four for a reason, don't make me regret my decision. (*Keshio*): Hmph. *Keshio takes a seat at the desk next to Namari. The fireball disappears. Rosken walks next to Namari facing Taku. Taku holds out another photo* (*Taku*): Otara Misugami. *Keshio and Namari jump back in their seats, Rosken takes a step back. Stuttering* (*Ro*): Otara?! ArE yOU sUrE tHATt's ThE rIgHt NAME? (*Keshio*): He must be gathering up the strongest people so he can have a massive sadist battle or something. (*Savanna*): Quiet down, you're not even old enough to know what that means. (*Keshio*): Hold on, how do you know how old I am? (*Taku*): That's not the point, do you know where to find her, Rosken? (*Ro*): Ye-, yeah. *Rosken turns around and starts walking towards the door* (*Taku*): Do you think you need Savanna for her? (*Ro*): No, I can manage her. *Rosken leaves the room once more* (*Keshio*): Wait, how did you just use Kosai, you can't even use Magic in this area. (*Namari*): I said the same thing. -Keshio says something undefined- (*Savanna*): Hmph, please refrain from calling Taku that. *Keshio looks at Savenna then Taku* (*Keshio*): Sure, your highness. *Savanna scoffs of the remark* **Flech**: I'm going to skip to the part where Misugami arrives because nothing happens for thirty seconds. (Display): (**Keshio**): Speaking of Magic, doesn't Otara . . . have a permit? (**Namari**): They never gave her one because . . . actually I'd rather not say. *The door opens. A shorter girl with silver hair enters the room next to Rosken* (**Taku**): Otara Misugami, good to see you in the flesh once more. *Otara stops while Rosken continues walking. Rosken then stops and looks at Otara* (**Otara**): Taku. (**Keshio**): Woah, you've even managed to get Otara surprised. If that's the face she makes when she's surprised. (**Taku**): Would you mind taking a seat for me, Otara? (**Otara**): I'd rather stand. (**Taku**): Suit yourself. (**Otara**): Savanna too. (**Savanna**): Otara. *Otara looks at Namari* (**Otara**): What happened to the others? (**Namari**): Somehow, they're able to use Magic. (**Otara**): Hm. *Otara faces Taku* Okay. How many of us will there be in the end? (**Taku**): Four. *Rosken walks up to Taku. Taku takes out the last photo* (**Rosken**): Him? Okay. *Rosken turns around* (**Taku**): Rosken. *Rosken stops* (**Rosken**): Yeah? (**Taku**): Once he's here you don't have to enter the room again. (**Rosken**): Okay. *Rosken exits the room for the final time* (mTV)**Flech**: I'm going to fast forward the video again because nothing happens until Yashi Taramasu is about to enter. (Display): *The door opens and one boy enters* **Keshio**: Taramasu's here, haha what. (**Taku**): Take a seat and close the door. *Yashi slowly pushes the door closed behind him and walks to an empty seat next to Otara and sits* I don't have all day before those Balancers arrive. (**Keshio**): Alright, all four of us are here, you mind starting off on why you attacked the school? *Savanna moves forward slightly and Taku instantly puts his hand in front of her* (**Savenna**): But, Taku. (**Taku**): If the kid wants to know, he can know. *Savenna nods before standing upright* (**Taku**): I know you've heard quite a few rumors that I'm a Fallen Dicipient, correct? Well, that is true. Now, I wouldn't go as far as saying I attacked you. It was more like me walking in here with Savenna, requesting for you four, and then getting attacked myself. **Reine**: Well, I wouldn't say that Taku, hahaha. (Display)(**Taku**): So, Keshio, I don't recommend you start calling names, alright? (**Keshio**): Yeah, whatever. (**Taku**): As you know, by looking at the ones around you, that you all have some of the highest Oplitals and Elilament ratings at this school. (**Keshio**): 'Bout time someone noticed what I'm capable of, but uhm~ *Keshio turns his head towards Yashi* (**Taku**): As hard as your pride deceives you, you are the strongest. (**Savanna**): Taku, the sensors have just been activated. We need to get going. (**Taku**): Before we leave, are there any of you who want to stay? I'm not forcing you to come with me. *A bright white box appears in Taku's hands* I'm sure you know, once you come with me, you won't be able to attend this Academy anymore. If you're coming, stand. *Yashi stands, Keshio stands, then Namari* (**Taku**): Nice. *Taku throws the box at the ground in the middle of everyone. The door gets kicked right open and lands right behind Otara's legs* (**Balancer**): Stop! (**Taku**): Hey Balancer, tell your Generals I got some new recruits, but what I'm doing shouldn't concern them. They will end up thanking me!

^Spirals from the box cover all of them, the Balancer fires a spear at the spirals. Savanna casts a Barrier on the outside of the side that the attack is coming from. The spear hits the Barrier. The display turns off after multiple lines that look like broken glass cover the screen while bright white lights cover the lens's vision* (mTV)**Flech**: The recording that you heard was really contradicting what many theorists had, but a rumor that spread from Sablein, Bushido reformed to be exact, claimed that Taku was now a Fallen Dicipient. **Reine**: Media, hahaha. (mTV)**Flech**: There's no direct source of where it came from, but everyone who has spoken about it says that it originated from Sablein. Based on the dialogue from the video, the four students Keshio Revalorese, Namari Katsuni, Otara Misugami, and Yashi Taramasu, each decided to join Taku of their own will. Whether this classifies them as treasonous is still up for debate once the Generals are notified of his whereabouts. On the side, there were no casualties from the . . . kidnapping? Only light injuries from those who attempted to attack them by Savanna. Based on public opinion, the majority still find it hard to believe that Taku is 'out for good' is impossible. Particularly, in our Droxima. What do you feel about this matter, Tsuno? *The bathroom door quietly opens. Yashi slowly walks in with his cloak on and looks at the conjoined beds* **Yashi**(thts): You just had to, didn't you? *Yashi looks at the mTV* **Yashi**: Reine? *Reine doesn't hear Yashi. Yashi sits on the bed next to Reine also watching the news* (mTV)**Tsuno**: The basics are true. Taku's a Fallen Dicipient. And coincidentally during the Demon King's consistent attacks? Every five to six years now, Korosi invades a Seira. Maybe Macadamia will finally have its turn. What can we look at, he abducted some of the highest potential students at Jurono Academy. With what we've recently seen from Taku, the last thing he participated in was not even that bad. He ran through a gate in Yasis, Kyunn'Ku, which was 1-13. And if you want to talk about destruction, that was a year ago in Sablein, 11-5. Two communication towers, but still there were other Dicipients, so it could not have been him. Do you honestly think he would solo in invasion himself? In Macadamia? Please. Ever since Jurono, we immediately hit our cap of a hundred Balancers. More than half of the off-duty Balancers are now active once more. The whole population, in general, has exploded. Digona, Makatama, even the Western Seiras have all maxed out their Balancer count. One word that there is an attack in Macadamia, whoever it is won't be so happy. **Flech**: I see. We happened to mention that the four students that were taken by Taku were in Jurono's top ten of Elilament Effectiveness, and Great Trants Potential. Why do you think he took those four specifically? **Tsuno**: That could mean anything. I'm surprised that they all agreed to follow him. Even Misugami. When you first issued this case, Watashimono would have gotten it a day later. We talked to them recently before Otara's birthday, and they weren't shook in the slightest. Myungnia Misugami even told us not to bother them about the matter. It's hard to believe they don't care, or she can manage her own. I'd say the ladder. Namari Katsuni is a well-known tournament specialist and makes good grades. Keshio is more in tuned with his own style of training, and also fights in a public match or two, but they've never fought for their lives so to speak. Each of their parents were devastated, especially Katsuni's. They came to us before we could even process exactly what had happened. Revalorese's . . . I wasn't given permission to tell. Yashi, he's under an NDA much like the rest of the students who attend Jurono. He has the stats, but he is just a lone wolf. *Shakes head* It's all jumbled up into a complete mess. I'd say, them all working together could fairly out power Taku and Savanna, but as inexperienced as they are, fighting may not be their best option. *Flech*: This leads us to our next topic, something that is mind-boggling still to this day and is still in research. Yáshido's equal, Dia Kean, assaulted and nearly destroyed Kedum, Regra with other Dicipients. With further investigations and from data Regra have sent out, they lost a total of 32,049 civilian lives, and 12,450 migrant lives. The ending of the battle ended with an explosion causing 23,144 more injuries. The total debt for loss of buildings was about 780,000*Ca* or 500,000*Krislia*. *Flech pauses and looks around his room. His facial expression changes to a sad one* It is hard to believe Dia would do something so vague with no clear intentions. Someone who we thought would help the Hero defeat the Demon King turns around and does his bidding. Dicipient's clothes, and a new Dicipient in the mix. *Reine*: I find it hilarious how specifically it's basically the same news I've seen for at least three different times now. *Reine sighs* *Yashi*: You've seen this three times? *Reine looks at Yashi with a surprised expression* *Reine*: You must really want to get hurt, don't you? *Yashi*: What do you mean, did I scare you or something? *Reine*: Yes. I was this close to screaming. *Reine holds up two fingers and pushes them together* *Yashi*: Well, I'm sorry. *Reine*: It's okay. I probably was too focused on the TV anyway. *Yashi*: So, three times? *Reine*: At Taku's, when I went out with the other explorers, and now. *Yashi*: Hmph. *They look back at the mTV* (mTV)*Flech*: This time, the complete video file is properly working. Here it is now. *The screen behind Flech and Tsuno turns back. The video starts with someone downward looking at their shoes. Flech and Tsuno look back around to look at the screen* The one holding the camera is R'Xagario Joyce, and the girl who's about to appear later is Emi Ukitima. *Yashi feels a sharp pain rush down his spine. The feeling makes him jerk on the bed. Reine turns around to look at him* *Reine*: You're okay? *Yashi*: Yeah, yeah, it's nothing. *Both of them look back at the TV* (Display)(*R'Xagario*): There. It's on. *R'Xagario is running down a hall* I can't believe there's an attack going on now. ^A blast is heard outside and the building rumbles in response^ Crap, I still haven't found her! *R'Xagario takes a left still running* Emi! Emi, where are you! *R'Xagario starts to speed up his run* (Voice)(From Behind): Someone help! *R'Xagario stops* (*R'Xagario*): That's Emi! ^Another blast is fired from outside the building. As it hits the ground, people are heard screaming^ (*R'Xagario*): They're right by us! *The screen layout turns light blue as R'Xagario moves rapidly down the hall* (Voice)(From Outside): Die! You Dicipient!

While R'Xagario is running, a red line of energy comes from the right wall and cuts through the left wall nearly hitting him. R'Xagario stops for a moment realizing he could have died from the power of the attack. The camera starts to shake as R'Xagario continues to run down the corridor. Once reaching the end door he punches through it. R'Xagario panes around with the Mangole, but there's nothing in the room. Part of the wall is broken, exposed to the outside world (**R'Xagario**): Is she up one more floor? Or down? Emi, can you hear me!?! (**Voice**)(From Outside): There's a Regraian in there! (**R'Xagario**): Huh? ^The camera points up at the ceiling. A loud buzzing noise is heard before something dark comes through the ceiling into the floor R'Xagario is on. The Cast hitting R'Xagario's floor causes his and floor one above to fall. A portion of the building is heard falling and crashing into a building next to it. The screen fizzles a bit before returning to the scene of debris and two legs^ (**R'Xagario**): Ohm, I wasn't prepared for that. *R'Xagario stands up* That came from upstairs. That means Emi's down here. *R'Xagario starts to climb the debris. Once he's over it, people are heard screaming outside as another explosion happens, following the crashing of a building. Ice starts to freeze over something outside the building. R'Xagario starts to run around the small, connected rooms* Emi?! ^A blast in the next room hits a wall^ **Emi**: Xa! *R'Xagario goes around the corner. Emi is sitting on the floor with debris next to her. Two people in black clothing stand above her; one farther from Emi than the other. Next to them is a completely broken wall showing all the chaos ongoing outside* (**R'Xagario**)(Y): YOU STAY AWAY FROM HER!!! ^The two figures turn towards him. R'Xagario drops the Mangole. The Mangole hits the ground and spins in a full circle, still giving a perfect angle of everyone in the room; the same angle as before just on the floor. R'Xagario stands facing the two figures. The one closest to Emi backs away and stands next to the other shadowed person. R'Xagario raises his right arm with a balled fist at them. A blue frost spirals around his arm creating a much larger frosted fist^ (**R'Xagario**): Peace Savor! ^The icy fist gets blasted off towards the two figures. Both of them just stare until the last moment where they hold up their arms to block. The figure on the left stops blocking and takes a staff out from their back and hits the ice fist before impact. At the same time, ice surrounds R'Xagario's legs; He uses a Protojet that spins him in a circle as he activates Zoka Strength. Using this momentum, he kicks the ice towards the two fingers once more: And the fist ricochets off the staff downwards. The ice wave from R'Xagario's kick and his fist collide. Instead of exploding everywhere, it shoots towards the two figures. Covering that entire side of the room with ice. Blue smoke flows through the floor. Emi sits on the ground with her right leg nearly devoured by the giant ice brick. An exhaust is cut in half and it starts making a loud eerie noise. Gray smoke leaks from the exhaust and rushes upward to the ceiling. The two clouds of smoke maneuver out of the room through the partially exposed wall into the air. From the position of the camera, you can just barely make out the two figures in the ice. The tiny holes coming from the wall that got shot before R'Xagario entered enables him to see Emi. R'Xagario runs up to her^ (**R'Xagario**): Emi, come on! (**Emi**): Okay! *R'Xagario picks up Emi by her waist. Both of them start running to the way R'Xagario entered. Before they get out of the camera's sight, a crack forms in the ice. R'Xagario stops and looks back at the ice. Emi continues running but stops with only one of her legs still showing on camera. The crack widens in the ice^ (**Emi**): Xa, wh-, what are you doing? ^R'Xagario aims his hands at the ice blocks^ (**R'Xagario**): Go without me! (**Emi**): Are you insane?! *Emi runs to R'Xagario and pulls him back* (**R'Xagario**): They're going to escape-, (**Emi**): You idiot! Why are you trying to be a hero! ^The cracks spread to each end of the ice brick^ (**R'Xagario**): I already made my choice, Emi! Go while you still can! ^R'Xagario fires a large quantity of ice at the existing ice brick. Before it makes contact, the ice brick explodes in all directions covering the interior of the building in the snow. R'Xagario stops as he and Emi watch his attack curve around something^ (**R'Xagario**)(Y): Go!~ ^R'Xagario and Emi glow in a light blue color as they quickly vanish from the camera's sight, running in the opposite direction. A mCircle appears next to the curved ice and fires a wave of fire in the direction Emi and R'Xagario ran. The blast makes contact with something before exploding^ (**Emi & R'Xagario**): Ahh! ^The fiery flames of broken material land in front of the camera's sight. A person walks out from the left side of the ice wall wielding a staff and holding their other hand parallel to the ground. They lower their hand^ **Flech**: This scene is edited to get a better shot of the two attackers. Display: *The camera zooms in on them. The figure on the left has two long purple curls, red sparkly eyes, light brown skin, and an evil smile. The black clothes make them seem as if they were a deep bottomless pit floating in reality. The figure chuckles* (**Jyokumo**): Hahaha, finish them, Dia! *A figure walks from the right of the ice wall with nearly the same outfit. The camera zooms out and zooms in on them* **Reine**: Dia . . . Display: *Dia's eyes are closed, but once the camera fully zooms in, her facial expression turns into a displeased face. Dia's eyes open and she looks angry. Suddenly mCircles form on both of her sides, above her, on the ceiling, and on the flooring. All facing towards the direction R'Xagario and Emi are in* **Yashi**(thts) & (Display)(**Dia**): Catatróph! ^The mCircles rotate with an endless increasing speed as if something was about to come out, and the color pulses within a dark red. R'Xagario is seen crawling into the camera's sight from the left^ (**R'Xagario**): Dia? Is-, is that really you? *Dia looks over at Jyokumo. Jyokumo nods. Dia looks back at R'Xagario who is a foot away looking up at her* It is . . . *R'Xagario starts to cry* I don't believe it. Why are you with them? I thought you and the Hero were a team? ^Dia's legs glow within a red color as she raises her left leg slightly up. Dia then stomps the ground and R'Xagario goes back flying out of sight. R'Xagario slams against the wall as the walls shake and the Mangole turns onto its side. The red aura around Dia's legs disappears as she takes a deep breath^ (**Emi**): No! Stop! Why are you doing this?! *Dia turns her head away from them* (**Dia**):

Attack! ^The center of the mCircles glow with light before hundreds of Pure Energy blades shoot out in all directions. So many are being fired that it nearly covers up Dia's appearance. Dia turns back to Emi and R'Xagario's direction, then she looks at the camera directly as the building they're in is getting completely destroyed and slightly grins^ (Dia): I'm coming for you, Yashi! ^The camera zooms out as a blade goes straight for it. Before the blade makes an impact, the screen turns off. Yashi's hands ball up into fists^ Yashi(thts): How could you? I still can't believe this is even real. *Yashi glances at Reine and she is looking away from the mTV with her eyes closed and a squinted face. A tear rolls doing her face onto the bed as she fights back the tears. This causes Yashi to un-ball his hands* Niola . . . (mTV)Flech: As you can see, our accusation about Dia participating in this epidemic was not false. Tragic is the only word I can use to describe such, such actions. We spoke with Emuna, but she wouldn't answer our questions regarding Dia, however . . . it is clear that she is even more confused and shocked by the situation. The last sighting of Dia, Emuna, and Yáshido was in Hostel, Kedum, 4-11 through 4-13, so maybe this has something to do with the attack specifically damaging Kedum, the most out of all the shore cities of Regra. Civilians claim that Yáshido, Dia, and Emuna were a bit more serious than usual, causing many of them to believe that they were going to fight the Demon King, Korosi, for the first time. Yet, the Counsil, nor the Macadamian Generals were informed of the breach. Not that it matters, but just an interesting thing to note. *Clears throat* Sorting through some of the Edasian scanners, there was a teleport at 4-13 in Hostel, Kedum by Emuna . . . *Flech closely looks at the papers he's holding* to a marked off location, meaning Darku Mat'u or Yat'u. Leading to the theory that they did attempt to fight Korosi more believable. Tsuno: Excuse me one second, Mr. Flech. *Flech looks at Tsuno* Flech: Go ahead. Tsuno: First off, no doubt that they fought the Demon King. Let's get that out of the way for all those listening. Secondly, I understand and do pay my respects to those lives that were lost at Regra, but expanding out a bit, who should we be more concerned about here? Dia Kean, the Hero's partner, Trants, whatever you want to call her, or the Hero himself? I dove deeper into his punctuality while I was pondering through my thoughts. Before being seen at Hostel, he wasn't seen for a week. Dia was, however . . . and so was Emuna. It's been a week since the teleport was dated and again no sighting of the Hero. Emuna obviously being his Spawn, she's taking it quite lightly than you'd think, continuing her job and all. Plus, Emuna's the only source who claims she saw Yáshido, so unless Emuna wants his location to stay secret, I'd say he would be up to something himself. A plan of some kind. *Reine looks at Yashi* Reine: It's almost like he knows. Yashi: Don't make me paranoid. (mTV)Tsuno: We have to support our Seiras as a whole. The Demon King could attack, a Dicipient, Dia, we have a chance of stopping them. Let us remember, not to many decades ago, the 6th Hero died, and we didn't know till a year later. Of course, they would know something that we don't, so with that said, everyone should just calm themselves and wait it out. Bringing panic only makes the situation worse. *Tsuno rubs his chin* Hmph, I spoke with Emuna recently about Macadamian matters and she told me that the Hero is perfectly fine. We all know Emuna too well to even think she would lie to a Council member, anyone for that matter. Her career as an Alchemist is on the line as we speak. She's only still been working after Dia's first strike is because they need her, that's the only reason. No offense Ms. Levebrve. Korosi is still alive. It's been passed on for so many generations that if you didn't catch the last one, it would be extremely obvious. If the Hero or Demon King dies, a bright beam of light where the death happened will shoot up into the sky from that location. Massive amounts of Pure Energy would cloud the skies. Thirdly, regarding Dia, it is a possibility that she was converted directly by Korosi. In the video and pictures we have of her, she is wearing Dicipient clothing. What makes it strange is that it's not all of the Dermal. Even some of the survivors who encountered Dia stated that she didn't have that Dicipient aura, so I don't think it fully classifies her as a Dicipient, but that's not for me to make that decision now is it? *Yashi looks at the bottom of the mTV to see the time and gasps out of fright. Reine looks back at him* **Reine**: What is it? **Yashi**: It's twelve we need to go, I forgot to tell you that we're going to Menium. *Reine jumps up* **Reine**: Menium! That's so far! Why didn't you say something sooner! *Yashi stands* **Yashi**: We were going to leave when I got out, but you were distracted so I decided to watch it too. **Reine**: Haah~, we are going back through the West Gate, right? **Yashi**: Are you energized enough to where you won't drop me? **Reine**: That's not funny anymore. Honestly, why would I drop you, Yashi? *They stare at each other* **Reine**: Hahaha, I won't drop you, okay? **Yashi**: Good. Get your cloak. *Reine walks over to her cloak* **Reine**: Oh, Yashi, could you do me a favor and get my headband from the counter with the sinks? **Yashi**: You wear a headband? **Reine**: With this Casted hair? I'd look stupid with a headband on. It's for my natural hair. **Yashi**: Hm, that makes sense. *Yashi walks and opens the bathroom door. Reine turns off the mTV with the Mangole. Reine's headband is to the left sink. Once Yashi grabs it he looks at the reflection of the glass to see Reine reaching for her cloak then pausing looking at the bedroom door. Yashi turns around and looks at Reine* You okay? *Yashi walks out of the bathroom* **Reine**: I . . . I sense Balancers coming up here. **Yashi**: Balancers? *Yashi looks back at the door* **Yashi**(thts): That cannot be good. The girl at the front desk might not care much about knowing who we are, but when it comes to authority, she would have had to talk. **Reine**: Definitely Balancers, three of 'em. You never registered yourself, but I don't come here often to know if they have a body scanner on their doors. Which means we could have no chance at all of getting out of this without you turning into the Hero. **Yashi**: We can wing it and say that they don't have body scanners. I'll pretend that I'm taking a shower. Itilusion me. **Reine**: Are you sure? I know you're the Hero and everything, but you're just as vulnerable as anyone else without a Sustain. **Yashi**: We don't have time, if you don't, I might as well transform right here. **Reine**: Fine. *Reine sparkles as her Dermal disappears and her original hairstyle and color comes back. She looks at Yashi and snaps her fingers. Yashi starts to sparkle. Before anything else could happen, Yashi goes inside of the shower room closing both doors behind him. Once in, he turns on the shower and lays against the door with his eyes closed* **Yashi**(thts): All of this just to save some Oplitals. *In the bedroom, after the shower starts, the bedroom door knocks. Niola slowly walks to the door* **Balancer**(A): We know you're here. Open the door, we have questions for you. *Niola touches the door, and it fades away. Three Balancers stand in the corridor. Each one has a Macadamian Sword attached to their waists. Even though they have helmets on, all three of them seem to be staring directly at her* **Niola**: Balancers? What's up? **Balancer**(A): We came to question you about your recent entry into Dreium. **Niola**(m): Oh, you mean last night? **Niola**: Ha, your welcome inside. *Niola moves back away from the door. Two of the Balancers enter the room and another stands guard outside the door. The bedroom door fades back in. Niola looks at the numbers on each Balancer's back. The one talking to her before 371 and the other 377. In the shower room, the Itilusion around Yashi's body begins to reside. Yashi sighs before noticing something odd about what noise came out of his mouth. Opening his eyes, a long bang hangs down across his field of view. He looks down and his chest is bigger with more long brown hair over it* **Yashi**(thts): No. *Yashi looks at the wall mirror to his left. A shocked facial expression quickly washes over his face* NO. *Looking at himself, instead of the Gi he got from Namari, he has a long black tainted skirt with red leggings. There is an 'A' marking with a line going through the middle of it and a circle going around it on his skirt. Looking farther down, he has a pair of red heels on with the same marking on the tip of them. Yashi feels a tear drop down his face while grinning* I told her to use Itilusion, but she went a step further and used it with Sosa. Why couldn't she have made me into another boy or change my hair or something? She literally made me into a whole girl, and Kuki Sosa makes it to where I can actually feel . . . *Yashi stops* That scared me, at least Niola didn't go that far. *Yashi looks back at the mirror. The cloak still being on him highlights his appearance, even more* The sad part is that I'm not even mad. I'd probably have turned her into a boy too. How am I even going to get up? I've never worn shoes like this before. Yashi pushes himself up against the wall, slowly standing. Inside the bedroom. Niola is sitting on the bed, the two Balancers standing in front of her* **Balancer**(377): Take a look at this. *377 swipes the air in front of Niola and a Mangole appears. It has the latest entrances of Dreium by Niola. Niola reads the information* **Niola**: My specs, what about it? *371 points under Niola's name. Niola follows his finger and it leads to her density and weight checks. Niola sees the huge jump in numbers* **Niola**: Hahaha, that doesn't look normal. **Balancer**(371): That's exactly what we're thinking. Would you happen to know why? **Niola**: Well~, I did go through it with a friend of mine. **Balancer**(377): A friend? **Balancer**(371): I suppose they are the one in the shower? *Niola nods. 371 looks at 377. Both of them look back at Niola* That does not explain why the scanner only read you. As in, it completely negated your friend out of the picture. The system didn't catch a 'second person'. *377 swipes the Mangole to another screen* **Balancer**(371): Flight, Zoka Strength, Fukashi, Personal Casting, Barre, and Ikkasei were the Elilaments you used. **Niola**: Sounds right. **Balancer**(371): Last night, there was also an encounter with two individuals who fled from the probating Balancers along the same Gate. One with pink hair and brown. We assume that this was you and your friend? **Niola**: Yes~. **Balancer**(377): Why did you resort to running, especially being so close? **Niola**: She was afraid that you might say something about the unsigned weapon she had with her, which she was going to Dreium to get signed. Plus being shy, she wanted to just leave. *Niola looks at 371* I have to admit, it was a bit sketchy of me to start running away right in front of them and flying back through the gate with her, but I think that was a better choice than her making a scene. *377 sighs* **Balancer**(377): I told you she's clean. This was a waste of time. *377 turns towards the door* Let's go. **Balancer**(371): Wait a minute. *377 turns back around as 371 looks at Niola* I want to see this friend of yours. *Niola looks at the bathroom wall* I can wait, you can stand outside if you don't want to be in here, 377. **Balancer**(377): Fine by me. *As 377 starts walking towards the door, a loud banging sound comes from the bathroom as if something hit the floor really hard. 377 quickly turns around and 371 both look at the bathroom door* **Balancer**(377): What was that? **Balancer**(371): I-. *Both the Balancers look back at Niola. Niola is facing the opposite direction with a hand over her mouth. The sound of resisting air from escaping comes from her general location* Ms. Akimora, what's going on? *Niola takes a deep breath before turning towards the bathroom door* **Niola**: Siyo, are you alright?! *Inside the shower room. Yashi sits crooked between the door and floor* **Yashi**: Ahh~sss . . . **Yashi**(thts): How does anyone even walk in these things? I think I just broke my entire leg just now, and did she just call me Siyo? Yashi(**Siyo**): Yes, I'm alright! *Yashi moves the stand that sits to the right of him. He slowly moves up the wall and uses the stand to keep him from slipping again. Once completely up, he slowly slides across the floor to a sitting spot. Once seated, he starts to take the heels off. Inside the bedroom* **Niola**: Haha, she's okay. *371 looks back at the door, then 377, then finally back to Niola. 371 sighs* **Balancer**(371): Sorry for disrupting your time, we'll be on our way. Have a good day, Ms. Akimora. *371 turns around and begins walking towards the door. Niola follows him* **Niola**: Don't worry about it; I don't get visits from Balancers often. *377 touches the door and it fades away. The guarding Balancer is looking at a Mangole, but instantly vanishes it and stands back up as if he was doing nothing, then slowly looks at the two exiting Balancers* **Balancer**(C): Oh, I didn't hear you come out. **Balancer**(371): She's clean, 342. **Balancer**(342): Told you. **Balancer**(377): Hey, I was the one who said that. Don't make me tell her what you called her yesterday. *Niola stands at the door* **Niola**: What'd he call me? *342 quickly stands in front of 377* **Balancer**(342): Nothing, Akimora, hahaha. Nothing at all. *377 puts her left hand on his left shoulder* **Balancer**(377): My feet~. *342 looks down* **Balancer**(342): Oh, sorry. *342 stands between 377 and 371. 371 starts walking down the hall* **Balancer**(377): Thanks for helping out with Saramaenous yesterday. **Niola**: Did you get any information on him? **Balancer**(342): Hmph, yeah he spilled some quality information. There's a couple more awaiting by other Gates if you don't mind 'being bait' again. *Niola chuckles* **Balancer**(377): With that said, you and your friend stay safe, we need to get back in position. **Niola**: K, you too. *Niola waves as the Balancers leave. After Niola makes the door reappear, the bathroom door opens. Yashi storms out towards Niola, pinning her on the bedroom door* **Yashi**(**Siyo**): Change me back now! **Niola**(w): Shh! They may still be able to hear you. **Yashi**(**Siyo**): No you wiz, the rooms are soundproof. **Niola**(w): Oh, you're right. *Niola starts to furiously laugh in front of Yashi. Yashi backs away* **Yashi**(**Siyo**): This isn't funny, Niola. **Niola**: It's gold. *Niola wipes the tears of laughter off her face* Man, I don't know if this'll be weird to say, but I don't know which one of you is cuter. *Yashi awkwardly smiles as he loosens his grip* **Yashi**(**Siyo**): That is weird. Why didn't you make me into another boy? **Niola**: You didn't give me enough time to create a whole new body and stuff, so I just went with someone who I haven't seen in a long time. **Yashi**(thts): Siyo, I don't know any Siyos. **Yashi**(**Siyo**): So who am I? **Niola**: Look in the mirror and you'll notice right away. *Yashi sighs as he walks back into the bathroom. Niola enters behind him* Oh and imagine your hair as a silvery color. *Yashi looks at himself in the mirror and takes off the hoodie* **Yashi**(thts): Silver hair? *Yashi's eyes open as he realizes who he has been turned into* **Yashi**(**Siyo**) & **Niola**: Emuna. **Niola**: Yup, right before she became an Alchemist, and still was adventuring with me. *Yashi looks down at his hands* **Yashi**(**Siyo**): That's nice and all, but now I just feel even more uncomfortable. Mind changing me back now? **Niola**: One more thing. *As Yashi turns around, a Mangole is in his face. Niola holding it, leaning to the right of it smiling* Cheese!~ *A bright light shines from the Mangole before disappearing* Now I can undo it. *Niola raises her hand and snaps her finger. Particles form on Yashi's body starting at his feet raising all the way up until he is back to his normal self* **Yashi**(thts): What just happened? **Niola**: Hahaha, are you okay, Yashi? You look like you're amazed at something. *Yashi slams his fist into his palm while clearing his throat* **Yashi**: Get your cloak before I don't take you. *Niola backs away before walking to her cloak* **Niola**: Okay, okay, I'm sorry, but I was forced to lie using my innocence. *After putting the cloak on, Niola takes the headband that's next to Yashi and puts it on. Niola then closes her eyes as Particles start surrounding her body. Her hair turns purple, changes style, and her school uniform reappears* **Reine**: Ready. *Both of them put on their hoods before leaving the room and using the elevator to get back down to the main floor*

Chapter 14 - Admission from the Ranks

The main floor is empty other than the Receptionist who is rearranging some paperwork. Before Yashi and Reine could get to her desk **Receptionist**: You two had a good night? **Reine**: Yes! It was perfect! *The receptionist looks up with a smile* **Receptionist**: Great! I hope you two come back soon. *The receptionist waves back as they leave the hotel. Standing outside the door, the sidewalks and streets are populated with hundreds of traveling civilians. Yashi and Reine start walking towards the Tai River. Other people with cloaks on, hoodie or not, makes them look less suspicious. After crossing the Tai River, the area becomes extremely crowded with people carrying large baskets of fruit and other materials, mCarriages transporting heavy items, and more travelers. Reine tugs on Yashi's cloak from behind* **Yashi**: Yeah? **Reine**: I can use the bracelet now. **Yashi**: Nice, let's go. *Reine floats a little off the ground so she's able to put her arms under his arms. After succeeding, they begin to fly upwards. A few others are also flying above the crowded markets and shops. Reine goes a little higher as she activates Fukashi* **Reine**: Uhh~, forgot I can't use the Dermal when going through the Gate. **Yashi**: Welp. *Reine stops to Reverse her Dermal and covers Yashi with an Ikkasei of her aura with a Barre. Niola speeds up as they go through the gate. Turning right, after leaving the Gate, Niola goes even higher in the sky and casts her Dermal again* **Reine**: It's been a while since I've been to Menium. **Yashi**: I thought adventures had to get classified every month by their top General of the Seira they were born in? **Reine**: Yeah, well . . . not this one. *Reine's arms glow red as she activates Zoka Strength* I'd never thought one day I'd be carrying the Hero around Macadamia. It feels kinda cool. **Yashi**: I'm just happy you're not crazy about me, it makes this so much easier. **Reine**(m): I wouldn't say that. **Yashi**: What? **Reine**: Nothing.

-A few hours pass before they see the H.Q. of Macadamia's army-

Yashi: Oh~, we're here. **Reine**: In good timing too. *Reine slowly descends as they get closer to the gate. On the ground, a couple feet inside the forest* **Yashi**: How do you want this to go? Want me to transform here, or in front of them? **Reine**: I want to see you transform in front of the Balancers, haha. *Yashi and Reine start walking towards the gate* **Reine**(w): You still have some of my aura coming off you, it's like there's a tiny me in the area. **Yashi**(w): I couldn't, not a tiny you. *Silence as they walk* So, you're Dermal. What did you base it off of? *Reine looks up at the sky and puts her right index finger on her chin* **Reine**(w): Hmm~, if I remember correctly . . . Stamina conservative and it raises my base efficiency up. *As Reine finishes her sentence they stop. Two circles appear in the ground in front of them. Two figures come up from them. They're Balancers* *Balancer*(A & B): State your business. *Reine*(w): That's your cue. *Bright lights beam into the air from the bottom of Yashi's cloak, multiple different particles fill the surrounding area around him, the ground under him starts to slightly crack. Finally, the dark, purple Dermal overlaps his body. The waves from the transformation blow both Yáshido's and Reine's hoodies off. Looking up at the Balancers, they try to stand in position. Reine next to him has a thin Barre in front of her and Reverses it after Yáshido is done. Yáshido looks around himself* *Yáshido*: Did I go overboard? *Balancer*(A): Yáshido? Maybe a bit overboard. *Reine*: Hahahaha, they were so scared. *Balancer*(B): We were not! *Balancer*(A): Speak for yourself, I thought he was a Dicipient. I was literally going to Protojet a Void at him while he was transforming, and gratefully I am glad I did not. *Balancer*(B): Who's the girl? *Yáshido*: My Familiar. *Balancer*(A): You got a Familiar now? Nice. *Balancer B holds Balancer A by the shoulder and whispers something to him. Suddenly, both of them are back to being serious* *Balancer*(B): General Opaine has been expecting you. Follow us. *Yáshido*: With pleasure. *As they turn around, Yáshido can see their nameplates. 334 is the Balancer they just talked to and 399 is the aiding Balancer. The five of them enter through the gate. Once in, multiple Balancers stand guard at the top of the gate wall. From the inside, you can see a Particle Magic plating going all around the top with Fukashi on it. As they enter the main building, there are multiple groups of Balancers, talking about plans and recruits. In the middle of the land, there is a training ground much like the one Taku made, but rectangular and made out of a harder material. A few that Yáshido notices from before. With everyone they pass by, they nod down while covering their swords handle or just say 'Yáshido'. Yáshido greets them all equally. They soon enter another building where it is quiet enough to hear yourself breathe. A Balancer is spread out for each third door pin the corridor. Walking all the way down to the final door, 334 talks to the Balancer that stand there. 334 and 399 stand against the wall. The Balancer standing in front of the door opens it and 334 motions them inside as he walks in first. Above the door reads 'General Vius Opaine' in italics. Inside, the room has one yellow light aiming down at a table in the middle of the room. The table has many documents, maps, and Mangoles open that are organized in a way that only Zoka Vision could make sense of it. The walls have larger maps on them of Macadamia, Digona, Catalyst, and Zenni. A few Balancers are off to the sides working on their own tasks either using large Mangoles that are connected into the wall or a writing on documents. An mTV sits on the wall opposite the door, with someone in a chair, presumably General Opaine, looking at it. The door closes after the Balancer behind Reine enters. Not a single person in the room looks at them* *Balancer*(334): General Opaine, Yáshido is here. *With only a few Balancers looking over at them, the chair slowly swings around. General Opaine has a unique Dermal on. Red and purple with multiple designs and metals protruding from it, representing a Macadamian General and a

170

white wreath on his right shoulder representing an Edasian Council Member* **Vius**: Oh~, Yáshido, it's great to see that you're well. **Yáshido**: Yeah. *General Opaine's eyes shallow* **Vius**: I can tell by your expression, you didn't come here just to talk about all the mess that's going on, but you want something. **Yáshido**(thts): Woah, and I thought I was doing a good job trying to hide it. *The room becomes quiet* **Yáshido**: You've seen the news, so you know the gist of things. **Vius**: And I intend on knowing more. Enlighten me, please. First, start off with Dia. *Silence* **Yáshido**: I can only give you the benefit of a doubt and say that she hasn't gone to the bad side. **Vius**: Hmph, I see. So~, thousands of casualties, thousands of property damage placed on Macadamia, someone who has been with you since the beginning killing innocent lives, all of those things, but yet you still believe that she hasn't gone bad? *General Opaine laughs out of confusion* There's an entire recording of her doing it, she was even seen with other Dicipients, haha. *Suddenly, Yáshido feels a deep pain in his head. He remembers what happened with Moon before he left for Dreium. The pain causes him to stop breathing for a few seconds* I know you've seen it. No matter where you've been, the whole world has by this point. **Yáshido**: Let's say she has converted, what would that make of me? *General Opaine leans back in his chair* **Vius**: Good question. I can't answer because I don't know. It's not like I can make you accountable for her actions. Even so, you could be the reason. **Yáshido**: Everyone wants to know more about what's going on, right? **Vius**: Agreed. **Yáshido**: That category includes me as well. **Vius**: Even you? **Yáshido**: I can't give you a single thread of an idea on why she attacked Regra. I'm just as confused alright. I even talked to her after she did it, and still, she left me nothing about what she was planning, but what I got from it is that . . . it's something that she's hiding from Korosi. **Vius**: Hmph. *General Opaine's chair turns away from Yáshido* I've been alive long enough to tell you that that's not the case, boy. You might be the Hero, but you don't have the experience to know when you're being fooled. I'd say, she'll do it again. To another Seira. *Yáshido feels his hands ball up once more* **Yáshido**: I object to that. She wouldn't, not again. *General Opaine's chair swiftly turns back around* **Vius**: But who's stopping her? She clearly doesn't care what you think anymore. You said it yourself, you talked to her and still, she didn't tell you 'nothing. I feel remorse for Regra, attacked so ruthlessly and flawlessly. They recouped enough to not make the situation seem entirely bad from a nation to nation view. It's just that Dia did it of all people that's bringing chaos. Put Macadamia in its place, however, how would you feel then, Hero? **Yáshido**: Of course . . . I'd be angry. I would never be able to forgive Dia if she attacked Macadamia. **Vius**: But I thought you were supposed to protect all Seiras? That sounds very selfish of you. **Yáshido**: I try my best, I really do. It's impossible for me or anyone else to protect every Seira. **Vius**: And yet, you tell no one about your departure to Darku? *Yáshido starts talking with more tone in his voice* **Yáshido**: You're saying the problem isn't obviously me, but Dia, right? **Vius**: I think thousands of lives would agree with that statement, and the Generals of Regra. **Yáshido**: Sounds like to me . . . you could care less about Dia and want to take her down . . . **Vius**: You wouldn't think the same way towards anyone else who starts killing people for no reason? Some Dicipients I only meet once before they were locked away in prison for the rest of their lives. Why? We just do it right because their a Dicipient, working under Lark, right? But it's different when it's your 'girl' who you've been with your whole life? Why should I show any sympathy to a little girl who murdered someone on air?! **Yáshido**: Something you apparently wouldn't understand. *Vius clears his throat* **Vius**: Sorry, that was not necessary on my part. I do understand the grief, and I am sorry that this has occurred, but Yáshido I'm a General, a Council member, I'm thinking about the future of my civilians. However, I see that you don't want me expressing my current feelings about Dia, so I'll leave it at that. *Yáshido feels Reine's eyes scan over him* **Yáshido**: Thank you for taking my feelings into account . . . General. **Vius**: Let's get back to the main topic, why are you here? *Yáshido looks at all the Balancers looking at him without turning his head* **Yáshido**: I want to request a Flag Treaty under-, **Vius**: If you are referring to the name that's lingering in my head, I think you may as well leave now. **Yáshido**: Hear me out on this. *General Opaine leans up in his chair* **Vius**: Tsk, I knew it. The Fallen one has gotten to you first. *Yáshido takes a step forward* **Yáshido**: General, it's more complex than that. **Vius**: You honestly believe that I would give a Flag Treaty, Macadamian sacred property, land that has been passed down a thousand years to someone who has killed some of the very people who have made this civilization what it is today? **Yáshido**: I thought about the same thing, but you need to look past that just like I did. Think of the opportunities we may have from having Taku on our side in full. **Vius**: Look past it? What opportunities could a single Dicipient give us that could turn the tides in our favor? **Yáshido**: We'll never no unless you give it a shot. I alone can't give him what he needs, it could benefit me in helping defeat Korosi. **Vius**: So why hasn't he told you the information already? **Yáshido**: He needs a wider audience. It's not just for me as a scheme, but for everyone I suppose. *Vius sighs as he facepalms onto his wrists* **Vius**: Even coming from the Hero himself, the words you say are hard to believe. **Yáshido**: If it does not seem like something you want to do, I understand. There are Council members who could execute what I want. Who can see in which direction we could take this. *With Vius looking up at Yáshido with a stern expression, the tension in the room rises* **Vius**: To think you'd even have what it takes to speak to me like that. What makes you so sure that he's trustworthy, Yáshido? **Yáshido**: We both fought-, **Vius**: Let me stop you before you finish that sentence. I've never laid a sword on him. Every time I was close, that Trants Savanna had shown up and held me back. Annoying little knight she is, but I guess a good soldier is supposed to do exactly that. With that said, what makes you so sure he's trustworthy, Hero? **Yáshido**: About four days ago is when we associated. He told me nearly everything and concluded that he wants to go against Korosi. He's made it clear to the Jurono students, and me that he will explain everything once he has the proper attention. I just need you to do this for me, then Taku will willingly explain everything he knows. *General Opaine turns around* **Vius**: Go against Korosi, huh? **Yáshido**: The thing is, he's been training them with professionals who've already sought up in helping him achieve his goal. **Vius**: The students from Jurono, seriously? No joke? **Yáshido**: I stand by my word. Now to expand further, he needs a Flag Treaty. That's why I'm here now. With this, I might give us an upper hand on Korosi. **Vius**: Hm~ . . . Alright, this is what I like to hear. I'll tell you now. Maya's tearm in Macadamia has ended. She and Andreas have been monitoring you all for the past few days. I don't know much, but it really backs up your claims. What do I have to go by other than your pure honesty? That is a trait I am very fund of the Heroes. However, you know should be aware that I cannot simply just give you one on his behalf. He has to speak to me directly. **Yáshido**: That is doable-. **Vius**: Wait, I want to ask you a few questions that may alter me doing this early. *Yáshido nods as General Opaine turns back towards him* Has he told you specifically why he left Korosi? **Yáshido**: An invasion of some kind on Edasia. **Vius**: Hm . . . I assume that Taku has been to any of the Temples because of their current alias? **Yáshido**: Not that I know of. **Vius**: I see. Last question, was it his or your idea to come to speak with me? **Yáshido**: I did this under my own intentions. **Vius**: Major spaces indeed, but, I'll accept those answers. There's still daylight outside, lots of it, so how about you bring Taku here? *Yáshido slightly jolts forward trying to hide his happiness* **Yáshido**: SO, you're going to help? **Vius**: Am I going to help? Look at me Yáshido, I'm a Council member and a General, I'm going to do what's right for every Seira, Droxima, and every other place on this planet. **Yáshido**: And that's giving him a Flag Treaty, good. *General Opaine and few Balancers laugh* **Vius**: You have a good sense of humor. *General Opaine rubs his chin* That was actually so funny that I'll send one of my elites with you to bring him back. *Even more Balancers starts to laugh* HTB, this is your task. *A Balancer comes from the left of General Opaine* **HTB**: Affirmative. **Balancer**(C): Really, General Opaine? I thought you were joking? **Vius**: It's only right for him to be invited and have him be at his most comfortability. *HTB walks in front of Yáshido and they nod at each other. They start walking towards the open door* Taku has till the day is over to show his face, HTB. **HTB**: Affirmative. *After leaving the complex and walking out of the building's view, Yáshido stops* Where are we heading, Hero? **Yáshido**: A small part between Distome and Ruby. **HTB**: Oh, that's, that's pretty far. *They continue walking* **Yáshido**: We can fly if you want to, HTB. **HTB**: We can walk until we get to Hina. **Yáshido**: Hina's still in Macadamia? I thought she had been transported to Zenni? **HTB**: I thought the same thing. Turns out Zenni had sent multiple requests for teleporters before her, and a few actually decided to accept it before Hina could even get registered. General Gordon gave her a new contract that paid her a little more since she's closer to the base than before, so really it was a huge benefit for her. **Yáshido**: Does she teleport the same as before? **HTB**: Whew, I'm glad she doesn't. She can teleport back and forth now. **Yáshido**: General Gordon did a nice job with that contract. Surprised she never reformed it herself since the first was . . . was her doing her own thing. **HTB**: Everyone has said that, and I don't know why. I guess only a few knew Hina had problems with the Council. **Yáshido**: Really? My first time hearing this. **HTB**: Yeah, I was there when it happened. When was this . . . It was before she was registered as a Teleporter so around seven years ago. I was an intern guard or something like that for the Edasian Council meeting in . . . Adenine. She was called in because of unlicensed teleporting. It was nothing too bad because it was between two peaceful Seiras, but she still wasn't supposed to be doing it, so they took off multiple abilities that she had requested when she finally wanted to be registered a couple weeks later after the incident. One of them was back warding teleports. **Yáshido**: Hm, well, that sucks. I never knew that though. All these years, I just thought she was ignorant. **HTB**: Hah, you sound like the majority. *While walking, HTB peeks back at Reine* **HTB**: So, I assume you're Yáshido's first Familiar. What's your name? **Reine**: Reine. **HTB**: How do you spell it? **Reine**: Yáshido, how do you spell my name? **Yáshido**: R. E. I. N. E. Reine. **HTB**: Oh, okay. What did Yáshido make you specialize at? **Reine**: Kosai. *HTB looks at Yáshido* **HTB**: You're going to be an easy target if all you use is Kosai for all your main Elilaments. **Yáshido**: I kind of slide in Pure Energy in there, but no one has really taken advantage of that. **HTB**: What about Teoka? **Yáshido**: That was a practice match, and plus it was the only thing I was using the entire match, and no one has since then . . . really. **HTB**: You don't want to jinx it now. *Yáshido and HTB laugh* When we get there, do you want me to close my eyes or something? **Yáshido**: No, in a few days everyone's going to know about it. **HTB**: I see, you're that confident that General Opaine is going to give Taku a Flag Treaty? **Yáshido**: I can only hope at this point. I'm not the type to control everything like some of the Heroes before me, and I've been establishing that since I became the Hero. Whether he arrests him, interrogates him, or gives him one. They see all those options as a benefit. **HTB**: Well Hero, I have hopes for the guy as well, so I do hope he gets it. And, that's just more uh~, strong allies, right? **Yáshido**: Yeah, exactly. **HTB**: I feel a bit sympathetic for the General. Being the first General to be in the Edasian Council too, I see on a daily basis on how much work he puts in. And the way he is makes people you know, 'afraid', I guess. **Yáshido**: I know what you mean. **HTB**: Right? But the time I've got to grow up under him, gaining my status and all that, he does have a soft spot for emotional situations. **Yáshido**: That's good to hear. **HTB**: Hey, I'm just saying, it's no secret to say that people are scared of General Opaine. **Yáshido**: And being a past Dicipient is supposed to make them less scared? **HTB**: Yeah, possibly. I don't know. **Reine**: What about you, are you scared of him? **HTB**: Me? Not of him, but what he might do too bad people caught. I've witnessed some crazy things after becoming a Balancer, and General Opaine has at least three spots in the top ten. By the way, have you seen the new interrogation room? Man, I feel creeped out just by thinking about it. **Yáshido**: I heard another Balancer talk about it, is it that bad? **HTB**: Ooh boy, you'll have to take time out and see for yourself, Hero. **Yáshido**: Definitely when I get the chance. *Yáshido feels nearby auras, but can't tell if they are friendly or foe. Continuing to walk, Reine stops in her tracks looking into the right of the forest* **Reine**: Yáshido, I think we have a problem. **Yáshido**: A problem? You must feel that too, Reine? **Reine**: Yeah. *HTB also looks to the right* **HTB**: That aura is all bundled up, but it feels familiar. *Yáshido spectates as he watches Reine's eyes turn gray* **Reine**: They're . . . some kind of bandits . . . using Aced Fukashi. **HTB**: I see them now too. **Yáshido**(thts): This is why Ace matters. **Reine**: They're not facing us. *Looks at Yáshido* What do you want to do? **Yáshido**: Since I can't see them, HTB, Protojet a Celestial at them. Try not to make it obvious. **HTB**: Affirmative. ^Without a second thought, HTB glows red with the combination of light blue around his arms and instantly throws a spear into the forest. They all watch the spear break apart before a purple Barre appears covering that section of trees^ **Reine**: Ca-, camouflage? **HTB**: Wait, a completely unnoticeable Barre? **Yáshido**: Aced Uhnyoi, so it wasn't a hold, and the auras are gone? **Reine**: No time, let's check it out before they get away! ^All three of them glow in blue light as they dash over the collapsing Barre. Reine beating everyone to the bodies, she tapes on it before it breaks into pieces soundless^ **Reine**: These are, ragdolls? *As Yáshido lands next to Reine, two all-black ragdolls about the same height as he lay motionless on the ground*

Chapter 15 - Intruding Dicipients

HTB: This is strange. Was this meant to be a trap or something? ^HTB points at the opposite end and another path is on the other side from where they just came from. As Yáshido looks at the second path. He hears movement behind him and instantly summons a Barre surrounding the three of them. A second later and something powerful hits the Barre moving the entire Magical device backward. Yáshido is still holding his hands up, supplying the Barre so that it won't fade away. Yáshido feels something slowly freezing over the Barre starting from the direction of contact with the attack^ **Yáshido**(thts): The ice and the aura, it's got to be Povroca. **Yáshido**: It's an ambush, summon your weapons now! **Reine & HTB**: Okay! **HTB**: Maca Sudo! ^A long sword appears in HTB's hands. A large amount of fire shoots out from Reine's back into two tekCircles that float next to her. A fiery color oozes around her body like an aura. The freezing on the Barre becomes more intense as it starts to crack on the sides. Then, another blast comes from behind Yáshido and hits that side of the Barre. The cracks become larger as the Barre starts to leak water from the outside in^ **Yáshido**(thts): That must be Nvonka then. **Yáshido**: Two Dicipients, Povroca and Nvonka. **HTB**: Yeah, I'd recognize those auras from anywhere. **Reine**: You jinxed it. **Yáshido**: But just in case I'm wrong, you two take the fire user, I'll handle the ice user. **Reine & HTB**: Got it! *The Barre completely breaks* **Yáshido**: Jeshika! ^Yáshido already has his sword in a slashing position as he comes out of the Particles. Nearly hitting the figure in front of him, he activates his highest stages of his Zokas. His sword collides with the figure's ice and freezes over. Getting a good look at the figure, they have a sadistic smile^ **Yáshido**(thts): It is them. ^Yáshido comes back down with multiple attacks, Povroca guards by throwing blocks of ice or dodges. After one attack, Yáshido lowers one of his hands while swinging and fires an electric charge right through the ice as Povroca makes a wall of it. The electric sparks crack through the ice and shock Povroca. Yáshido plows right through the remains of ice wall and Povroca is stuck in mid-air with the electricity flowing all around his body^ **Yáshido**: Collision Breaker! ^The ice melts off of Jeshika and she glows with a yellow stream of light in all directions. Yáshido flashes from multiple spots before right in front of Povroca about to hit him^ **Reine**(Protojet): Hero! Behind you! ^Instead of doing a direct hit, Yáshido splits the move into a spin by using Protojet in a circle. A large fireball gets knocked away into a tree, and Povroca becomes mobile again dodging before Yáshido could hit him. Both Povroca and

Yáshido land a couple feet from each other. As Yáshido measures and tries to guess what Povroca will do next, then notices Povroca's casting something^ **Yáshido**(thts): Is that another blast, wait no that's a-, **Povroca**: Haha! I didn't expect to run into you, Yáshido. Unfortunately for me, I don't have enough Oplitals to take you down right now! But Dia will be quite pleased to know you're still in Macadamia. Come on, Nvonka! ^Yáshido gets kicked into the ground from behind. Yáshido immediately jumps towards Nvonka who is flipping in the air, but she has two hands pointed at him casting two more fireballs. Instead of attacking, Yáshido blocks the two incoming attacks. The fireballs hit his forearms as if they absorbed them. Nvonka lands behind Povroca holding his shoulder^ **Povroca**: See you on the flipside! ^Multiple colors of energy enter the palms of Povroca's hands as he points them at Yáshido. An immense wave of energy fills Yáshido's view, but nothing hits him. The white light fades and he is in a Barre. Still standing up as if he was going to eat the attack head-on, he turns around to see Reine and HTB also in the Barrier^ **Reine**: Haha, what are you doing? **Yáshido**: What do you mean? **Reine**: You were just standing there like that wasn't going to do anything to you. **Yáshido**: It wasn't. **HTB**: Hm, well that means you're alright then. *The Barre quickly fades away. All the trees in an eleven-yard radius from the exterior of the Barre are gone and trees up to twenty yards are scorched. The crust of Edasia around the Barre was completely exposed in a ring-like shape* Tsk, pesky Dicipients, I didn't even get a hit on her. **Reine**: Same. **Yáshido**: Well, I hit Pov with a Stage I Denki shock, so he still has to recover from that. **Reine**: Yáshido, remember what I told you I could do. *Reine's aura starts to appear* **Yáshido**: Wait, so you know where they went? *Reine stops her Ikkasei* **Reine**: I didn't get a lot, but Nvonka. If you want to go, we need to go now before she gets too far. **Yáshido**: Okay, we'll follow your lead, Reine. *Reine nods as she flys up above the trees. Yáshido and HTB follow. While they are flying speedily* **HTB**: What a great Familiar you have, Hero. **Yáshido**: Hmph, thanks. *Reine dips down through the leaves. They follow down into the branches. On the ground, the three of them use Fukashi. **Yáshido**(w): Details? **Reine**(w): Well, they are opposite us, but further right. Seems as if Nvonka is healing Povroca. This time they're just using Stage II, so you can see them now. **Yáshido**(w): Good. *Yáshido activates Fukashi Vision and Uhnyoi while scanning through the forest opposite of them. He spots where they are. Nvonka's hands are hovering above Povroca. With Uhnyoi, Yáshido can sense that Nvonka is using Stage I Patchi Tekiyo and Stage III Konseitsu while Povroca is using a Stage II Fukashi* **Yáshido**(thts): He's holding the Fukashi while she's healing. Hmm . . . **Reine**(w): But Balancers are coming. **HTB**(w): Balancers? *HTB and Yáshido look down the path and sense three auras and each with the Flight Elilament coming towards them* **Yáshido**(w): Either . . . HTB could go out there and tell them what just happened and form a counterattack, or we could wait till they pass. *Reine looks at Yáshido* **Reine**(w): How would the former work exactly? I don't think we'd have enough time for that, Yáshido.

Yáshido(w): So just wait? *Reine*(w): Just wait. *Looking down the path, three Balancers start slowing down before stopping right between the Dicipients and them. Two of the Balancers are Macadamian Balancers, but the other has a blue color with a completely new style* *Yáshido*(thts): Zennian Balancer? *Balancer*(Zennian): Flipping flip, I don't know what happened down there, but it looks like it's over. *Balancer*(A): Watch your tongue, 117. *Balancer*(117): Yeah, my bad. *Balancer*(B): Felt like Yáshido, HTB, and someone else was fighting them. *Balancer*(117): You're crazy. There's no way he would be here coincidentally when there would be Dicipients. *Balancer*(A): He could be right, 117. General did say that Yáshido stopped by not too long ago. *Balancer*(117): Well never mind then. *Balancer*(B): I still can't believe we lost them. *Balancer*(A): True. *Balancer*(117): You think they ran because they were outnumbered? *Balancer*(A): If that's the case, why'd they attack us first? *Balancer*(117): Good point, but it could be that they thought we knew they were there. *Balancer*(A): Hey, you think we should report back while they're still in our Proxima[City]. I mean, they are Dicipients, in Macadamia. *Balancer*(117): That's our job, no? Actually, you and I will keep searching. 378, you can sound the alarm. *Balancer*(378): That's perfect, we just flew right past one. *378 levitates before flying back off in the direction they came from. Yáshido looks back at Nvonka and they seem to be watching the two remaining Balancers. Suddenly they vanish from Yáshido's sight* *Yáshido*(w): Woah, what just happened? *Reine*(w): They canceled out the waves of a Fukashi Barrier with another Barrier that has . . . Fukashi? That's insane. *HTB*(w): What?! That's impossible! You can't do that with a Barre, not even with a Personal Cast. *Yáshido*(w): Can anyone still see them? *HTB*(w): No. *Reine*(w): Wait, I can. Ace. *HTB*(w): I have Ace, and I can't. *Reine*(w): Reverse it and cast it as a *carry*. See if that works, that's what I just did. *Reine slowly starts moving down the forest trying not to disturb the surroundings as she watches the two still Balancers* *HTB*(w): Hm, still nothing. *Yáshido and HTB follow Reine* *Balancer*(117): Come on 390, let's go. *Balancer*(390): Right. *117 and 390 lift up off the ground and continue their search down the path. They fly slow enough that Yáshido's group can keep up* *Reine*(w): They're getting awfully close. If they're planning to attack, it would be any second now. *Yáshido*(w): I got a plan. *HTB*(w): Speak your mind, Hero. *Looking at HTB, the way his helmet is aligned towards Yáshido, he looks so as serious as one can get* *Yáshido*(thts): Haha, what. I've never heard anyone say that before. *Yáshido shakes his head to get back focused* *Yáshido*(w): Elilament Adapt. *HTB*(w): The ice from your sword? *Yáshido*(w): Yeah. When they attack, you two go out, and I'll be able to freeze one of them. *Reine*(w): Freezing them? *HTB*(w): Slightly easier capture. *Yáshido*(w): It'll take a minute to make sure there's no way they can cancel it out, so you both might be fighting for a while. Are you two okay with that? *Reine*(w): I get to fight Dicipients already? *HTB*(w): I'm up for it. *Yáshido*(w): Pick your targets. *Reine*(w): I want the fire user. *HTB*(w): Guess that leaves Povroca to me. *After a minute of following, the quiet siren rings through the forest*

Reine(w): Nvonka's moving fast. *Balancer*(117): Good that's the siren, let's go up now. *Reine*(w): GO!!! *Yáshido stays put as Reine and HTB disable their Fukashi, glowing with a mixture of red and light blue, and jump out of the forest towards Nvonka and Povroca. As the two Balancers start flying up into the sky, Yáshido watches Nvonka Protojet from her side of the forest with a dense pocket of fire in her right palm about to hit Balancer 117. Before Nvonka lands the hit, Reine reaches her first and gets a powerful blow with her fist in the right side of Nvonka's stomach. Reine doesn't hesitate and immediately shoots a long wave of fire into Nvonka's side. The controlled Kosai in Nvonka's hands flys off and combusts in the air away from everyone. The Balancers look down in amazement as they watch someone hitting a tree and ricocheting towards them before hitting the ground under them. The smoke covering Nvonka gets pushed away immediately as she stands with Reine's flames still scorching around her body. Everyone in the area can feel the flames taking the small bits of Sustain from her. Nvonka huffs and a powerful wind comes from her body blowing away the small flames. A white smoke leaks off her clothing. Another explosion happens higher up in the air as HTB lands back down with his left arm completely covered in ice. The other two Balancers land behind him. A Barre suddenly surrounds everyone blanking out the siren sound* *HTB*: Barrier? Did you do that, Reine? *Reine*: No. *Balancer*(390): HTB? *HTB*: No time to explain, I'm going to need you two to help me take them down. *Balancer*(117): Of course! Zaten Naga! *117 summons a Naginata* *Balancer*(390): Maca Sudo! *390 summons a sword similar to HTB's. Povroca lands next to Nvonka with a smug look on his face* *Povroca*: Ha! Trying to call more Balancers to make this easier, are you? I admit, you all caught me off guard before. Now you seem to be failing at the only occupation you're able to achieve. *HTB*: Hm, you can't win, Povroca. *Povroca*: What seriously?! I'm not weak like Saramaenous. Haha, all of you combined couldn't even defeat me. What makes you think you can hold us both? *HTB*: I'd just say you're a bit too cocky. *HTB stands guard* *Povroca*: Oh really? Why don't you show them, Nvon-, *Povroca pauses as he looks at Nvonka* Nvonka, are you alright? *Nvonka*: The girl . . . she hit me. *Povroca*: What? The Familiar? *Nvonka clenches her fists* *Nvonka*: Yes. *By Reine* *Reine*(w): Is she talking about me? *All of the Balancers turn towards Reine* *Balancer*(117)(w): Well, you're the only Familiar over here. . . and girl for that matter. So who knows. *Reine*(w): She is talking about me! *Reine looks back over at Nvonka. When they make eye contact, Nvonka has the meanest look on her face. A red flame goes through Nvonka's eyes and she lifts up her head and runs a finger across her neck. Reine jumps back in response* *Reine*(Y): DID YOU SEE THAT?! *HTB*: No, what happened? *Reine*: She just-, *Povroca*: Hey, Familiar! *Reine*: Ye-, yeah? *Yáshido facepalms* *Yáshido*(thts): Why would you respond, that's the last thing you'd want to do with a Dicipient. *Povroca*: Looks like you made my friend here quite mad, and now she wants to fight. *Nvonka*(m): I'm going to burn her. *Povroca*: She's going to burn you. *HTB points his sword at eye level towards Povroca* **HTB**: I don't think I'm going to let that happen. *Povroca raises his hand covering the left side of his face. Ice starts to form on Povroca's wrist and bundles up his hand making a long ice blade* **Povroca**: Woah there, don't think you're going anywhere, other than fighting me. Make your choice, before I help her. **HTB**: Help what? Burn the Familiar? **ovroca**: What else could I be referring to? **HTB**: You think you're trying to be funny Povroca, but we all know you can't burn people with ice. **Povroca**: What do you mean you can't, of course you can. **HTB**: With ice? No, you can't. Frostbite doesn't count, Povroca. **Povroca**: Nvonka, tell them you can burn people with ice! *Nvonka is still staring at Reine* **Balancer**(117)(m): What about with salt? *Povroca turns back to the Balancers* **Povroca**: Hyah!!! *A wave of energy disperses from Povroca's body. Throwing any loose objects outward. A couple seconds later and he is surrounded in an icy blue color with small snowflake-like particles in his aura* There's only one way to find out. Now come on! Before I really change my mind! *Povroca jumps several dozen yards behind Nvonka. HTB looks back at Reine, she nods. HTB and the other Balancers follow Povroca and jump over Nvonka* **Povroca**(Y): Go Ahead And Start It Nvonka! **Nvonka**: Finally! Ha! ^Another Green Barre comes from Nvonka covering and causing the existing Barre to separate into two, one surrounding each group. At the same time, Nvonka's body surrounds itself in a deep red flame. It circles her until it reaches the top of her hair. The circling flames disappear, but the flames, in general, continue to grow until reaching the top of the Barre. The air pressure is so intense that Reine starts to slide backward even after holding up a guard. A tree next to Yáshido detaches from its roots and completely disintegrates in the hot air. The flames focus on the outline of Nvonka's body as her body appears as if she was melting. The golden light increases the temperature drastically in the Barre. The flame wall disappears, but the melting illusion of Nvonka stays. The ground under her begins the melt away into tiny particles that also disintegrates when it goes up into the air. Still golden, Nvonka arms stretch outward, and she creates fists with her hands. Two daggers appear around her arms, each one with two different blade-like structures on each end. The golden light shining from her slowly fades away. Once it all vanishes, Nvonka has a tiara on. The symbol of a skull with a flame around it sits on the front end of the tiara. As her pupils flash between multiple colors^ **Yáshido**(thts): Her Stage I Dermal. Hmm~, if Reine still uses the same Dermal from last time, this could be problematic. **Nvonka**: Hehehehe, hahahaha, HAHAHAHAHA. *As Nvonka stops laughing, she smirks* Not so confident now our we, Familiar? *Closer to the edge of the Barre than before, Reine looks down at how far she sled before lowering her guarding arms* **Reine**: Whoever would have said that? **Nvonka**: Let's see what you can do, I want to be entertained before killing you. *Reine angrily frowns* **Reine**: Sadly for you, I don't think that will happen. **Nvonka**: Hehehehe. ^Nvonka slashes her right dagger diagonally, right to left, downward. ^Yáshido sees about five fireballs appear above Reine, all flying down at her really fast.

With little time to counter, Reine uses Zoka Swiftness to instantly move out of the way, barely dodging the three fireballs. Nvonka forces the three fireballs to explode as they pass Reine. Reine gets rocketed across the Barre. To lighten the fall, Reine summons a Particle-Block that her back hits and she lands softly on the ground before her aura becomes dominant once more. Looking back at the other two fireballs, they hit the edge of the Barre, exploding back inward. Reine turns back around to see Nvonka landing closer to her^ **Reine**: Fine then. My turn. ^Reine's body levitates off the ground. Suddenly, bursts of fire spas off of her like ripples in water, but they only go so far before disappearing into thin air. Reine's entire body soon becomes enveloped in flames. This sudden appearance of fire causes a huge sound wave that nearly causes Yáshido to slide backwards^ **Yáshido**(thts): Woah. *Nvonka stands still watching Reine; Not intimidated at all. The flames around Reine shrink as if her Dermal was absorbing it. Still with a fiery aura, once all of the flames have been devoured, the back of her hair is a bit longer and shifts into a red tone. A plate of armor goes around her forehead, causing her front curls to go up and over it; making them point sideways. Reine's Dermal is also more Familiar-advanced as if she was a Charlie. The same fingerless gloves appear on her hands that she wears in her Adventurer outfit. Two tekCircles unwrap from the remaining flames and float above Reine's open palms* **Yáshido**(thts): That is one big upgrade for a Familiar Dermal clone. It just barely rivals Nvonka's current state from raw potential. But fighting wise, I can judge, and Nvonka isn't using her highest output Dermal. My best choice would be to attack before Niola is too far hurt. *Yáshido's sword is surrounded by ice and rapidly shaking. He puts a Konseitsu around himself and ups his Fukashi once more to keep his sword from giving away his location* **Nvonka**: I was going to ask who's Familiar you are, but it's clear that you're actually not even a Familiar. **Reine**: What makes you say that? **Nvonka**: Your aura. *Reine steps back* **Reine**(m): What? **Nvonka**: Hahahahaha, so it turns out that more people can manipulate other people's aura other than Dicipients. Observe. *Nvonka's body visible shifts as if there was a second her and now her aura emits as it was Vekfla's* **Yáshido**(thts) & **Reine**: How? **Nvonka**: Impressed? Hahahahaha. Too bad you made me angry, I would have told you a little bit about it. Now I'm going to finish you quickly. *Reine grins* **Reine**: Yeah? **Nvonka**: Hahahaha. *As Reine's grin goes away, they stare at each other. Nvonka changes her stance to a fighting one. Reine slowly leans her arms back. Each of their flames brightens in luminosity. Nvonka closes her eyes* ^Without warning, Reine aims the tekCircles at Nvonka and fires a tremendous number of fireballs. Nvonka slices and dodges through them while moving forward^ **Reine**: HA!~ ^Reine's tekCircles double in size, and so do the fireballs balls shooting out of them. Loud cannon sounds immerse from each fireball being shot out. Nvonka surrounds herself with a ball of electricity. When the fireballs hit Nvonka, it just fades away. Reine stops firing and reverts the size of the tekCircles back to normal as they float behind her back. Reine points her arms forward and makes fists with her hands. A light of energy runs down both of her arms and down off her balled hands. A short metal scythe appears in each of her grasps. Nvonka comes out of the fireball with a spinning kick. While kicking, flames surround her leg and at the end of the kick the flames continue on as their own wave. Reine jumps over the wave. Coming back down, Nvonka is mid-air charging towards her. Each of their blades collide. Reine thrusts her arms with a Protojet outwards after the collision which causes Nvonka's arms to spread open. Reine attempts to directly hit Nvonka in the chest with her Scythe, but Nvonka surrounds Reine's hand with a rope made out of Particle Magic. Nvonka aims at Reine's face then jolts her blade right at it. Reine holds up her left forearm to block the incoming hit. The block stops the momentum, but the blade still goes through Reine's guard knocking Reine's head back. Nvonka pulls the rope downward, but Reine Protojets backward diagonally higher in the air. Looking for Nvonka, Reine suddenly feels something squeeze her waist and constrict her movements. Looking down, two arms wrap around her with the hands overlapping each other facing towards her stomach. The grip tightens. Trying to turn around, Reine knows it's Nvonka^ **Nvonka**: This will end sooner than I thought. ^Reine's aura increases in size, but Nvonka's overlaps it^ **Reine**: Get off! ^Reine tries to elbow Nvonka. Successfully hitting Nvonka in her right abdomen, Nvonka's anger intensifies^ **Nvonka**: HA!~ ^Nvonka squeezes even harder, cracking Reine's Dermal around her waist. Nvonka's hands emit fire which slowly turns the contacting portion of Reine's Dermal red hot. Reine stops struggling to escape^ **Yáshido**(thts): What's going on? Why did she stop? **Nvonka**: Hahahaha. You gave up already?! I'm not even at Ace yet! **Reine**: Ahh~!!! ^Nvonka's Zoka Strength increases to Ace as she squeezes Reine almost at full power. Particles come from Reine's burning Dermal^ *Yáshido slowly stands up* **Yáshido**(thts): Crap, she's not going to make it. **Nvonka**: Let's see if you can take this. ^Nvonka's Dermal starts to shine^ **Nvonka**: Huh? ^Nvonka notices pink orbs float from Reine's feet. Nvonka also feels Reine's body vibrating. Reine's aura starts to reemerge^ **Reine**: No . . . not this easily! ^A burst of fire covers both Nvonka and Reine^ **Nvonka**(Y): You Think Your Fire Is Hotter Than Mine! How Wrong You Are! Eat This!!! Pairable Infernos!!! ^Nvonka's hands still attached to Reine's stomach grow vertical waves of fire that look like small galaxies. The red flames soon turn into purplish flames. Nvonka then crosses her legs around Reine's legs^ **Nvonka & Reine**(Y): HAA!!! ^The entire flame surrounding them turns purple as it grows in all parameters to a point where they are no longer seen. Then two more explosions happen inside the already giant holocaust, spreading even more fire outwards. Yáshido looks away from the immense light. The spreading fire goes over the trees, setting every tree inside the Barre on fire. Yáshido slides back as the flame roasts the bushes in front of him and hits him. Staying inside the warmth, Yáshido summons a small Barre and puts more ice inside of his already beaming sword. The light dims down as the ground stops vibrating. Yáshido looks up to see a body falling to the ground with dark smoke trailing it. Doing a barrel roll before standing up and turning around, the figure is Reine. Reine has a very angry facial expression while she stares at the spot she just came from. The bottom half of her Dermal is missing and multiple cracks are seen in her chestplate^ *Yáshido*(thts): I'm just now noticing, Niola's Oplitals are low considering what I felt from her max. That's not a good sign. *Yáshido puts even more of the ice Elilament inside of Jeshika. As the aftershock clears, Nvonka floats in the same location as before. She has the same face, but a more annoyed side to it. Reine's aura is faintly seen around her, but her power is still at its peak. Nvonka's aura hasn't changed one bit* *Nvonka*: That was one move you pulled, Niola. *Reine*: It's Reine. *Nvonka*: Reine? That must be your fake Familiar name. Took me a while to get it, but after tasting your aura myself, I couldn't not know who you were. *Reine*: All the more reason for you to be afraid. *Nvonka*: Afraid? Hahahaha, you might be strong for an adventurer, but you'll never rival a Dicipient. Especially not this one! *Reine*: Are you trying to make me go full out? I haven't even used my actual weapon. *Nvonka*: You're just asking to be killed? Aren't You?! Ha~! ^Nvonka charges down at Reine. Too fast to see, Reine gets hit in the chest before being slashed to the ground. Reine spins around to block Nvonka's next strike. As their blades collide, a huge ring of fire explodes outward. Reine backflips lands on her feet with Nvonka separating. Before Reine hits the ground, Nvonka Protojets toward her. Their blades collide again with a loud metal scratching sound. Strike after strike, Reine is slowly being pushed back. Nvonka comes in from the side, instead of dodging, Reine tries to impact Nvonka directly. Before making contact, Nvonka disappears. Reine's attack hits the air as her momentum continues and gets stunned from missing the powerful strike. Reine quickly looks up, to her left, and to her right. Suddenly, Nvonka appears in front of her. Nvonka knees Reine in the helmet then kicks Reine in the chest after spinning in a circle. Reine gets pelted away and lands back first in the ground. An explosion of electricity occurs from the blow^ *Yáshido*: A critical?! Why now of all times! ^Reine leans up with static around her body. A moment later, Nvonka stomps on Reine's chest from above. Rocks burst into the air. Nvonka grabs Reine and tosses her into to the air. Reine doesn't defend herself being stunned from the relentless attacks from Nvonka. Nvonka stabs Reine in the back after flying to her, and the blades pierce out onto the front of Reine's Dermal. A large amount of Pure Energy bursts from the front and rear of Reine's Dermal. Nvonka elbows Reine in the back of the head before casting a Particle-Block that Reine slams against. The Particle-Block explodes, knocking Reine back to Nvonka. Nvonka does a backflip kick, landing it on Reine's face. Reine plummets towards the ground before her stamina comes back. Reine flips facing Nvonka while in the air. Reine is visibly in pain as her entire Familiar Dermal is gone. Sje stares at Nvonka breathing heavily^ *Nvonka*: To think you could even think of beating me. *Reine*: Heh, well Miss Overconfident, I haven't been trying myself, but now you might have actually made me mad from that little stunt you did there. ^Nvonka points at Reine then points at herself^ **Nvonka**: Then show me your fire inside of you. ^Reine points at Nvonka^ **Reine**: You asked for it. ^A wave of wind sprees from Reine as hair shortens back and turns into its natural pink color. Another wave of wind comes off of Niola with a small amount of energy. She's back to her normal self. The Barre is nearly back to normal temperature, but Nvonka aura keeps it steadily warm. Niola holds her right arm out as far as possible holding it open facing away from her^ **Niola**: Nelion! ^Energy forms in her palms as she closes it, gripping the energy. A long-shadowed Scythe forms with Niola's invisible Dermal^ **Niola**: This is all I need. ^Niola's Scythe emits a dreadful sense of power as both Nvonka and Yáshido feel a visionless aura pass over them^ **Yáshido**(thts): Nelion, Niola's weapon of choice. An Aced Celestial Scythe. It feels so . . . dangerous. Nvonka's definitely going to go Ace her Dermal now, and Nvonka's Zoka Swiftness advantage isn't helping Niola out at all. **Nvonka**: Hahahaha, glad you're back to your pitiful self, Niola. *Rapidly, shards of fire in the shape of lightning bolts into the sky from Nvonka. The entire Barre fills with a bright dark blue light that shifts into white about five seconds in. Niola and Yáshido shield their eyes while Nvonka laughs in the background. The light vanishes all at once with Nvonka in her Aced Dermal. A mixture between a Dicipient's Dermal and her own personal Dermal. The tiara on her head has been replaced with a helmet. Niola's face has become slightly more frightened from the huge potential increase. However, Niola hides this fear as Nvonka turns toward her* I'll be happy to show you something with the Magic we have before you die. ^Nvonka's body shifts again as her aura changes to Niola's^ **Niola**: You're me now? How's that gonna benefit you? **Nvonka**: Turns out, using other people's aura while using their Pure Energy is almost double efficiency. With that, I can also do this. Nelion! ^A massive wave comes from what feels like Niola, two Niola's in two separate locations. In front of Nvonka, the same scythe Niola has started to form, but with flames around it. Nvonka grabs the Scythe with her right hand after blade around her right hand disappears. Niola takes a defensive stance^ **Niola**: That's problematic. **Nvonka**: You think so-, ^Instantly, a stream of blue light rushes for Niola. Using Aced Zoka Vision, Niola blocks the incoming attack. A loud sound of two powerful weapons colliding echoes throughout the Barre^ **Niola**: You can try as much as you can, but you're never going to beat me now. ^Niola swiftly kicks Nvonka away from her with neither Nvonka nor Yáshido seeing her move having Aced too. Lounging after her, Niola slices Nvonka by swinging her Scythe from her left. The blade of the scythe goes completely through Nvonka's Dermal. Niola then slices downward and Nvonka hits the ground chest first. The ground under Nvonka completely shatters and raises up in the air. Nvonka heals herself with Patchi Tekiyo before bouncing up and landing on her feet. Her facial expression emits nothing but pure hatred towards Niola^ **Nvonka**(Y): If Only That Did Anything! ^In a flash, Nvonka dashes over the thirty meters to Niola and stabs her right in the stomach with her one remaining blade, but Niola kicks her away and slices through her sides^ *Niola*: Hm! ^Nvonka removes herself from Nelion and disappears again. Coming from the right of Niola, Nvonka punctures and pushes the blade deeper in Niola's Dermal, however Niola barely swings around her Scythe stabbing Nvonka in the side before the pain rushes through her body^ *Nvonka*(Y): DIE!!! ^Flames rush down Nvonka's arms into Niola's Dermal exploding on contact. Niola smacks against the dirt in front of the crater Nvonka made earlier before falling inside of it. Taking a few seconds, Niola flys back up into view. Nvonka surrounds herself in flames and Protojets towards Niola. Niola blocks three attacks with little time to react between them. Niola slices down again, but Nvonka blocks it with her Nelion. In just under a half of a second, Niola Protojets to the top of the Barre and back down with a kick. However, Nvonka grabs on to Niola's leg before Niola hits her and swings Niola down even faster, but Niola rings Nelion around Nvonka's neck. Niola puts and Atoskito under them causing them to fall faster and they both smash against the ground. The impact becomes direct damage as both of them backflip away from each other and land on their feet^ *Nvonka*: Hehehe, someone's running out of time. *Niola looks at herself* *Niola*(m): She's right. *Niola makes slight eye contact with Yáshido before looking back at Nvonka* *Nvonka*: I've tarnished your Sustain, hahahaha. Not to mention it seems you were unprepared to fight in the first place. If you haven't noticed, this Barre you're in has been sucking you dry this entire time, and I've been absorbing it, hahahaha. *Niola*: You tell me why? *Nvonka*(Y): You were doomed to die from the beginning! ^Nvonka bolts toward and behind Niola. Niola blocks the strike as she turns around. However, Nvonka's strength suddenly increases and Niola takes a blow to the top of her chest. Niola's guard breaks as another loud noise spreads from the point of contact. Niola quickly hits the Barre at nearly two hundred and twenty miles per hour. Niola bounces off and lands a few yards from the Barre and almost twenty feet from Yáshido on her chest. Niola slowly stands up using her knees and arms to support her. Nvonka lands about twenty feet from Niola^ *Nvonka*: Hahahahaha. There's no escaping for you. ^Nvonka starts to walk towards Niola. Niola's tekCircles grow in size behind her. Both of them start to spin before decreasing to a tiny speck^ *Nvonka*: You still have more to give? ^Niola's scythe turns into Particles and appears attached to her back. Taking a deep breath, Niola opens her eyes and raises both her hands towards Nvonka^ *Yáshido*(thts): Don't do it, Niola. You'll be out of Oplitals and Nvonka won't hesitant to kill you. Niola's Sustain can't even take one more hit. I have to go now. *Nvonka*: Accept defeat and prepare for annihilation; you know at this point simple attacks don't work on me, and by what you have left, unfortunately for you, simple attacks is all you can do. *Niola*: Once again, you're assuming things. ^Nvonka is about ten feet from Niola. Nvonka slows her pace down Reversing her Nelion. Yáshido starts to make his way behind Nvonka^ *Nvonka*: What are gonna do then? *Niola*: If you keep walking towards me, you'll find out. *Nvonka*: Bluffing only makes your situation worse, Niola. ^Niola watches as Yáshido comes out from the burning collapsed trees as he Reverses his Fukashi. Yáshido stops a couple feet behind Nvonka^ **Niola:** Hmph! ^Niola shoots a small fire blast at Nvonka. Nvonka simply takes the hit and comes out of it walking unscratched^ **Nvonka:** A bluff it was. ^Nvonka shoots two rows of fire waves parallel to each other. The waves continue moving up the Barre after lining up the ground surrounding Niola in a rectangle. Nvonka has a direct path to Niola. Nvonka holds her hands out to her sides. A flame courses from her feet to her head, her flaming aura becomes purple^ **Nvonka:** My fire . . . is the hottest of them all . . . as if I had the sun itself embedded in my palms, only hotter. ^Nvonka stops five feet from Niola and she raises the hand that contains the immense power towards her. Niola feels invisible pulses of heat from Nvonka^ **Nvonka:** Niola, your career ends here. A life full of exploration and adventure ended by yours truly. Any words before you die? **Niola:** A few. Thanks for the battle, it was fun. I wish it could have lasted a little longer though. *An unsatisfied expression appears on Nvonka face* **Nvonka:** I'll~, enjoy killing~, you~. Bye-, bye! ^Another galaxy like disk forms at the palm of Nvonka's hand covering Niola's from Yáshido's view. Niola watches as she feels the strength of the attack running against her Dermal and pushing her back against the Barre behind her. Large gusts of wind spread from Nvonka's body blowing away loose rubble. As the spinning disk gets bigger in diameter, it starts to split the ground under it as it spins^ **Yáshido(Y):** Cold Tears, Nvonka! ^Yáshido unleashes all the Kori that has been building up in his Sword. The massive amount of exportation shakes the entire Barre as Yáshido thrusts towards Nvonka. Nvonka instinctively turns around with her left hand doing the same attack. Yáshido's sword penetrates through the Cast with ease because of its required time to finalize. Nvonka then tries to swing the already summoned attack over, but her left hand grabs touches the frosty blue sword. The ice quickly consumes her, freezing from her left hand over her entire body. The galaxy of flames slowly vanishes in thin air. Nvonka is fully concealed inside a thick layer of ice. Yáshido can no longer feel her aura. After the remains of the small galaxy disappear, the fire surrounding Niola and Green Barre vanishes all at once. Niola falls to the ground catching her breath. Yáshido swiftly runs to her^ **Yáshido:** Good job, Niola. I'm sorry you had to go through that, but you really stood up to her. *Yáshido starts to heal Niola* **Niola:** Man, my heart's beating so fast. I guess slacking around really does lower your stamina. I was thinking I would pass out before she'd do something to me. **Yáshido:** Well, we don't have to deal with her for a while. **Niola:** Oh~, my Oplitals. They're so low. How could she drain them so fast? **Yáshido:** For one, you were emitting so much from using Ikkasei alone, and then she directly absorbed a lot when she grabbed you. **Niola:** I know that, but before even fighting. My Pure Energy was lower than what I would expect. I mean, I haven't done much except for being in those two Dermals that don't even eat up Oplitals if I were to wear them for a whole week.

Yáshido: I noticed the same thing. *As Yáshido crouches above Niola, he scans around her hair with Zoka Vision* *Yáshido*(m): No way. *Niola looks up at him* **Niola**: What is it? *Yáshido slowly grabs a small patch of Niola's hair. It's purple. Instantly he starts to heal it. Once it's gone* **Yáshido**: There's more of that crystal stuff in your hair, Niola. **Niola**: What?! I thought I got it all?! **Yáshido**: Well, it seems to . . . *Both Niola and Yáshido look at the hole to their left at the same time. They both stand and fly over and hover above the hole* **Yáshido**: What are the chances. **Niola**: You've got to be kidding me. *In the hole, a dark light-reflecting purple crystal sits at the center of the pit. Yáshido activates Denryoku, the crystal's aura lushes throughout the entire hole* **Yáshido**: How rare exactly is this stuff? And you've had that on you for about four days now? I hope none of your Oplitals have been completely destroyed. *Niola's eyes open up* **Niola**(Y): MY MAX CAN ACTUALLY LOWER BECAUSE OF THIS STUFF?! *Yáshido looks at Niola* **Yáshido**(thts): I forgot she doesn't know that much about it. **Yáshido**: Yeah, the longer it's on, the more it takes, and after a real long time, it could start lowering the maximum amount of Pure Energy you can hold. *Niola hugs herself* **Niola**: I'm going to start taking showers with Patchi Tekiyo, and thanks for healing me up a bit. Yáshido fires Kosai destroying the crystals* **Yáshido**: No problem. *Yáshido flys back over to the frozen Nvonka, Niola follows him* First in a long time where I used Elilament Adapt. She looks out. *Reine walks closer to the frozen Dicipient. Nvonka's position looks like a warrior statue. Niola gently pokes it and the smallest bit of ice falls down and lands on the top of her shoe* **Niola**: Ha-, Ah! *Niola jumps back behind Yáshido* **Yáshido**: You're not scared are you? She's completely frozen. **Niola**: No, it's not that. You know how we've been fighting under nothing but heat? **Yáshido**: Yeah? **Niola**: That ice hit my shoe and the top layer is thin, so I felt it. **Yáshido**: Hahahaha, that's one way to get jump scared. **Niola**: It's not funny, I nearly blasted my foot. **Yáshido**: Do you think you can handle her if she unfreezes? *Niola pauses as she stares at Nvonka* **Niola**: Yeah. **Yáshido**: Good, because I have to help HTB with Povroca. **Niola**: Go ahead, I got this. *Inside HTB's Barre. 117 and 390 are badly injured. HTB is in front of them. A striped line across his Dermal up the chest plate. Povroca has multiple strikes across his Dermal, but his posture makes him seem like he's taken no stamina loss at all. HTB is breathing extremely heavily with pauses between his breaths* **HTB**: Nvonka's down, Povroca. **Povroca**: I forgot the Hero was with you, I should have warned her. To be honest, I forgot about him entirely. She especially couldn't win against him and another, but you didn't stand a chance against a one v. three. ^Povroca rushes towards HTB with the final blow, but while he's in the air, the remaining Barre breaks and Yáshido counters the attack. Povroca gets thrown back to where he was. Povroca looks up in disgust as Yáshido stands in front of HTB^ **Povroca**: Crap. **HTB**: Right on time. **Yáshido**: Yeah. *Dozens of other Balancers start flying in and surround them in all directions* It's over, Povroca. **Povroca**: You might have taken Nvonka down with no casualties, but this will be different. ^Povroca immediately Protojets towards HTB. Yáshido activates Zoka Swiftness attempting to slash Povroca as he intersects him. Yáshido misses by a few feet. At the last second, Balancer 117 and 378 summon a Conjoined Barre in front of Povroca^ **Povroca**(Y): HA!~ ^Povroca thrusts through the Barre as if it was nothing. Before HTB gets hit, he puts the last of his energy into an electric shock towards Povroca. Povroca's ice blade pierces through HTB's chest, but HTB's last attempt at getting a hit makes contact with Povroca. HTB gets tossed dozens of meters against the ground. His Dermal disappears off of him as he lays in pain. Povroca watches the other two Balancers charge at him as his movements are heavily restricted by the Aced Denki from HTB. Povroca barely manages to take a step back. Before 117 lands a strike^ **Povroca**: Glacier! ^Povroca's body is quickly engulfed in a red aura as he lifts his hands. A large mountain of ice rises from the ground in between himself and the Balancers. For that moment believing he's safe, Povroca Reverses his Zoka Strength and starts healing himself. Around this time, Yáshido is just now turning around^ **Yáshido**(thts): He's wide open! ^Yáshido lets go of Jeshika and she floats to his sides. Yáshido aims his hands toward Povroca with immense balls of Raito at the edge of each of his fingertips. However, before firing, the iceberg gets sliced in half^ **Povroca**: What?! ^Balancer 117 has cut the iceberg in half while 378 Protojets through it attacking Povroca^ **Yáshido**: Consecutive Repulsion! ^Instantly, dozens of lightning strikes hit Povroca in the back from Yáshido's fingertips. Although each bombardment takes a hefty amount of Oplitals from Yáshido, Povroca takes a considerable amount of damage to his Dermal and Sustain. So much damage in fact that Povroca's Dermal vanishes after fifteen hits, which hit him at a speed in under three seconds. Loud powerful thumps explode through the Barre in a low pitch from each hit. Once Yáshido is done, 378 gets a perfect slash against the defenseless Povroca. Povroca gets slingshotted towards Yáshido^ **Yáshido**: No chances. ^Yáshido puts up his offhand^ **Yáshido**(Y): Disappear out of my sight~! ^A blue smoke comes from Yáshido's hand as Povroca's back beams straight at him. Yáshido's hand, his entire body starts to turn blue from inside out. Povroca screams in pain. Yáshido throws his sword up in the air and stabs Povroca right through his back. Povroca Sustain and completely burst off of him following a patch of blood. Yáshido lands and Povroca falls on the ground in front of him, unconscious. The Balancers move in to capture the Dicipient. Yáshido takes his sword out as he turns towards Niola's last spot and he sees her flying backward towards him as if she was knocked away. Barely catching her with his arms, Niola has Nelion equipped^ **Niola**(Y): She's Free! ^Yáshido looks at Nvonka and she's floating above the trees with her Aced Dermal once more and her aura visibly pulsing with Ikkasei through the air. Yáshido sets Niola down as he looks at Nvonka* **Nvonka**(Y): THERE'S NO WAY I'M GOING TO BE CAPTURED!!! YOU'LL HAVE TO KILL ME!!! ^Nvonka raises her hands towards the sky as flames start to form a giant galaxy. The power she is using causes what feels like an earthquake^ **Yáshido**: Niola, help them get our allies. *Niola nods as she goes to assist* ^Bits of Earth's crust come up from the ground. The fiery disk takes up nearly seventy feet in diameter before coming to a stop. Nvonka makes direct eye contact with Yáshido^ *Nvonka*: Let's See If You Can Stop This, Hero!!! ^The wind from the giant move causes the Balancers to summon a Barre shielding everyone^ *Nvonka*: HAA!!!~ ^Nvonka swings her arms down and with it rushes the giant galaxy towards Yáshido, including everyone behind him. The attack covers Nvonka, but Yáshido can sense that she is in the same spot putting more pressure down on her attack to cause more damage^ *Yáshido*(thts): She's not going to give up! Fukashi Deamsou! ^Yáshido's body glows a spacious white color. Without hesitation, he scopes right through the attack, aiming for Nvonka. Before hitting the flaming rotating circle^ *Yáshido*: Lapathos Strike! ^Yáshido's sword brightens as it is surrounded by Pure Energy. Contacting the flaming galaxy, Yáshido gets halted, seeming as if he would have to put more energy into it. Suddenly, as if the galaxy suddenly got twice as strong, Yáshido starts to slowly go down with it^ *Yáshido*(thts): Come on, Jeshika!~ This is nothing to you! ^Yáshido stops descending and hovers about fifteen feet from the ground^ *Yáshido*(thts): There's just too much power in it. Maybe I can take the blow entirely. ^Yáshido feels someone coming up to his left. Reine comes next to him and places her hands surrounded by fire on the massive swirling attack^ *Yáshido*(m): Reine? *Reine*: You got this, Yáshido! ^Yáshido slowly feels himself going upward back towards Nvonka^ *Yáshido*(thts): You heard her, Jeshika, we got this! *Yáshido & Reine*: HA!!!~ ^Both Yáshido and Reine's body glow in red light as they use Aced Zoka strength. Yáshido using Aced Ikkasei while Reine is using Stage I. Jeshika slices through and the galaxy of flames quickly explodes afterward. Coming through it, Nvonka is seemingly going straight for Reine with her dagger. Reine makes a Barre in front of herself, but Yáshido jumps right into Nvonka's path. The blade makes contact with Yáshido's chest, but hits it as if it was an impenetrable wall^ *Nvonka*: Wha-, ^Nvonka looks up at Yáshido as she becomes parallel with him^ *Yáshido*: Begone! You squalling Dicipient! ^Yáshido sword pierces Nvonka's Dermal in her stomach. Loose saliva empties from Nvonka's mouth by the shock of the blow. Yáshido levitates Nvonka in the air above him with his sword and throws her down to the ground with all his strength. While still falling, Yáshido beams downward towards the ground with his sword aiming directly at her. Before they crash against the ground, Yáshido's sword invades her Dermal once more. They smash against the ground. The area gets filled with smoke and another crater appears on the surface. Once the smoke clears, Nvonka is lying on the ground in agony without her Dermal. Yáshido is standing with his sword still in her stomach area. Nvonka is holding onto Jeshika with her left hand as if she was clinging on to her life. Blood starts to pour out from the intersection^ *Yáshido*: Done. ^Nvonka's right eye barely opens looking at Yáshido's face^ *Nvonka*(m): Damn it . . . I hope you burn in an endless pit of fire, Yáshido. *Yáshido*: I appreciate that, Nvonka. ^Right as Nvonka mouth opens, Yáshido thrusts his sword out of Nvonka. Nvonka's mouth closes as her entire body clenches, her mouth opens again for one long exhale. Nvonka's Sustain bursts off of her once she finishes. Yáshido takes a knee and puts his finger on her neck and another on her chest^ **Yáshido**(thts): I didn't want to kill her, so I'm glad she's still breathing. *Yáshido stands up. A group of five Balancers rushes up to them. Three of them start to lock up Nvonka's limbs with Dicipients' Whips. Another surrounds her in a Hydro-Block and lifts her into the air. **Balancer**(A): Good work, Yáshido. *Yáshido nods* **Balancer**(B): Wait till they hear about this one. *Yáshido turns around to see multiple mCarriers, and nearly all the Balancers are surrounding them. One is closed, and as Nvonka is placed into the other it closes too. Yáshido faintly feels Reine's aura and spots her on the ground with four Balancers and HTB crouched over her. He activates Zoka Swiftness as he dashes to her. Once near her, she is awake but on the ground as if she was out of stamina. The Balancers make room for Yáshido except for HTB who stays crouched* **Yáshido**: You okay, Reine? **Reine**: Hah, yeah. My last attempt really took a lot out of me. **HTB**: We can give her some X Potency if you allow it. *Yáshido looks at Reine* **Reine**: That's fine. **Yáshido**: Yeah, I'd appreciate it. *Soon after, a Balancer comes back with a glowing capsule. He gives the capsule to Yáshido* **Yáshido**: Thank you. **Balancer**(C): Don't mention it. *Yáshido sits Reine up against him and feeds her the Potency. Once the tube is completely empty, Yáshido and Reine stand up* **Reine**: The wonders of Alchemy, I feel completely restored. **Balancer**(D): It should get you the rest of the day without you having to Reverse her Yáshido. *HTB puts his hand on Reine's shoulder. Reine looks at him a little confused* **HTB**: Everyone agrees that Reine here did excellent today? **Balancers**(All): Yeah!!! **Yáshido**: We all worked as a team. To defend Macadamia! **All**: Yeah!!! *Everyone with a weapon raises their weapon. After celebratory spoils, everyone walks back to the mCarriers. HTB starts to talk with another General there, Yáshido starts walking to them. By HTB. General Uro is looking him up and down* **Uro**: I see they were a bit of a problem, huh, Conner? **HTB**: We have our good days and our bad days, General Uro, but Povroca sure has strengthened. **Uro**: Times are getting rougher out there, I'll be happy to see some more of those good days. *Yáshido joins them* **Yáshido**: General Uro. **Uro**: Yáshido, his Familiar. *Yáshido and Reine nod* Thanks for your efforts out there, I know it was a bit of a surprise, seeing you're probably just now getting back out on things, but it's good to see you're okay. **Yáshido**: It's no problem, I'm just doing what I'm here for. **Uro**: Right. Uhm, HTB already told me what your situation was so I'd be happy to give you a ride to Hina. General Maikeru has everything under control here. **Yáshido**: Yeah, that would be nice. **Uro**: Great, follow me.

Chapter 16 - Taku's Directive

General Uro takes Yáshido, Reine, and HTB to a separate mCarrier. General Uro enters in the front with Yáshido in the passenger seat. HTB enters the second row, and another Balancer, 313, is already back there. In the final row is Reine who stretches across the whole row since there is no one back there. The walls of the interior of the vehicle turn completely transparent. Reine leans up looking out of the window. The vehicle starts to rise into the air. Some of the Balancers rise up with them and wave them off. General Uro waves them off before he speeds up. Looking in the rearview mirror, Yáshido watches as the other two mCarriers rise up in the air and start going back towards Macadamia Army H.Q. General Uro sighs **Uro**: Things have been so busy since you know what. I can't even sit down for coffee without having to get back up to attend to something else. **Yáshido**: I saw it when I was inside of the Menium. **Uro**: You came in on the low end. There were so many Balancers here about three days ago, we had to send more to patrol around Macadamia. **HTB**: Thirty went to the cross between Catalyst. **Uro**: Yeah, and I bet their Generals didn't like that. *As they come to a small building, General Uro lowers the mCarrier. Yáshido looks at the sun and it's on its way to sunset. At ground level, Yáshido and Reine exit the mCarrier* Alright, Yáshido. See you later. **Yáshido**: See you, General. Oh wait, can I ask a question? **Uro**: Yeah-, sure. **Yáshido**: Would it be alright if you did not mention Reine in the battle? I don't want her to be announced to everyone in the world just yet. **Uro**: Yeah-, okay, sounds simple. I'd be able to do that. **Yáshido**: Thanks. **Uro**: Stay safe and keep protecting. **Yáshido**: You do the same. *General Uro and Yáshido put a thumbs up at each other. General Uro and HTB nod at each other as HTB gets out. Once the three of them are out, General Uro flys back up in the air and goes back into the direction they came from* **Voice**(Feminine): Yáshido?! Is that you?! *Yáshido turns to the building to see Hina running out of it towards him* [Hina has short light blue bangs in the front which shifts into a purple hue in the hair behind her head which reaches halfway down her back. Her clothing makes her seem like she's some type of maid, but a crystalline 'T' that dominates the middle of her shirt defines that she's a Teleporter. Hina is also carrying a staff that holds three different crystals around a bright white orb at the end of the stick. Hina is taller than Reine but shorter than Yáshido] *Hina slows down her pace as she gets closer. Hina stops about seven feet away* **Hina**: It is you! **Yáshido**: Hey, Hina. **Hina**: Man, it's been a while since I've seen you. You've grown up and gotten so much taller. You even look better with that Dermal now. **Yáshido**: Haha, thanks, Hina. *Hina starts walking towards Yáshido again before seeing Reine* **Hina**: Fa-, Fa-, Familiar? *Hina's eyes and mouth open in astonishment. Reine smiles too* You have a Familiar now?! *Yáshido*: Yeah~, it's been about a week now. *Hina looks at Yáshido with a bawdy face and chuckles* What's with that face? *Hina*(m): Nothing. *Hina covers her mouth with her wrist as if wiping above it. Then the face goes away, and she looks at Reine* *Hina*: What's your name? *Reine*: Reine. *Hina*: Kosai as the main, right? *Reine*: Ye-, yeah. How'd you know? *Hina*: Your master here said his first Familiar was going to be a Kosai main. *Yáshido*: You still remember that? *Hina*: How could I forget? And there was such a big joke going around that if your first Familiar was a girl, you'd let a select few pat her hair. *Yáshido*(m): Oh~, no. *Yáshido*: And you were one of them, weren't you? *Hina*: Yup. Only if Reine wants me to. *Both of them look at Reine. Reine laughs while looking at Hina* *Reine*: Go ahead. *Hina*: Really?! *Hina runs to Reine and her hands immediately but gently rubs Reine's dark purple hair up and down. Hina stops violently rubbing then sits her hand in the middle of Reine's hair* *Hina*: Oh~! It feels so amazing. *Reine*: I'm glad you like it, haha. *Hina*: Make sure you keep your hair healthy since you are a Type Two Familiar. *Reine*: I will. *Hina*: That means no prolonged fighting with Reine after seven, Hero. *Yáshido*: Like I could ever do that to poor Reine. *Reine has a big smile* *Reine*: Hehe~. *Hina steps back and then takes an extreme gasp* *Yáshido*: What now? *Hina*: Can she show me how strong she can get? *Yáshido*: Like, her fighting Dermal? *Hina*: Yeah. *Yáshido*: I don't know about that, Hina; she just got done using all of her Oplitals. *Reine*: It's okay, Yáshido. I can show her. *Reine looks at Hina* You're the first to ever ask how strong I can get Hina, so it excites me a little. *Yáshido*(thts): Reine . . . *Hina comes up to Yáshido with her hands together* *Hina*: Can she? Please?~ *Yáshido*: If Reine's okay with it, so am I. *Hina*: Great! *Hina lifts her staff up and a large Barrier spreads around them and under them* There. Let's see what you can really do, Reine! *Reine*: Okay! *Reine raises her hands in front of her and balls them up. Looking down at them, she closes her eyes. Both Hina and Yáshido can already feel Reine's efficiency rise drastically using Uhnyoi. A quick flame curls around Reine's arms. Seconds later, bursts of fire fragments come off of her. Some of them touch Yáshido's Dermal. The ripples continue to get spread faster before suddenly the exportation stops and the flames flow around Reine like it's an aura. The drastic increase of power puts a crack in the Barre above Reine. Also, it slides Yáshido and Hina away from her. Hina surprised, almost slips* *Hina*: Woah. *As Hina catches her balance, Reine looks at her pausing with the flames still pulsating from her* Don't worry about me, keep going, Reine. You're doing great! *Reine smiles before closing her eyes again and the smile goes away into a more concentrated look. Reine puts more energy into the transformation. Brighter blue flames mix in with the still-dominant red flames. The curls in the front of Reine's hair begin to rise upwards while it all turns into a bright yellow. The curls in the back of her hair expand halfway down her back straightening out. The same yellow light curves around Reine's forehead as a metal plating appears on it. Different parts of her Dermal glow before sizzling away looking more rigid, compact, and denser. The yellow light then appears on her wrists, going halfway up all her fingers, leaving the tips of her fingers exposed. The yellow light around her fingers turn into red fingerless gloves, but they seem to animate as if they were flames. The constant flame around Reine's body separates into two tekCircles that lay above her palms after she opens them* **Yáshido**(thts): So, that's what it looks like up close. Even though she's holding back, her peaks can rival Dia. *Reine opens her eyes* **Reine**: Finished. *Both of them look at Hina. She has the most exciting face ever* **Hina**: You're amazing, Reine! You managed to top out a Stage I Dermal! **Yáshido**: She was nearly keeping up with Nvonka with this Dermal. **Hina**: Really?! I don't know which is crazier? The fact you let her fight a Dicipient or the fact that you were fighting a Dicipient?! **Reine**: Em~, hm~, I could try going for an Aced Dermal now, but as Yáshido said, I'm kind of going off of a supply right now. **Hina**: Hahahaha. *Yáshido watches as a sinister smirk washes over Hina's face* **Yáshido**: Hina, I know what you're thinking and no. *Hina's face turns into a confused one before she chuckles* **Hina**: Oh, hah, you got me. **Reine**: What was she gonna do? **Yáshido**: She likes to test your reflexes with a super-fast jab with her staff. **Reine**: That's all? I think I can take it. **Yáshido**: That's not it. This attack is really fast. I mean, one of the fastest attacks in the world. It's as fast as Protojeting after a Zoka Swiftness launch into a Raito strike. **Hina**: I activate as many things as possible that can boost up my swiftness all at once, Reine. Both wings included. The attack lasts for about eleven-three milliseconds. *Reine's aura goes away with one swift blast upwards* **Reine**: Ele-, that's insanely fast. **Yáshido**: The catch is, some of what takes her to speed it up actually requires her to make it a lot stronger as well. That power plus the speed can really damage a person with low Sustain or Oplitals. *Yáshido moves his arm in front of Reine* Reine's off-limits, Hina. **Hina**: What!~ You don't think I would really hurt your Familiar~, Yáshido? When was the last time I did it without asking when someone was with you? *Yáshido sighs* **Yáshido**: Good point. *Yáshido lowers his arm* **Reine**: Has anyone ever blocked it? **Hina**: There was one kid. He kind of looks like your master, but shorter. I don't know where he vanished though. **Yáshido**: I blocked it once, Reine. **Reine**: If you could do it that means I can. **Yáshido**: Maybe when you have Oplitals and an Aced Dermal, Reine. **Reine**: Iah~, okay. **Hina**: Not only did he block it, he dodged it too. In front of all his people that one time too and it made me look bad. I'm still kind of salty about it, but ever since then, he has declined me. **Yáshido**: And I will continue declining until you get faster. *Hina puffs up her arms as if she was Yáshido* **Hina**: Until you get faster, hahahaha. Thanks, Reine. You can use your Base Dermal now. **Reine**: Okay. *Within a small light of energy, Reine is back to her Base Dermal and her features turn back normal. The Barre around them breaks as she does this* **Hina**: Now, where will I be taking my two customers? *Yáshido stretches out his hand towards Hina. Hina grabs Yáshido's wrist and closes her eyes. A white-blue triangle appears for a couple seconds* Hm~ . . . yeah, okay got it. *Hina opens her eyes and lets Yáshido's wrist go. Looking behind Yáshido she sees HTB* **Hina**(w): There's a Balancer here. *Yáshido turns around* **Yáshido**: Oh, HTB. I forgot you were with us. **HTB**: It's alright. **Hina**: He's with you? **Yáshido**: Yeah. *HTB stands close. Hina walks in between Yáshido and Reine. Hina takes her staff and plants the bottom of it in the ground. A circle forms under them and overlaps them into a sphere. The inside of the orb is displayed with an ocean. Making it seem like they are in a glass facility underwater* **Yáshido**: Ocean themed? **Hina**: Pretty cool, right? **All**: Definitely. **Yáshido**: Hopefully you don't scare anyone with this. **Hina**: I thought about that. Knowing that if you fall into the ocean, uhm~, it's basically your life. No one has yet to pass out, and the Generals haven't said anything about it so~. **Yáshido**: I'm surprised you're not busy too. **Hina**: Yes, I am, Hero. I teleported those Balancers to you. And before I got them, I had three others and after the Balancers I-, **Yáshido**: Okay, I get it. You're pretty busy. **Hina**: Hmph, darn right. *The scenery unwinds as Yáshido notices they're in front of the entrance of the woods to get to Taku's base. Looking along the path that path on their left and right, there's no one in sight* **Yáshido**(thts): I hope they're okay. **Hina**: Are you coming back? **Yáshido**: Yes, we need about five minutes. **Hina**: Okay, I'll be waiting right here. *HTB, Reine, and Yáshido start walking towards the forest. Hina summons her Mangole before disappearing into Gray Particles. **Yáshido**(thts): I wish I had teleportation. **Hina**: I heard that. *Yáshido turns around to see Hina's head levitating with Particles surrounding her neck and going up into the air* Haha~, so you did say something in your mind, didn't you? **Yáshido**: Hina, please. **Hina**: Haha. *Hina vanishes once more. While they are walking through the forest* **HTB**: Interesting location. He must have known our routes or something. **Yáshido**: He said something about it. **HTB**: This passage was the last on our list to search, haha. **Yáshido**: Now that you mention it, he did tell me that he knew about your search patterns during a conversation with him. *After walking for a while, they spot a small clearing and soon Taku's house. While they approach the house* **Reine**: Hina seems like a fun person to be around. **Yáshido**: You don't say. **Reine**: Maybe I should convert her into an adventurer. **HTB**: Hahaha, that'd be a sight to see. **Yáshido & Reine**: Her contract probably doesn't let her leave though. *Reine and Yáshido stop and look at each other before they both laugh* **Yáshido**: I can't believe we were both thinking the same thing. **Reine**: Me neither, hahaha. **HTB**: She is your Familiar after all. You're going to have to get use to that. *When they get to the stairs, Yáshido stops before turning around towards Reine. Reine and HTB look back at him* **Yáshido**: Reine, can you do me a favor and tell Taku what's going on? **Reine**(m): I guess I could. He already can feel your presence with Denryoku. **Reine**: Okay. **Yáshido**: I'm going to be in our room so when you're finished-, **Reine**: I know~, what you want~ . . . Yáshido. *Yáshido feels his dignity wash away as Reine smiles at him* **Yáshido**(thts): Why, why. Especially in front of HTB. *Yáshido sighs* **Yáshido**: You're going to falsely accuse me around everyone, aren't you? **Reine**: What are you talking about, Yáshido? *Staring at each other* May~, be. **Yáshido**: I'll be in the dorm.

Yáshido flys over Taku's house **HTB**: I can tell, for his first Familiar, you give him a hard time, don't you? **Reine**: Without me, I'd say he'd be a mess. *Reine knocks on the door. By Yáshido, in the air looking at the dorm* **Yáshido**(thts): What? It's so huge now. It doubled in size. *Yáshido looks at the surrounding tree line* It's almost reaching the top of the trees! Savenna is not playing around. *Yáshido feels the presence of the other four occupants of the dorm* No new people it seems like. *Landing on the dorm's steps, he walks to and stands in front of the door* I want to clear things up with Moon. I don't remember much but . . . I can't just not address it. *Raising his left hand to the door, it opens inwards and Moon is standing there with her hand on the inside knob. Her face instantly widens* **Moon**: Ky-, Kyon? **Yáshido**(thts): The timing couldn't have been more perfect. *Yáshido lowers his hand* **Yáshido**: Moon. **Moon**: You're back already? How was it? **Yáshido**: Well, General Opaine seems like he'd give it a try. Reine's talking to Taku about it now. **Moon**: That's good. *Moon looks at the door before stepping back as if gesturing Yáshido inside. Yáshido enters, and Moon closes the door behind him* **Yáshido**: Moon. **Moon**: Ye-. Yeah? *Yáshido turns around and looks at Moon* **Yáshido**: I remembered what happened *A frown appears on Moon's face before looking down* **Moon**: I'm sorry, Hero. I was taken over by anger and . . . couldn't control my actions. I just . . . didn't know what to do. **Yáshido**: That doesn't make it your fault, okay, Moon? *Moon looks back up at Yáshido. Her eyes are watery. A picture of when they first had this conversation appears in front of Moon, covering her face with that angry expression she had before. Yáshido clearly remembers the deaths of her family by Dia and how Moon attacked him, and how he pushed Reine out of the way. That picture soon drifts out of reality, showing the present Moon. Yáshido feels a tear form in his eye thinking about the situation more deeply* Dia killed your family. The last you had to relate to you. Someone who you thought was full of justice and righteousness, killed not only your family but innocent lives. Your idle, changed in a way you never would have thought possible. I can understand why you were governed by your emotions. Anyone sane would have done the same thing. That's why you attacked me. The person who would have had full control over how she formed her morals and acted was standing right in front of you. Denying that she had turned . . . evil. The person who was her partner nearly all of her life, somehow let her go into the darkness. Said that killing thousands of lives, with others who have been possessed by this darkness didn't change how he felt towards her. That's why you attacked me. *Moon wipes her face with her wrists and palms* I'm not ashamed to say that I would take full responsibility for what Dia did. For your sake, Moon. *Yáshido and Moon sit in silence with Moon's soft snuffles* Yet, there's still my feelings in the matter. Which I would want to express as my main objective. The feelings I have towards Dia rejects the cruel reality that I'm being faced upon . . . Moon. It's saying, in order to believe it, I have to hear it for myself. I want to hear Dia tell me that she's converted upon her own will . . . anything that would suffice that means she is no longer working for good . . . but for evil intentions. *Yáshido looks at his open hand* Until then, I can only hope that she hasn't. That there's still some good in her. That I can save her, and I want to take the chance to say there is. Do you understand, Moon? *Slowly looking back up at Moon, her facial expression is filled with sincere sadness. Her mouth slowly opens* **Moon**: Yes, I understand. *Still sniffing her nose, Yáshido walks over to Moon and gently hugs her* **Yáshido**: I know losing your family to the Demon King, and now Dia, puts a lot of endless stress on you, and you want revenge . . . or something like that. Having my parents killed by the Demon King as well, I also have a bone to pick with him. *Moon's eyes widen* Dia, I'll let you have your way with her, only if she has converted. But until then, I'll handle this, okay? *Moon hugs Yáshido back* **Moon**: Okay. **Yáshido**: Good. *After hugging for a few more seconds, they separate. Moon uses her magic to clear the tears off of her and the tears she cried on Yáshido's shoulder* Thank you for understanding Moon, and I would like to deeply apologize for your loss. *Moon does nothing but nods as it seems as though she is holding back more tears* If you need anything ask, I'll be in my room. *Moon pushes herself to speak* **Moon**: Okay. Thank you, Hero. *Yáshido goes down the hall and enters his room. The lights automatically turn on and he locks the door behind him. Lying on the one bed next to the window, he looks at the ceiling* **Yáshido**(thts): I haven't been in one of these situations in so long. Especially not as one so closely related to me, but now Moon should be satisfied. For now. *Yáshido gets back up and enters the bathroom, in front of the sinks and Reverses his Dermal* **Yashi**(thts): All of the Pure Energy I allocated was used to fight Povroca and Nvonka, so it's like I did nothing at all. I'll have to remember to visit Emuna for a refill. *Stretching out, Yashi feels his bones crackle* Iah~, there we go. *Looking at himself in the mirror* Regarding what Povroca said, does that mean Dia is planning on physically visiting me, or was he just saying that? Even if that's what he meant, it doesn't matter now that he's captured. Well no, because they'll newscast the situation. Hm~ . . . *Yashi sits on his bed. A couple of minutes later, someone knocks on his door. Yashi clears his throat* **Reine**: It's your Familiar. *Yashi stands and walks to the door* **Yashi**: How do I know it's you? **Reine**: What was the name of my Cast again? Oh yeah, Solar!~ **Yashi**: Okay, okay. *Yashi opens the door, Reine runs past him and jumps into the bed* **Reine**: Are we going back out to Dreium once we're done? **Yashi**: Before we get into that, what happened? **Reine**: Well, it was a bit, how does one say, slow. Savenna nearly had a heart attack when she saw I brought HTB here because she didn't have her Sustain on. Taku came running to her to cool her off and then I had to explain everything. Now they're going back to Menium. **Yashi**: Wait, we didn't tell Hina that 'We' wouldn't be coming back, but 'THEY' would. **Reine**: Oh yeah~, that could cause problems. **Yashi**: I might still have her on my Mangole. *Yashi nb casts his Mangole and quickly searches through his contacts* Yeah, I do. *Yashi taps on her name under Yáshido[the Mangole automatically readjusts his voice to Yáshido's when he taps calls this way] and turns his face camera off. It starts calling her. A second later, Hina appears on the screen* **Hina**(M): Yes? **Yashi**: We actually won't be coming back with HTB. **Hina**(M): Ow. **Yashi**: But he'll be coming back with Taku and Savenna. *Hina's face gets closer to the screen* **Hina**(M): The Dicipient Taku and Savanna?! **Yashi**: Don't worry, they're on our side. You'll be taking them to the Army H.Q. HTB will clarify everything I'm sure. **Hina**(M): This is all too sudden. You couldn't have told me sooner? **Yashi**: Ha, my bad. Just try not to make it awkward. **Hina**(M): Got'cha. I think I see them now, thanks for prepping me, I guess. **Yashi**: I don't think you'll have to teleport him back, because he can teleport himself. **Hina**(M): Okay, bye Hero, they're here. **Yashi**: Talk to you in a bit, Hina. *The screen fades back to his contacts list, and he Reverses it* That solves that. About leaving, when Taku comes back, then we can go back for maybe a day or two. **Reine**: Good. **Yashi**: You must have plans? **Reine**: My brother and sister are here. They wanted to meet up. **Yashi**: Oh, cool. *Yashi does more stretches as Reine watches him* You don't have to stay in that Dermal, Reine. **Reine**: We still have to go back, right? **Yashi**: Yeah, but like I just said, you can get out of that Dermal. *Reine leans up* **Reine**: Oh~, I get it, you miss Niola~, don't you? **Yashi**(m): I just don't want you to lose your Oplitals. **Yashi**: Let's go with that. *Reine's body sparkles before the Familiar is gone* **Niola**: Iah~, so much better. *Niola raises up her arms* I can just feel the nutrients and energy flowing through my body. **Yashi**: That's exactly what it feels like. *Niola lays flat across the bed towards Yashi* **Niola**: Wake me when Taku gets back. **Yashi**: Okay. *After a while of standing and stretching, Yashi starts meditating* **Yashi**(thts): General Opaine never did say I couldn't watch as a spectator. Hm~ . . . This should be good. *Without standing back up, Yashi makes his way onto the bed. Sitting up, he looks out of the window, the sun is setting. He sighs* I'm usually not impatient, but it's been about an hour. What's taking them so long? *Yashi lies back on Niola's legs* Uh~, so bored.

To Be Continued

Lore

At youth, the average number of Oplitals is 10,000, and the average of an adult is very vast with some people reaching 400,000 while others barely over 200,000.Alchemists calculate Oplitals by taxing an individual with Stage III Efficiency Z Zoka Strength, as they documented Zoka Strength to be the first ever Elilament.

Elilaments are classified by how many Oplitals they use while in Stage III Efficiency Z mode compared to Zoka Strength, the percentage of people who have it, and how difficult it is to achieve high Efficiencies. Many Elilaments between the Basic and Novice are interchangeable but are in that particular order from a common trend Alchemists found between them.

Efficiency is calculated by subbing each alphabet as a number based off of 'A'. Z would be 0/25. Marking the efficiency for Stage III Zoka Strength is as follows. {14 chains all Z's. 0/25 x 14 = 0, Max Efficiency would be 0%} This means that although the individual would gain strength, it would be hardly noticeable, and they would be consuming a lot of Oplitals per second to   where they would almost run out immediately.

Each Elilament has its on specific chain that is named Efficiency once in use. Alchemists denote each chain through the alphabet A-Z. Z is the worse efficiency to have while A is the best. With each Stage, the amount of chain increase. For example, a raw Stage III Zoka Strength will have 14 chains {ZZZZZZZZZZZZZZ}. A raw Stage II Zoka Strength will have 24 chains {ZZZZZZZZZZZZZZZZZZZZZZZZ}. Efficiency carries over per Stage. Stage III {YYYYYYYYYYYYYY} 14/350 M.E. 4% > {YYYYYYYYYYYYYYYYYYYYYYYY} 24/600 M.E. 4%

Stage III {UUVVXXYYYYYYYY} 26/350 M.E. 7.4% > Stage II {UVXXYYYYYYYYYYYYZZZZZZZZ} 20/350 M.E. 5.7%. Chains are not always in order from the example from above. Realistically, they would look like the following: {XYZYYZZYYYXZZXYZZYZZYZZXXYYZ}.

Some Alchemists prefer to lowercase the z to count the 'Real' inputs. With a chain advancing to the next Stage, no one conversion will be better than another if they are the same Efficiency. The difference in having a Stage I and Stage II with the same Efficiency of

60% Zoka Strength is that the individual with Stage I will be able to achieve a greater power at the cost of using more Oplitals. If the Stage I and Stage II individual used the same 60% efficiency, the Stage I user will be using less Oplitals. Both Stages with equal Efficiencies of 60%, gives a strength force of 47x Newtons. Stage I can use 73x Newtons of force at 60% and use more Oplitals.

An individual does not need a specific Efficiency to get the next Stage of the Elilament. Gaining Stages is a genetic, mental, and physical based achievement. Once the genes detect that a body can withstand even more energy and that the user is confident in their ability to use the Elilament, the next Stage is unlocked. Just because someone has a higher Stage doesn't mean that they are necessarily stronger than someone else. If they both hit fists with their highest outputs, the person with the higher Stage over Efficiency will win the impact, but battle styles, knowledge, Efficiency difference, or physical features all impact the victor of a fight.

Many fighters in Divine Credence try to mimic their opponent's output to conserve their own stamina and Oplitals. Even though someone may have a higher Stage than someone else, they limit their Efficiency and only raise it when needed, especially if they have a higher Sustain.

Having a Sustain active emits your aura. This aura can be see only if the user uses an Ikkasei or an individual looking at them uses Denryoku or Kenesu. Lowering the Efficiency on Sustain decreases the range of being detected by Denryoku. People can stay hidden even though next to someone using Denryoku if they go Z mode until that individual uses Denryoku or Kenesu as a *hold*. Lower the Efficiency of a Sustain does not impact how much damage you can take but will decrease casting times.

Casts can be used in three ways with a *hold* being the most effective, *sustain* in the middle, and a *carry* as the least effective. MultiCast allows an individual two cast two separate *holds* at the same time, the same goes for the other two choices of casting. In Divine Credence, you see that multiple characters are using more than one Elilament at one time, but they are actually using separate *sustains* at different intervals allowing them to use Zoka Strength and Zoka Vision simultaneously. However, this drains a lot of more Oplitals than if someone were to MultiCast two separate *holds* of Zoka Strength and Zoka

Vision.

To increase the Efficiency of an Elilament, some of them require you to concentrate on using it specifically, while others are literally randomized. An individual's Max Efficiency can never drop, but they call willingly use a lower Efficiency. Each Stage of an Elilament has its properties demining them as separate Magics. Aced Zoka Strength is a lot more powerful than Stage I Zoka Strength, but in return you use a lot more Oplitals.

No one has ever achieved Max Efficiency.

The Elilament Elemental Void has a chain count of 132 at Stage III making it one of the hardest Elilaments to master.

People who are born with Magic don't start off with Magic right away. Around the age of 5 is when their Sustain becomes active.

For those with a Sustain, you must have it enabled in order to use magic, but some people unfortunately have Sustain as a Locked Magic which enables them to trigger the use of Elilaments without one at birth. Everyone does not simple learn a new Elilament. Each Elilament that an individual possess is already coded into their genetic make-up. Locked Magic can only be obtained by preforming a Trants.

Majority of Alchemists believe that Trantsing should not be an active trait that should be possible. It was determined during the mid-5th Generation that it would never be classified as an Elilament.

Their planet, Edasia, has eruptions of Pure Energy that comes from the absorption of Particles on the surface that eventually transitions into the planets on Oplital count. Once a certain threshold is broken, an explosion occurs through the Dispositor.

Dispositor/Dispensers are like volcanoes that erupt Pure Energy instead of lava. Each existing one has been concealed with technology that can indirectly and directly transfer Pure Energy into electronics and other forms of energy in its region since the early 6th Generation. Generation 1 is when the first Hero, Yáshido, fought the Demon King, [REDACTED], for the first time. However, neither of these terms became apparent until the 3rd Generation. Neither the exact date of Yáshido casting the first Dermal ever, which made him the first Hero.

Generations 1-2, 3-4, and 5-7 are splits apart from each other due to Dispositor eruptions.

Dispositor eruptions fill the air with toxins and disable able Magic abilities after standing it in for too long. The after effects of Dispositor Eruptions last more than 17 years which in return split the Generations into sections.

Generation 1 is when the first Hero, Yáshido, fought the Demon King, [REDACTED], for the first time. However, neither of these terms became apparent until the 3rd Generation. Neither the exact date of Yáshido casting the first Dermal ever, making him the first Hero ever.

While in Anzen, Yashi and Dia have captured a total of seven Dicipients. After becoming the Hero, Yashi started to delay his fights with Dicipients until the age of sixteen.

Balancers have a choice between becoming a Council Balancer, General, or remaining a Balancer once the opportunity is presented onto them.

Each Seira was limited to 100 Balancers each by the 5th General Council to prevent military strength from becoming too power for any Seira. The Western Seiras all share the 100 Balancers threshold.

Watashimono has no Balancers.

The Council consists of one member from each Seira. Each member is required to learn the customs, Generals, and languages of all Seiras.

There are a total of five languages. Atiro, what you would call English, one for the upper-right portion of their world, two for the lower-left, and one for the lower-right.

A Lost Friend Characters

Only characters that have spoken or have done a reasonable amount of actions are labeled below. Ages are refined by the final chapter.

Pg- Prologue Cp- Chapter Name (Balancer Number)- (Chapter) (Gender), (Age), (Born In), (Status)

63 Characters

Aran(348)-(Cp11)Boy, 26, Macadamia, Balancer

Arylia Jade-(Cp13)Girl, 27, Macadamia, Assistant-Master at Jurono Academy

Aosra-(Cp2)Girl, 23, Macadamia, Attends Jurono

Dandred-(Cp18)-Boy, 45, Kastopia, Early 6th Generation Dicipient

Dia Kean-(Pg)Girl, 17, Macadamia, Expisimist(Anzen), Trants of Yashi

Deven-(Cp2)Boy, 20, Macadamia, Attends Jurono

Doridan-(Cp1)Boy, 42, ???, Early 6th Generation Dicipient

Emi Ukitima-(Cp7)Girl, ???, Regra, Victim from the Regra Attack

Emuna Levebrve-(Cp1)Girl, 28, Macadamia, Teleporter, Alchemist, 7th Generation Spawn

Euvex Misugami-(Cp4)Boy, 60, Watashimono Delshigo, Father of Tera

Flech-(Cp13)Boy, 28, Macadamia, News Reporter

Hamsley Rans-(Cp13)Boy, 40, Macadamia, Elilament Dec'crador at
Jurono Academy

Haraku Yetirsere-(Cp2)Boy, 18, Macadamia, Attends Jurono

Hina -(Cp14)Girl, 20, Macadamia, Teleporter

HTB(384)-(Cp14)Boy, 30, Macadamia, Balancer

Iragaru-(Cp2)Girl, 16, Macadamia, Attends Jurono

Jyokumo-(Cp7)Girl, 34, Alma, Mid 6th Generation Dicipient

Kamira Exna-(Cp3)Girl, 19, Macadamia, Inside Specialist

Kata-(Cp4)Boy, 35, Regra, Mid 6th Generation Dicipient

Kato Taramasu-(Pg)Boy, 24, Macadamia, Yashi's Brother, Assist-Cast Dermal Armor
Designer

Keshio Revalorese-(Cp2)Boy, 19, Macadamia

;Kokoa Exna-(Pg)Girl, 20, Macadamia, Cross Seira Tracer Manager

Kyoka Exna-(Cp8)Girl, 24, Macadamia, Resource Manager

Laito-(Cp4)Boy, 19, Bushido(Sablein), Boyfriend of Kamira

Lark Korosi-(Cp1)Boy, 50, Poronku, 6th Generation Demon King

Latarea-(Cp2)Girl, 18, Adenine, Attends Jurono

Mokea-(Cp2)Girl, 18, Macadamia, Attends Jurono

Moon(Monaka Ukitima)-(Cp10)Girl, 20, Alma, Friend of Taku

Namari Katsuni-(Cp2)Girl, 18, Macadamia, Tournament Specialist

Neitseka-(Pg)Boy, 34, Macadamia, Shop for mLetters

Niola Akimora-(Cp1)Girl, 19, ???, Adventurer

Nvonka-(Cp15), Girl, 25, Late 6th Generation Dicipient

Okama-(Pg)Girl, 61, Macadamia

Ota'Nomi Misugami-(Cp4)Girl, 27, Watashimono Delshigo, Otara's sister

Otara Misugami-(Cp2)Girl, 17, Watashimono Delshigo, Holder of the
Book of Apara

Ozumi-(Cp12)Girl, 23, Kyunn'Ku, Niola's Friend, Lost Magic Abilities

Pehegima-(Cp2)Boy, 33, Macadamia, Teacher of Jurono

Povroca-(Cp15)Boy, 30, Kyunn'ku, Mid 6th Generation Dicipient

Reine Taramasu-(Cp7)Girl, 19, Macadamia, Familiar of Yáshido

Rita(374)-(Cp11)Girl, 25, Macadamia, Balancer

Rosken-(Cp2)Boy, 15, Macadamia, Attend Jurono

R'Xagario Joyce-(Cp7)Boy, ???, Regra, Victim of the Regra attack

Savanna Miskatae-(Cp2)Girl, 25, Takamaru(Sablein), Partner of Taku

Savenna Miskatae-(Cp2)Girl, 25, Yato, Trants of Taku

Taku Avalance-(Cp2)Boy, 29, Takamaru(Sablein), Fallen Dicipient, Trants of Savenna

Tamari Sutherland-(Cp2)Boy, 19, Macadamia, Attends Jurono

Tatsumi-(Cp3)Boy, 18, Macadamia, Otara's Friend

Tera Misugami-(Cp4)Girl, 39, Watashimono Delshigo, Mother of Otara and Ota'Nomi

Tirahi Colduiat-(Cp2)Boy, 19, Macadamia, Attends Jurono

Toby Misugami-(Cp4)Boy, 43, Watashimono Delshigo, Father of Otara and Ota'Nomi

Tsuno-(Cp13)Boy, 33, Makatama(Makatama Akima), Council of Edasia

Uro-(Cp15), Boy, 35, Macadamia, General, Balancer Allocator

Vekfla-(Cp1)Girl, 29, ???, Mid 6th Gen Dicipient

Vius Opaine-(Cp14)Boy, 42, Macadamia, General, Council of Edasia

Yashi Taramasu-(Pg)Boy, 18, Macadamia, Trants of Dia, 7th Generation Hero

Balancer(117)(Cp15)-Boy, 28, Zenni, Balancer

Balancer(313)(Cp16)-Girl, 31, Macadamia, Balancer

Balancer(334)(Cp8)-Boy, 32, Macadamia, Balancer

Balancer(342)-(Cp11)Boy, 31, Macadamia, Balancer

Balancer(371)(Cp13)-Boy, 27, Macadamia, Balancer

Balancer(377)-(Cp14)Girl, 28, Macadamia, Balancer

Balancer(378)-(Cp15)Girl, 29, Macadamia, Balancer

Balance(390)(Cp15)-Boy, 33, Macadamia, Balancer

Balancer(399)-(Cp11)Boy, 34, Macadamia, Balancer